THE DISTRICT GAZETTEER OF
JHARKHAND

THE DISTRICT GAZETTEER OF
JHARKHAND

Editor

S.C. Bhatt

GYAN PUBLISHING HOUSE
NEW DELHI-110 002

THE DISTRICT GAZETTEER OF JHARKHAND

ISBN: 81-212-07774-6

Published in 2002 in India by
Gyan Publishing House
5, Ansari Road,
New Delhi-110 002
Phone : 3282060, 3261060, Fax : 3285914
E-mail: gyanbook@del2.vsnl.del.in
Visit Our Web Site At http:\\www.gyanbooks.com

Laser Typesetting at: Power Photocomposers, New Delhi
Printed at: Chawla Offset Printers, New Delhi

CONTENTS

PREFACE

Importance of Gazetteer is wellknown. The district Gazetteer of Jharkhand has unique place for various reasons. Jharkhand has 18 districts. Detailed information about all the districts is peresented here with a concise but exhaustive history, the people inhabiting it, its geography, social and economic development, administrative set-up and indeed much more.

A team of eminent scholars worked under my Editorship just after creation of Jharkhand State to collect and collate the available information. All the facts and figures have been carefully and authentically assimilated in this work.

In Jharkhand State, there are eighteen districts. During the fifty years since Independence, the Jharkhandi land and the Jharkhandi people have been in a process of being reduced to shambles in several aspects. The region consists of 79,714 sq kms of land with 2,69,09,428 population of whom 30 per cent are indigenous Adivasis, whereas they were, 60 per cent at the start of last century. Due to displacement process the indigenous people of Jharkhand are perhaps the worst hit, otherwise this region is the richest region in the whole country in terms of natural resources, viz. timber and several kinds of minerals drawn from far flung areas.

Our nation comprises of States and Union Territories and each State or Union Territory in turn, consists of many districts. If Mahatma Gandhi was right in saying that India lives in its villages, a study of Jharkhand without knowing the eighteen districts in detail would result in an incomplete work. It is this lacuna that this study seeks to fill as it offers complete relevant data about each district.

Hopefully, this volume would prove to be immensely useful and become an invaluable academic companion to all researchers and scholars, administrators, planners, tourists librarians and all those who wish to gain micro-knowledge of this tract of our sub-continent. Undoubtedly, this work would also be beneficial to all people who are interested in the history, developments and future of the new State.

I feel much beholden to the Resident Commissioner Jharkhand, professors, librarians, the state information centres and those connected with the government for their valuable material they could make available to me. For the preparation of this work I have consulted a large number of published works and drawn from them. I owe a debt of gratitutde to all those publishers, authors, editors and compilers.

S.C. Bhatt

INTRODUCTION

The Parliament passed the Bihar Reorganization Bill on 2nd August 2000 to create the state of Jharkhand. The genesis of demand can be traced to early 1900s when Jaipal Singh, the Oxford educated hockey captain of the 1928 Olympics, mooted the idea of a separate state consisting of Southern districts of Bihar. After a prolonged agitation, spanning over 50 years by the people of tribal dominated areas of southern Bihar and spear-headed by Jharkhand Mukti Morcha. Jharkhand, the 28th state of the Indian Union, came into existence on 15th November, 2000 the birthday of the legendary tribal freedom fighter Birsa Munda.

The state comprises eighteen districts of the erstwhile Bihar:- Bokaro; Chatra; Deogarh; Dhanbad; Garhwa; Giridih; Godda; Gumla; Hazaribagh; Kodarma; Lohardaga; Pakur; Palamau; Ranchi; Sahebganj; Singhbhum (East) and Singhbhum (West) districts. With an area of 74714 sq. km. the new state is bordered by Bihar, MP, Orissa; and West Bengal to its north, west, south and east respectively.

Jharkhand meaning "the forest area", is geographically known as the Chhotanagpur Plateau, forming the north-eastern portion of peninsular plateau of India. It is a region of great unevenness consisting of a succession of plateaux, hills and valleys drained by several large rivers such as Damodar, Barakar; Subarnrekha; Brahmani, Baitarani; and Mahanadi. Jharkhand is one of the areas rich in minerals with huge reserves of coal, iron ore, mica, bauxite, and limestone, and has considerable reserves of copper, chromite, asbestos, kyanite, china-clay, fire-clay, statute, uranium, manganese, dolomite, tungsten etc. Coal is found in the Gondwana rocks of the Damodar basin. The famous coal fields of the region are Jharia; Raniganj; Ramgarh etc. It is said that about 44 per cent of the total coal reserves in the country lie in Jharkhand.

Damodar valley is famous for coal reserves, while Singhbhum is known for the uranium, copper, chromite, asbestos, kaynite, china-clay, manganese etc.

This area was the homeland of aboriginal races such as the Santals Mundas, Oraons, Hos, Gonds, Khairas, Bhuiyas, Bhumij, Birhors, Dom, Turi, Sadaus, Kamar, Kumhars, Kurmis, Tamaries, etc. These indigenous people of the area are known as *adivasis* literally meaning "Original settlers" or the earliest settlers. They have their own distinct culture and identity which they are determined to preserve. These groups comprise about 85 to 90 per cent of the total population of Jharkhand. They have been worst hit by the large scale exploitation of the natural resources of the region through the development of industries, mines and commercial exploitation of forests. The majority of them live in a state of semi-starvation throughout the year. The remaining 10 to 15 per cent of the population of the area are immigrants who have come here for commercial purposes.

Development of Jharkhand is getting momentum due to fast industrialization. It was in 1774, when the first mining industry was established at Ranigunj. In the year 1843, the first joint stock company M/s Bengal Coal Company was formed. After this a chain of collieries was established on the left bank of Damodar river. The famous Jharia coal fields in Dhanbad District are the richest treasure house of Indian metallurgical coal. The work at Jharia, Bokaro, and Karampura coal fields had started in 1856. The beginning of coal mining in Dhanbad area during the second half of the 19th century and the establishment of the Tata Iron and Steel Company in Jamshedpur in 1907 marked the beginning of the large scale exploitation of mineral and other industrial resources in this area.

Iron ore is the next important mining industry of the region. A big deposit of good quality iron ore is found in Singhbhum. Mining in this area was started during early 20th century when Martin burns company began iron ore mining operation in Ankua range. At present large scale mining is going on at various places in this area like, Gua, Jamda, Noamundi, Chiria, Manoharpur, Kiriburu. The total production of these mines is about 40 per cent of the total production of the country. Most of the production of iron ore is consumed by steel plants at Jamshedpur, Bokaro and Durgapur. Mines in Noamundi area are fully mechanised and their annual production is estimated about 2.5 million tonnes, these mines are owned by TISCO.

Eastern Singhbhum area is famous for copper. It is said that this area was the main mining area for copper from 2000 BC to 6th century AD.

Mica belt of Kodarma, occupied an area of about 150 sq. kms. This region itself supply about 71 per cent high quality mica production of the world's high quality sheet mica. The dressing industry of mica and mica godowns located in Jhumri Tilaya, Kodarma, Domachanchy and Giridih.

Lime stone deposits of Jharkhand are located in Singhbhum, Hazaribagh, and Ranchi districts. It is the chief material in cement. Kyanite an important mineral found mainly in Singhbhum district. Bauxite quarries are located in Pat region in the Ranchi district. China-clay deposits are found in Singhbhum Palamau Ranchi and Santhal Parganas. Fire-clay industries have developed in Jharia and Raniganj area. Manganese, apatite, chromite, quartz, silica, steatite and asbestos processing have developed on a large scale in various parts of Singhbhum district. Uranium processing plant is located at Jadugora in East Singhbhum and mining points for uranium are Bhatin, Narwapahar and Turamdih in Singhbhum district.

Industrial development of Jharkhand mainly around Jamshedpur, Rourkela, Ranchi, Bokaro and in the coal mining areas of Dhanbad and Ramgarh is very fast and impressive. The large scale industries of these areas are famous not only in India but their products and production capacity are famous in the world market.

Jamshedpur with Tata Iron and Steel Company is the most important industrial centre of the region. Ranchi is another industrial centre which is famous for Heavy Engineering Corporation. Cement factories at Japla in Palamau, Jhinkapani in Singhbhum, Sindri in Dhanbad, Khalari in Ranchi and Rajganjpur. Fertilizer factory at Sindri refractory works at Dhanbad and Ramgarh, glass factories at Kandra (Singhbhum) and Bhurkunda (Hazaribagh), mica industries at Jhumri-Telaiya and Giridih, coal washeries and cokeoven plants in Hazaribagh and Dhanbad districts. Medium and small scale industries are located at various places in the Jharkhand areas like, Chaibasa, Chakradharpur, Daltonganj, Gumla, Muri, Dumka, Latehar, Chatra, Ghat Sila, Kunti, Chandit, etc. are other important features.

Electricity generating plants (thermal) of large capacity are located in Bokaro, Patratu, Chandrapura and Sindri in the Damodar basin and at Jamshedpur in Singhbhum. At Konar, Pachet, Maithon and Telaiya, Hydro-electricity is generated.

In the beginning of 20th century, there were very few townships in this area. But after independence this region has registered phenomenal growth in urbanization. According to the census report there were only 8 towns in this region in 1872 while by 2001, it was 152.

The Jharkhand history and its references goes back to the 13th century. Jaysingh Deo, a king of Orissa, in 13th century, had declared himself to be the king of Jharkhand. Jharkhand is also mentioned in the copper plate of that period. Chaitanya, the great Vaishnava reformer of the 15th century also mentioned this part of land as Jharkhand. In 1585 during the time of the Akbar, the king of Chhotanagpur was a tributary ruler under

Akbar. "In Akbarnama", the region of Chhotanagpur is described as Jharkhand (Jangal Pradesh). The Jharkhand region was also famous by another name Khukhra during the time of Mughals, which was known for its Diamonds.

In 1605, after the death of Akbar, this area witnessed a very bad law and order situation and was declared independent by local chiefs. In 1616, during the period of Jahangir, Ibrahim Khan was the governor of Bihar. A battle was fought between the 46th king of Chhotanagpur, Raja Durjansal and Ibrahim Khan.

Raja Durjan Sal was defeated by Ibrahim Khan and was imprisoned in the fort of Gwalior. During his imprisonment, Raja Durjan Sal got impressed with the Hindu rulers of that area. In 1628, Raja Durjan Sal was released, as a tributary king.

In 1765, during the time of Shah Alam II, East India company became the revenue collecting agent of the Mughal emperor. This was the period of internal disturbances in the Chhotanagpur region. In 1771, Jharkhand came under the East India company. In 1760, Midnapur also came under the East India company. Due to the exploitation of landlords and the Company's agents, the farmers of that area were facing the menace of poverty.

The following are the most important historical events pertaining to this area that provide a background for the development of the Jharkhand Movement Later.

1765 The East India Company become the Revenue Collecting Agent of the Mughal Emperor Shah Alam II.

1771 Jharkhand came under the East India Company.

1780 Formation of the Military Collectorship of the Ramgarh Hill Tract.

1797 The Munda Uprising of Bundu (under the leadership of Bisu Manki)

1798-99	The Bhumij Revolt of Manbhum.
1800	The Chero Uprising of Palkamau (under the leadership of Bhukan Singh).
1807	The Munda Uprising of Tamar (under the leadership of Dukhan Manki).
1819-20	The Munda Uprising of Tamar (under the leadership of Rudu and Konta).
1832-33	The Kol Rebellion (under the leadership of Singhray and Bindray Manki).
1833	Introduction of the Wilkinson's Rule under Regulation XIII of 1833. Formation of the Non-Regulation Province of the South West Frontier Agency (cf. Regulation XIII of 1833) after abolishing the Military Collectorship of Ramgarh Hill Tract.
1834	The Bhumij Revolt (under the leadership of Ganga Narain).
1845	Introduction of Christianity in the area.
1854	Agency administration abolished (cf. Act XX of 1854) and the powers of the Agency vested in an officer appointed by the local government, known as Commissioner, placed directly under the Lieutenant Governor of Bengal. The area continued to be a Non-Regulation Province, but with a new name: Chota Nagpur Division, consisting of the districts of Birbhum, Lohardaga, Hazaribagh, Manbhum, Singhbhum and the tributary states of Chang-Bhakar, Korea, Surguja, Jashpur, Gangpur and Bonai.
1855	The Santhal Insurrection (under the leadership of Sidhu and Kanhu). Santhal Parganas formed into a separate Non-Regulation District, under a separate Commissioner of Bhagalpur Division (cf. Act XXXVII

of 1855).

1856-57 The Sepoy Mutiny (under the leadership of Bisnath Sahi, Ganapat Rai, Sheikh Bhikhari and Budh Bir).

1859 Introduction of the Sale and Rent Law in the Chota Nagpur Division.

1869 The Chhotanagpur Tenures Act.

1872 The Santhal Parganas Settlement Regulation.

1874 The Non-Regulation Districts were changed into Scheduled Districts (cf. Scheduled Districts Act).

1875-95 The Sardar Movement in Chhotanagpur.

1878 Indian Forest Act.

1879 The Chhotanagpur Landlord and Tenant Procedure Act.

1886 The Santhal Parganas Rent Regulation.

1895-1900 The Birsa Movement.

1903 The Chhotanagpur Tenancy (Amendment) Act, introducing restrictions on transfer of land.

1908 The Chhotanagpur Tenency Act. The Santhal Parganas Settlement (Amendment) Regulation, also introducing restriction on transfer of land.

1912 Separation of Bihar and Orissa from Bengal (cf. R.D. Munda, 1988, pp. 25-28).

The movement for autonomy of Jharkhand was started mainly by the tribals. The initial phase of the movement, starting at the turn of the 20th century, saw the rise of the institutions designed to introduce reforms and to stimulate development among the tribes mainly along denomination and even along inter-denomination lines. Christian Association had been formed in 1898 for the promotion of education. In 1912J. Bartholomew on his return from the students' Conference at Dacca, founded a branch of the Dacca Students' Union with the objective of raising funds for the education of poor Christian students. The Munda-Oraon Education Conference, founded by a non-Christian leader, and the Ranchi Union undertook the promotion of education among the urban tribals.

1920 The Chhotanagpur Unnati Samaj : For the upliftment of their bretheren various educated and politically conscious Adviasi leaders now started organising themselves into societies. In July 1920, a meeting of leaders from different tribal communities was held at Ranchi under the leadership of Rev. Joel Lakra, and the Chhotanagpur Unnati Samaj was formed. The objectives of the Samaj were: (a) to uplift Chhotanagpur from its backward state and, (b) to improve the social, political and religious conditions of the tribals. They also published a magazine called "The Adivasi". This movement sought to secure employment for educated tribals, reservation in the services and legislative bodies, and formation of a sub-state attached to Bengal or Bihar. The members of this movement submitted a memorandum to the Simon Commission asking for a separate state and demanding special privileges for the tribals.

1931 Formation of the Kisan Sabha : The Kisan Sabha was originally started in Chhotanagpur by Swami Sahajanand Saraswati. Its first president was Theble Oraon and its secretary was Paul Dayal. Some of the members of the Chhotanagpur Unnati Samaj left it due to difference of views and joined a parallel organisation called the Kisan Sabha to focus the farmers problem.

1935 Formation of the Chhotanagpur Catholic Sabha : The Catholics had kept aloof from these organisations. The Anglicans and the Lutherans were ahead of them in the political field. In order to forestall indifferentism and to safeguard their interests, the Catholics formed the

Chhotanagpur Catholic Sabha with inspiration from Bishop Severin. The Catholic Sabha set up candidates for the General Elections in 1935. Two of them won defeating the candidates of the Kisan Sabha and the Unnati Samaj. Ignes Beck was their representative in Parliament.

1938 Formation of the Chhotanagpur Adivasi Mahasabha : The general secretary of the Chhotanagpur Catholic Sabha Ignes Beck who had great political influence in the area, realised that unless the Advasis presented a common front setting aside all denominational differences, their salvation from economic, political and social exploitation would never be achieved. Under his persuasive leadership the *Unnati Samaj,* the *Kisan Sabha* and the *Catholic Sabha* formed a united front during the municipal elections in 1938 and all their candidates won their seats. The second conference of the Mahasabha was held under the presidentship of Jaipal Singh. The movement gradually became militant and several clashes occurred.

1950 Formation of the Jharkhand Party : Under the leadership of Jaipal Singh, the influence of the Adivasi Mahasabha spread all over the Chhotanagpur plateau. The members of the Adivasi Mahasabha gradually realised the need for making it more broad-based by including non-tribals also. To press this view, Justin Richard organised the United Jharkhand Block in April 1948 at Chakradharpur. Justin was a colleague of Jaipal Singh. After the Kharsawan firing of 1948, Justin lost faith in Jaipal and they parted company. Jaipal Singh, seeing that the wind was being taken out of his sails by the formation of the United Jharkhand Block, formed the Jharkhand Party as the political wing of the Mahasabha in early 1950 at Jamshedpur. The general session of the Mahasabha held at Jamshedpur decided that, though the Mahasabha would remain essentially a tribal organisation, its membership would be extended to non-Adivasi Jharkhandis. Thus from a tribal organisation the Mahasabha became a regional political party. Following the establishment of a democratic form of government in India based on adult franchise, the Jharkhand Party emerged as a full-fledged political party in 1951. In the first General Elections of independent India in 1952, the party adopted the cock as its symbol, symbolising 'day break' or 'tribal awakening'. The party won all the 32 seats in the Bihar Legislative Assembly which it had contested. It emerged as the main opposition party in the state.

1955 Demand for Jharkhand Prante before the States Reorganisation Commission : In January 1955 a memorandum was submitted by the Executive Committee of the Jharkhand Party to the States Reorganisation Committee (SRC) emphasizing the economic, political and cultural imperative for the formation of a separate Jharkhand state. The memorandum stated that the Adivasis were distinct from the non-tribals ethnically, culturally and linguistically. Besides there was also a certain geographical contiguity and administrative separateness which more than justified the claim for a separate state. The proposed Jharkhand state was to be made up of six districts of Bihar and nine districts of Bengal, orissa and Madhya Pradesh. Their demand was turned down by the SRC who pointed out that the Jharkhand tribals did not have a common language.

1957 The decline of the Jharkhand Party begins : As a result of the non-fulfilment of their demand for a separate Jharkhand state the tribals began to set disillusioned with the Jharkhand Party. One of the reasons for the people's discontent was that the leaders were far away from them and had lost contact with the masses.

1963 Merger of the Jharkhand Party with the Congress : In September 1963, the Jharkhand Party was merged with the Congress party. The leaders of the Jharkhand Party thought that their main objective of a separate Jharkhand state would only materialise if they merged. They were tired of sitting in opposition.

1967 Fourth General Elections: Fragmentation of the Jharkhand Party : Following the merger in 1963, the Jharkhand Party was characterised by a number of factions and cleavages. By the time of the 1967 elections many groups came up claiming that they represented the Jharkhand Party. Some of these groups were led by tribals while others by non-tribals. Thus Lal Harihar Nath Sahadeo, a local Hindu advocate from Ranchi, claimed that his group represented the Jharkhand Party. Another group led by Paul Dayal also claimed that they represented the old Jharkhand Party. Two other claimants were P.K. Lakra, an employee of TISCO and Justin Richard. Such claims posed a problem before the Election Commission in 1966 regarding the allotment of the popular symbol of the cock of the old Jharkhand Party. Ultimately, it was given to none of them and they fought the election with various independent names and symbols. After the fourth General Elections had decimated the Jharkhand Party many attempts were made to unite the various splinter groups - without much success.

1967 Formation of the All India Jharkhand Party : On 28 December 1967 the All India Jharkhand Party was formed. It declared that the merger of 1963 with the Congress was unconstitutional and void as it was not approved by the General Body. This party began to split again in 1969-70. One faction led by Bagun Sumbrui, a Ho, retained the name All India Jharkhand Party. The other group led by N.E. Horo, a Munda, kept the name of Jharkhand party.

1967 Formation of Birsa Seva Dal : This organisation was formed by a group of young men, named Lalit Kujur, Prem

Kujur, Moses Guria and Pius Lakra. It was an urban group of educated tribals, centred at industrial complexes, to demand jobs for tribal youths in industrial undertakings. In the beginning it used violent methods of struggle to secure tribal rights. Birsa Seva Dal demanded the creation of a separate state, expulsion of the Non-Chhotanagpuris, agrarian reforms and measures against money lenders. At present the Birsa Seva Dal has almost ceased to exist except in Jamshedpur where it shows some activity now and then.

1968 Formation of the Hul Jharkhand Party : Before the mid-term elections of 1969, Justin Richard, the leader of one group of Jharkhand activists, renamed his party Hul Jharkhand Party and got it recognised by the Election Commissioner. Justin Richard took advantage of the anti-money-lender activities of Sibu Murmu, a leftist Santhal worker, who had gone underground. The party concentrated its activities mainly in Santhal Parganas. It was able to bag seven seats in the 1969 elections.This party split up into two in 1970. The break away faction led by Sibu Murmu formed the Bihar Progressive Hul Jharkhand Party.

Factionalism in tribal politics : After the merger we notice that the Jharkhand Movement began to develop on factional lines. Thus the All India Jharkhand Party led by Bagun Sumbrui drew its support mainly from the Hos of Singhbhum. The Jharkhand Party led by N.E. Horo had its followers among the Mundas. The Hul Jharkhand Party headed by Sibu Murmu became a party of the Santhals.

1969 The Naxalite Movement in Jharkhand : In the forested regions of Jharkhand the Naxalite activity started around 1969. There were many cases of murder and violent clashes. By the middle of 1971 the movement was suppressed and the leaders arrested.

1973 Formation of the Jharkhand Mukti Morcha (JMM) : From 1972 onwards the Jharkhand Movement began to take a new turn. For the first time both the industrial workers and the peasants came together to fight against the exploitation they were undergoing. The struggle began to take the form of a class struggle.

1973 On February 4, 1973, at Dhanbad, the Sonat Santhal Samaj of Shibu Soren and the Shivaji Samaj led by Binod Bihari Mahato merged together and formed the Jharkhand Mukti Morcha (JMM). It launched an operation to recover alienated lands from money-lenders and big peasants. After its formation it organised forcible harvesting of crops standing on lands illegally taken from Adivasis, Kurmis, Harijans and poor Muslims by the money-lenders. Under the leadership of JMM the tribal peasants, landless labourers and industrial workers started a popular movement against exploitation. Their objectives were: (i) For recovery of land illegally taken from the tribals by the money-lenders and the *mahajans.* (ii) For obtaining employment for local tribals in the public undertakings established in the area. (iii) The *jangal katai andolan* against the anti-people forest policy of the government. (iv) For the formation of a separate Jharkhand state.

1978 The Forest *andolan* in Singhbhum : In the year 1978 the Kolhan-Proahat area of Singhbhum district witnessed the outbreak of a well-organised and formidable *andolan* known as the *jangal katai andolan* started by the Adivasis of this area. This area is covered with some of the best Sal forests in the country. The andolan took the form of felling of trees in these forests by the Adivasis as a symbolic protest against the threat to their livelihood and identity. It spread like wild fire in the whole area and vast areas of forest were cut down by the Adivasis. Their argument was that these lands once belonged to them and were illegally taken away by the Forest Department.

1981 The emergence of the Kolhan Raksha Sangh : For the first time in the history of tribal movements in Jharkhand an attempt to form an independent nation for the HOs of Kolhan (Singhbhum) was made by an organisation called the Kolhan Raksha Sangh under the leadership of Narayan Jonko. Their demand exists in this area.

1985 Demand for a Centrally Administered Territory : On September 25, 1985, a demand for declaring Chhotanagpur and Santhal Parganas as a Centrally Administered Territory was placed before the Home Minister at Patna when he was meeting more than 50 MLAs from this area to find out the problems of the region. A formal letter regarding this demand, signed by 50 MLAs and MPs from this region belonging to all parties, was sent to the Prime Minister and the Home Minister on March 22, 1986. The leadership of this move was given by Devendra nath Champia, a Congress (I) MLA from Singhbhum.

1986 Formation of the All Jharkhand Students' Union (AJSU): On June 22, 1986, under the leadership of Surya Singh Besra, All Jharkhand Students Union (AJSU) was formed.

1987 Formation of the Jharkhand Coordination Committee: In order to establish a common front, a conference of delegates of all political, social, cultural and literary organisations supporting the Jharkhand november was held at Ramgarh from September 11-13, 1987. It was attended by 429 delegates who represented 49 organisations. Four more organisations joined later, making the total number 53. The Jharkhand Coordination Committee (JCC) was formed at this conference and Dr. B.P. Kesari was appointed the convenor of JCC.

1988 Demand for a separate Vananchal state by the BJP : The BJP jumped on the bandwagon demanding a separate Vananchal state consisting of Chhotanagpur and Santhal Parganas. This provided a lot of electoral advantage to the BJP.

1989 Formation of the Committee on Jharkhand Matters: It was in the backdrop of these developments that the Centre decided to act. In August 1989 a Committee on Jharkhand Matters (COJM) was formed. The COJM was asked to examine and recommend modalities for meeting the just aspirations of the people of this region within the framework of the Constitution. The Committee submitted its report to the Union Home Minister on May 18, 1990, suggesting three possible solutions to the Jharkhand problem: (1) Statehood, (2) Union Territory and (3) Jharkhand General Council within the State of Bihar.

1991 Formation of the Jharkhand People's Party : On 31st December 1991, the Jharkhand People's Party (JPP) was formed as an associate political party of AJSU. Dr. Ram Dayal Munda was chosen as the first President of the party and Surya Singh Besra as its Chief Secretary. The first convention of the party was held at Jamshedpur where it was decided that AJSU would work as the student wing of JPP.

1994 Jharkhand Area Autonomous Council Bill passed by the Bihar State Assembly : On August 9, 1995, the Jharkhand Area Autonomous Council was sworn in.

1997 Resolution for the creation of a separate Jharkhand state passed by the Bihar Assembly.

1998 Vananchal State announced by the BJP government at the Centre.

Victims of Development

The basic fact about the Jharkhand is that the wealth of this area is being usurped by a few rich for their own vested interests. The gap between these few rich and the majority who are poor is ever widening. Further there is little hope of any better life for the deprived masses. This systematic dispossession of the indegenous masses of Jharkhand in the name of "development of national interests" has reduced them to a situation of extreme poverty. They live in a situation of starvation squalor and disease. Further for their survival they are forced to function as cheap casual wage labourers for the large scale capitalist exploitations of the wealth of this area.

Wealth gives power to those who already possess it. In present society economic power is synonymous with political power. The political power in turn is used to increase economic power and hence remains the monopoly of the rich. Money-power brings power to control the live of the others.

Because of their extreme poverty the masses have been marginalised and are discriminated against and exploited by the dominant in society. They have become amorphous, powerless objects for the use and abuse of their exploiters. The rich use this economic and political power to promote and perpetuate their own vested interest, viz, to become more welathy and more powerful of course.

S.C. Bhatt

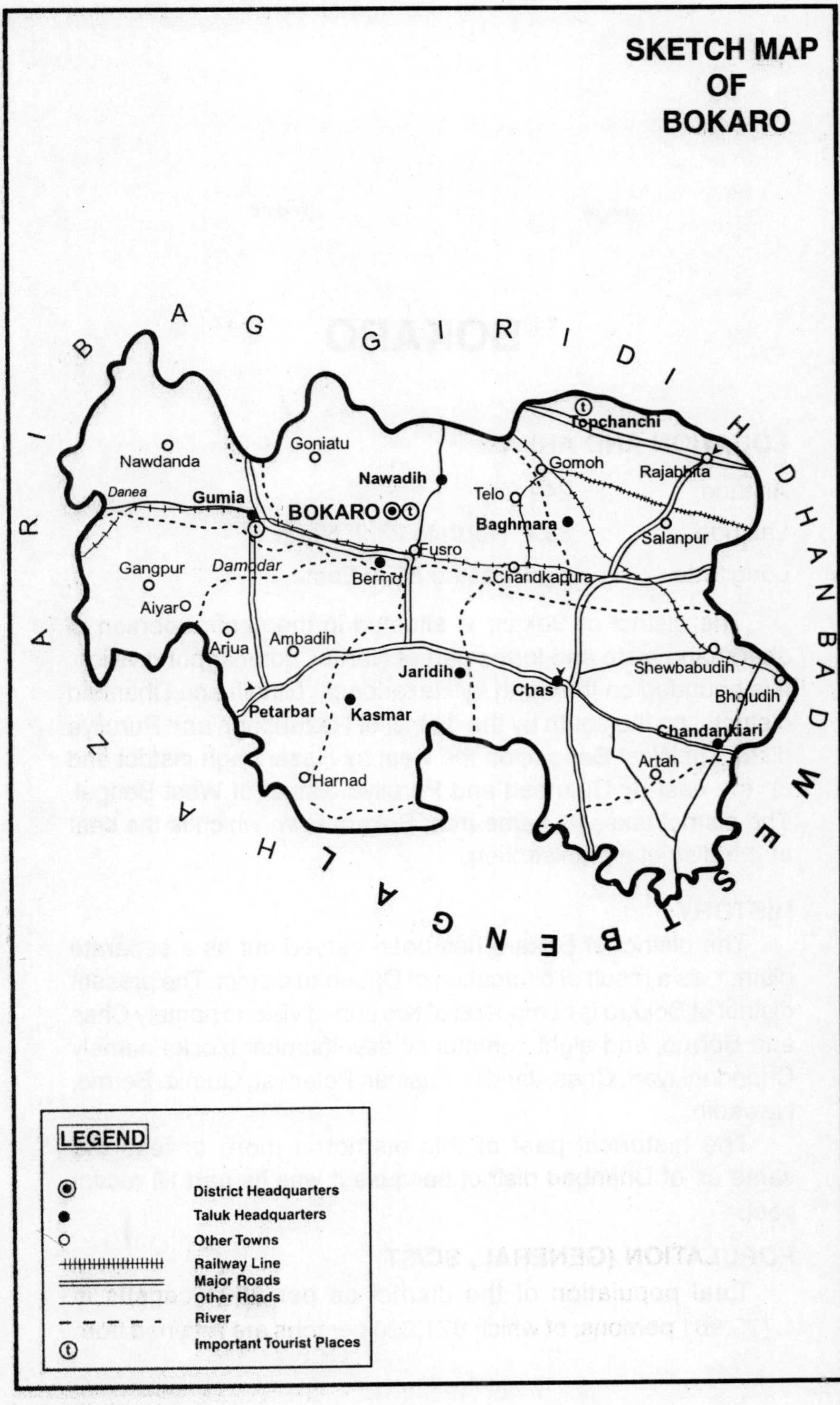
SKETCH MAP OF BOKARO
HAZARIBAG
GIRIDIH
DHANBAD
WEST BENGAL
Topchanchi
Rajabhita
Gomoh
Goniatu
Nawdanda
Nawadih
Telo
Danea
Gumia
BOKARO
Baghmara
Salanpur
Fusro
Gangpur
Damodar
Bermo
Chandkapura
Aiyar
Arjua
Ambadih
Jaridih
Shewbabudih
Chas
Bhojudih
Petarbar
Kasmar
Chandankiari
Artah
Harnad
LEGEND
District Headquarters
Taluk Headquarters
Other Towns
Railway Line
Major Roads
Other Roads
River
Important Tourist Places

BOKARO

LOCATION AND AREA

Altitude	:	242 (m)
Latitude	:	23.4° North to 23.9° North
Longitude	:	85.6°East to 86.4° East

The district of Bokaro is situated in the central portion of Jharkhand state and forms part of North Chotanagpur division. It is bounded on the north by Hazaribagh, Giridih and Dhanbad districts, on the south by the district of Hazaribagh and Puruliya district of West Bengal, on the west by Hazaribagh district and on the east by Dhanbad and Puruliya district of West Bengal. The district takes its name from Bokaro town which is the seat of the district administration.

HISTORY

The district of Bokaro has been carved out as a separate district, as a result of bifurcation of Dhanbad district. The present district of Bokaro is comprised of two sub- divisions namely Chas and Bermo, and eight community development blocks namely Chandankiyari, Chas, Jaridih, Kasmar, Petarwar, Gumia, Bermo, Nawadih.

The historical past of this district is more or less the same as of Dhanbad district because it was its part till recent past.

POPULATION (GENERAL, SC/ST)

Total population of the district as per 2001 census is 1,775,961 persons, of which 971,220 persons are retained from rural areas and the remaining 804,741 persons from urban areas.

Community development block-wise population distribution of this district as per 2001 census is given in the table on next page. It gives rural- urban break of general population, and the literacy rate.

The Community Development Block-wise, population distribution with sex ratio and literacy rate of this district is given below:

	Sex ratio		Literacy rate		Population	
C.D. Block	Rural	Urban	Rural	Urban	Rural	Urban
BOKARO DISTRICT	**927**	**858**	**48.56**	**79.47**	**971220**	**804741**
Nawadih	941	-	49.29	-	158,009	-
Bermo	883	858	56.71	75.21	30,128	220,098
Gumia	959	897	42.45	72.27	132,543	65,975
Peterwar	915	-	46.58	-	113,608	-
Kasmar	938	-	48.33	-	76,145	-
Jaridih	920	859	52.95	73.02	81,065	7154
Chas	908	853	50.06	82.49	200,221	497,855
Chandankiyari	926	845	48.67	73.35	179,501	13,659

LANGUAGES AND RELIGION

Main languages spoken in the district are Hindi, Bengali, Punjabi and Urdu.

Separate religion-wise breakup of population is not available because it was the part of Dhanbad district at the time of census taking. The combined figures in this regard are provided in case of its parent district

GEOGRAPHY AND PHYSICAL FEATURES

Annual Rainfall : 1570 mm

Temperature : Max. 43.40°C and Min. 6.0°C

In shape, Bokaro district is horizontally located in the map of which the western and eastern sides are of greater length than the northern and southern sides. The district has three broad natural divisions, viz., (i) the north and north-western portions consisting of the hilly region, (ii) the uplands containing coal mines and most of the industries, and (iii) the remaining uplands and plains lying to the south of the Damodar river consisting of culturable flat lands and includes the Bokaro Steel Plant and the industrial-cum-mining complex surrounding it.

In the north, a branch of the Parasnath hill runs through Topchanchi (Community Development Block) and Tundi of Dhanbad district. The southern part of the district is largely comprised of undulating land. The general slope is from west to east.

Forest in the district are largely confined to the north, bordering on the districts of Hazaribagh and Giridih. Sal, sisoo, siris, palas, mahua, jamun, simal and bamboos are the important trees in the forests.

RIVERS, CANALS AND WATERWAYS

Damodar is the main river of this district. It rises in the Palamu and flows eastward. It is joined by the Bokaro, the Konar and the Barakar rivers. The Damodar river enters Bokaro district at its confluence with the Jamuria, a stream which marks the western boundary of Bokaro with Hazaribagh district.

TOWNS, VILLAGES AND AMENITIES

The district is at present comprised of two sub-divisions and eight Community Development Blocks. It has sixteen towns.

COMMUNICATIONS

The district is well served by road as well as rail communications. The Grand Trunk Road runs through the northern part of the district. The other important roads maintained by the Public Works Department in the district are Gobindpur-Chas-Jamshedpur roads, Raghunathpur-Chandankiyari-Chas road and Pathardih-Chandankiyari-Baramaria road. As regards rail transport, the Grand chord line of the Eastern Railway passes through the district interconnecting with the neighbouring and distant important towns.

AGRICULTURE AND IRRIGATION

Paddy is the main crop of the district and covers the major portion of the gross area sown. Other important crops are wheat, sugarcane and oilseeds.

The main source of irrigation is Bundhs and Ahars due to hilly areas. Rain water is stored in Ahars or reservoirs and then led to the field by channels and sub-channels. Uplands are not irrigated ordinarily.

ANIMAL HUSBANDRY

Like in other parts of the state, cattle, buffaloes, goats and pigs, apart from poultry birds constitute the main livestock population of this district. The variety of the livestock is, however, poor. The district administration has opened many veterinary hospitals and dispensaries at C.D. Block level which look after the welfare of the animals.

INDUSTRIES

Bokaro Steel Plant located in the district is one of the biggest steel plants in India. BASF India Limited is another major industry in this district.

BASF India Ltd. Bokaro Industrial Area. Bokaro. Jharkhand.

Manufacturer: Expandable and expanded polystyrene (thermocole), expandable polystyrene (styropor) tanning agents, leather auxilliaries, oil and well chemicals, leather auxillaries and finishing agents, pesticides basic production. The company also renders technical service in relation to various industries and markets dyestuffs and chemicals in relation to dyestuffs.

MINERALS AND ORES OCCURRENCES

Coal

Bokaro (23.8, 85.7) specimens of coal from a locality on the Bokaro River, 36 km. to the South East of Hazaribagh, were forwarded to the Asiatic Society of Bengal by Drummond in 1838. The field is divided into two parts: East Bokaro, East of longitude 85.7 and West Bokaro to the west. There are nineteen seams over 4 ft. in thickness. In the West Bokaro coal field the Baghlata River sections, four seams of coal ranging in thickness from 6 ft to 12 ft have been recognised in the Barakars. In the Bokaro River section two coal seams 6 to 8 ft have been recorded in the Barakars.

Corundum

An occurrence of corundum in 23.9°N and 85.7°East.

Limestone

Lime stone occurs near 23.9°, 85.5°; 23.7°; 85.4° and also at 23.6°, 85.5°.

TRADE, COMMERCE AND EXPORT

The table given below presents the most important commodities manufactured, exported from and imported in the four towns of the district.

Name of the town	*Most important commodities*			*Banks*
	Manufactured	*Exported*	*Imported*	
Bokaro Steel City	Pig Iron, Hot Rolled coils/plates/ sheets	Pig Iron, Hot rolled Coils, C. R. sheets	Food Grains Edible oil and Medicines	9
Chas	Steel products Images, Wooden furniture	—	Grain, pulse, vegetable and oils	5
Katras	—	Coal	Rice, Wheat and Mustard oil	2
Bhojudih	—	—	—	1

HOTELS (2000)

Hans Regency. (Government Approved), 3 Star. Access- 1 km from Airport, 10 kms. from Bokaro Steel city Railway station and near to Bus stand.

Hotel Blue Diamond (Government Approved) 3 star. Access- 1.25 kms from Airport, 8 kms. from Railway station and 1/2 km. from Bus stand.

Bokaro Hotel (Government Approved) 2 Star. Access-5 kms. from Airport, 13 kms from Bokaro Steel City Railway Station 6 km. from Bus stand.

Limcas Hotel Industries Pvt. Ltd. (Govt. Approved) 2 Star. Access-1 km. from Airport 10 kms. from Bokaro Steel City Railway station, Bus stop just opposite.

Hotel Malti Mahal, Access- 3 kms. from Airport, 10 kms from Railway station, 1.5 km from Bus stand, 1 km. from Bokaro Steel Plant.

TOURISM

Babudi. The village is contained in Chas development block. It is noted for a 75 feet high tower with 6 feet thick walls and diameter of 10 feet. It is said to be very old.

Bansa. The village which also lies in Chas Block, has a Sati-sthan with stone walls believed to be over 200 years old.

Thinjhipahari. The village is situated in Baghmara development block. It is said that an ancient temple of Lord Shiva was found when the mines here were being worked.

Bermo. It is a Census town, being the headquarters of the development block bearing the same name. The town lies on a railhead on the Gomoh-Barkakana section of the Eastern Railway. It is an important coal mining centre.

Bokaro. It is a census town situated on the Bokaro river near its confluence with the Konar river. The town is noted for its Thermal Power Station set up by the Damodar Valley Corporation.

Gumia. It is a township situated near Gumia railway station. The works of M/s Indian Explosives Ltd., the only one of its kind in the country, are located here. It is a modern township made up mostly of workers of the factory.

Tenughat. It is a place where a dam and reservoir have been constructed on Damodar river at a height of 166 feet. It covers an area of 30 sq kms. The reservoir supplies water to the Bokaro Steel Plant through a canal 29 kms in length. Due to its scenic view, Tenughat attracts large number of tourists every year. It is also a favourite boating place for the tourists especially during moonlit nights.

ZOO

Jawaharlal Nehru Biological Park (Medium Zoo)

FAIRS AND FESTIVALS

Important fairs and melas organised in various parts of the district are mentioned below:

Dussehra mela, Kartik Purnima mela, Makar Sankranti mela, Divali mela and Basant Panchmi mela.

EDUCATION

Primary and middle school education facilities are generally available in all towns. The following table gives details of different categories of, educational institutions including stadia and public library available in the four towns of this district.

Name of the towns	*Educational institutions*	*Stadia*	*Public libraries including reading room*
Bhojudih	Secondary/Matriculation School (1), Junior Secondary and Middle Schools (2), Primary Schools (2)	—	—
Bokaro Steel City	Higher Secondary/ Intermediate Schools (3), Secondary/Matriculation Schools (4), Junior Secondary and Middle Schools (23) Primary Schools (28)	2	PL : 2
Chas	Secondary/Matriculation Schools (2), Junior Secondary and Middle Schools (4), Primary Schools (9)	—	PL : 3
Katras	Secondary Schools (3), Junior Secondary and Middle Schools (8), Primary Schools (12)		

COLLEGES (2000)

B.S. City College, Bokaro (Established 1971). Enrolment 4153, Teachers 37 (Constituent College)

Chas College, Chas, (Established 1977) Enrolment 2196, Teachers 65 (Constituent College)

K.B. College Bermo, (Established 1977) Enrolment 2909, Teachers 22 (Constituent College)

Baghmara College, Baghmara (Established 1979) (Affiliated College)

BDA College Pichri, (Established 1986) Teachers 30 (Affiliated College)

Bokaro Mahila College, Bokaro (Established 1976), Teachers 55 (Affiliated College)

Chas Mahila College, Chas (Established 1984), Teachers 19 (Affiliated College)

Imamul Hai Khan College Bokaro (Established 1982), Teachers 10 (Affiliated College)

P N Memorial College, Gomoh (Established 1970) Teachers 11 (Affiliated College)

RVS College, Chas, (Established 1978) Teachers 49 (Affiliated College)

SS College, Chas, (Established 1984) Teachers 33 (Affiliated College)

Tenughat College, Tenughat (Established 1975) Teachers 36 (Affiliated College)

Visthapit College, Balidih, Teachers 24 (Affiliated College)

(Above named Colleges belong to Vinoba Bhave University, Hazaribagh, Established 1992).

MEDICAL

The table given below furnishes information regarding of medical facility available in the four towns of this distrtct including that of beds facility.

Name of the towns	Medical institutions (with number of beds)	
Bhojudih	Dispensaries (5, Hom 6) :	—
	Health Centres (2)	
Bokaro Steel City	Hospital (1) :	572
	Dispensaries (1, Hom-1) :	—
	Health Centres {5) :	—
	Family Planning Centres (5) :	—
Chas	Hospital (1, Hom-2) :	30
	Dispensaries (1, Hom-2) :	—
	Health Centres (6) :	—
	Family Planning Centres (3) :	—
	Nursing Homes (2} :	20
Katras	Hospital (2} :	19
	Family Planning Centres (2) :	—

MEDIA

(i) Rashtriya Dainik Nazar

(ii) Mangalwar Hindi Weekly

ADMINISTRATION

(i) Administrative Divisions :
Sub-division: Chas and Bermo.

Community Development Blocks: Nawadih, Bermo, Gumia, Petarwar, Kasmar, Jaridih, Chandankiyari and Chas.

Towns and Urban Agglomerations with their Population, Sexratio, Decadal growth and Literacy rate (2001)

BAKARO STEEL CITY UA	PHUSRO UA
Bakaro Steel City (CT) Bandhgora (CT) Gumia (CT); Chas (M)	Phusro (NA); Bokaro (CT); Kurpania (CT) Jaridih Bazar (CT); Bermo (CT); Tenu-Dam-cum-Kathhara (CT); Jena (CT); Chandrapura (CT); Sijhua (CT);
Dugda	(CT); Amlabad (CT); Bhojudih (CT)

Town	Population	Percentage Decadal growth 1991-2001	Sex Ratio	Literacy Rate
Bokaro Steel City (UA)	497,855	24.81	853	82.49
(a) Bokaro Steel city (CT)	394,173	18.13	850	83.20
(b) Bandhgora (CT)	6,759	-	893	64.10
(c) Chas (M)	96,923	48.64	862	80.77
Phusro (UA)	174,367	22.29	862	74.57
(a) Phusro (NA)	83,463	22.29	862	73.99
(b) Bokaro (CT)	36,419	28.38	852	78.16
(c) Kurpania (CT)	7,440	-	868	78.22
(d) Jaridih Bazar (CT)	30,091	13.29	863	74.57
(e) Bermo (CT)	16,954	-0.93	890	68.08
Gumia (CT)	45,532	10.26	897	73.74
Tenu Dam-cum-Kathra (CT)	20,443	17.55	897	68.81
Jena (CT)	7,154	-	859	78.02
Chandrapura (CT)	22,389	13.00	835	81.40
Sijhua (CT)	4,478	-	866	60.11
Dugda (CT)	18,864	24.03	848	77.06
Amlabad (CT)	4,723	-	808	77.06
Bhojudih (CT)	8,936	5.86	865	72.10

(ii) Parliamentary Constituencies and Assembly Segments

No. and Name of Parliamentary Constituencies:
46–Giridih, 47–Dhanbad

No. and Name of Assembly Segments:

Giridih

277. Gomia—Gomia police station and Petarbar police station (excluding G.Ps. Champi, Rohar , Chando, Pichhri, Angwali and Chalkari) in Bermo sub-division.

278. Bermo—Jaridih and Bermo police stations and G.Ps, Champi, Rohar, Chando, Pichhri, Angwali and Chalkari in Petarbar police station in Bermo sub-division.

281. Baghmara—Baghmara police station and Katras police 'station (excluding G.Ps. Dharkiro, Daludih, Rajganj, Bagdaha, Dhawachita, Nagri Kalan and Ramkanali- chardur) in Baghmara sub-division; and Jogta police station in Dhanbad Sadar sub-division.

Dhanbad

279. Bokaro—Chas police station (excluding G.Ps. Bijulia. A1kusa. Buribinor, Khamarbendi. Dudhigajar , Kura Dabartu-para, Jaitara, Pundru and Sardaha) in Baghmara sub-division.

286. Chandankiyarl (SC)—Chandankiyari police station and *C.Ps.* Bijulia, AlkUsa. Buribinor. Knarnarbendi. Dhudhigaj"ar .Kura, Dabartupara, Jaitara, Pudru and Sardaha in Chas poiice station in Baghmara sub- division.

OBSERVATIONAL ORGANISATION

Seismological Organization

This facility is available at Bakaro city. Data from this observatory is used for routine determination of epicentre of earthquakes, preparations of Bulletins, special study and research;

Hydrometeorological Stations for climatological purposes.

Latitude	:	23.8°N
Longitude	:	85.9 E
Altitude	:	242 m
Date of starting	:	11-9-1949

DISASTROUS WEATHER EVENTS

Coldwave

29-30 November, 1982 Severe

4-10 December 1982 Severe.

December (3rd and 4th week) 1984 severe, persons reported died in this area

9 December 1985, Severe.

27-31 December severe, people reported died in this area.

1-10 January 1990, severe coldwave.

January 1st and 2nd week, severe coldwave.

Heatwave

June 1st, 2nd and 3rd week 1981, Moderate to severe.

28 May to 2nd June 1983, moderate to severe.

6 June 1983 severe.

7 June 1983, moderate.

3 June 1995, severe.

Flood and Heavy Rains

July 4th week to October 2nd week, 1987, this area observed, Floods, Flash floods in the Rivers and also witnessed heavy Rains.

July 1996, there was floods in the rivers.

Lightning

10 July 1996, several people died in the locality.

ARCHAEOLOGICAL SITE

Bokaro	Bokaro	Handaxe (4.2) of green micaceous quartzite was picked up in 1865. Brown C.J., 1917 Catalogue of Prehistoric An tiquities in Indian Museum; Calcutta, Simla, p.67. Logan, A.C., 1906, Old Chipped Stones of India, Calcutta, pp.30-3

SKETCH MAP OF CHATRA

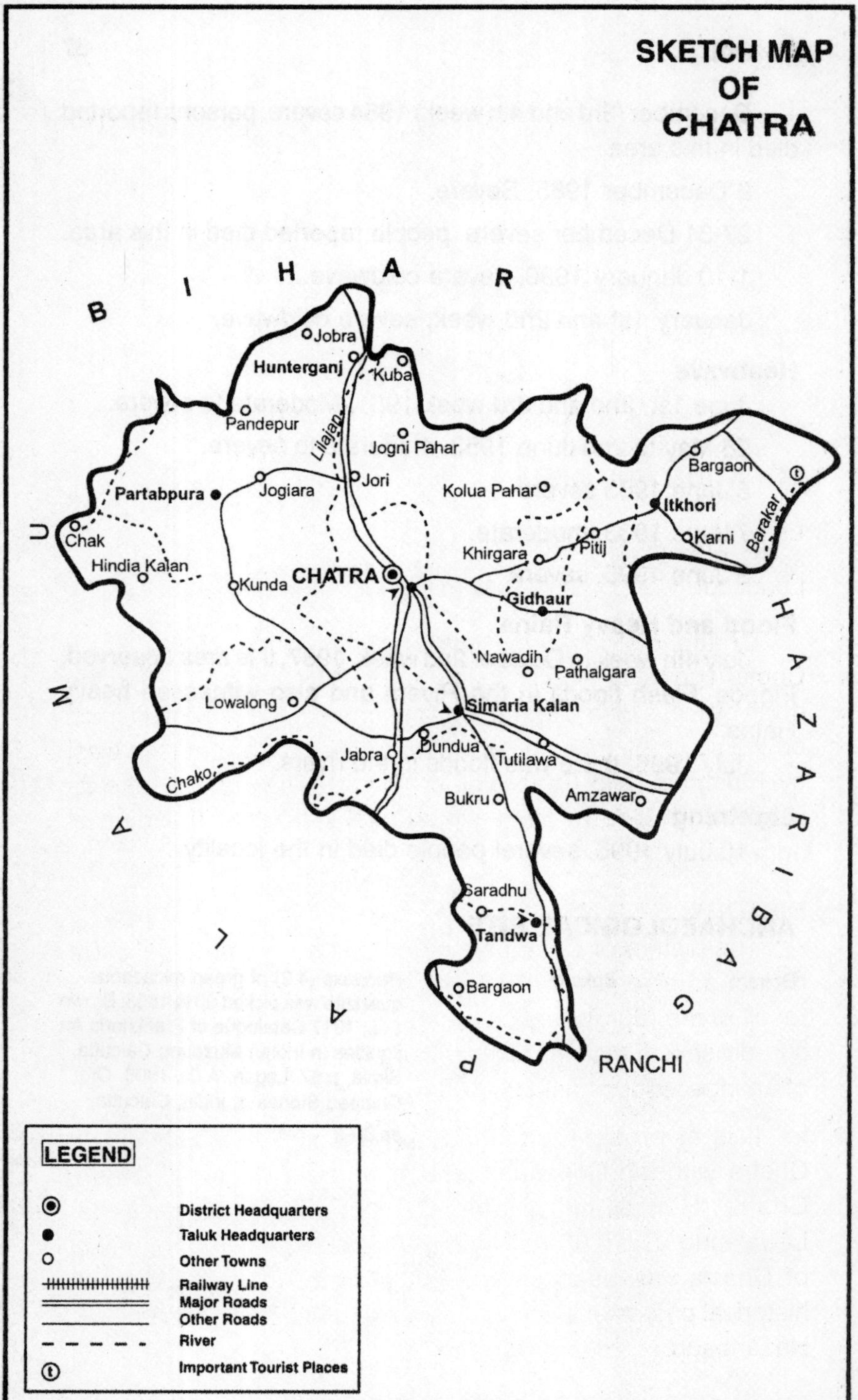

CHATRA

LOCATION AND AREA

Latitude : 23.6° North to 24.5° North

Longitude : 84.5°East to 85.3° East

Chatra district forms north-eastern parts of the North Chotanagpur Division of Jharkhand state. It is bounded on the north by Gaya district (Bihar), on the east by Hazaribagh district, on the south by Palamau and Ranchi Districts and on the west by Palamau, and Gaya district (Bihar). The district take its name from Chatra town which is the seat of the district administration.

HISTORY

The district of Chatra has been carved out as a separate district as a result of trifurcation of Hazaribagh district. As a result of the reorganisation of this district, Chatra which was a sub-division of erstwhile Hazaribagh district attained the status of an independent district.

It is at present comprised of one sub-division namely Chatra with ten Community Development Blocks viz. Itkhori, Chatra, Hunterganj, Pratappur, Simaria Tandwa, Kunda, Lawalaung, Gidhaur, Palhalgora. As stated above, the district of Chatra has been carved out of Hazaribagh district, its historical past is one and the same as of its parent district i.e., Hazaribagh.

POPULATION (GENERAL, SC/ST)

Total population of the district as per 2001 Census is 790,680 persons of which 748,690 persons are retained from rural areas and the remaining 41,990 persons are retained from urban areas. The Scheduled Castes and Scheduled Tribes population of this district as per 1991 census are 198,668 persons and 23,487 persons respectively.

The Community Development Block-wise, population distribution with sex ratio and literacy rate of this district is given below:

	Sex ratio		Literacy rate		Population	
C.D. Block	Rural	Urban	Rural	Urban	Rural	Urban
CHATRA DISTRICT	**969**	**880**	**41.29**	**78.53**	**784690**	**41990**
Hunterganj	971	-	39.10	-	143,464	-
Pratappur	945	-	36.79	-	18,771	-
Kunda	922	-	25.15	-	22,619	-
Lawalaung	929	-	28.30	-	38,770	-
Chatra	955	880	42.22	78.53	127,133	41,990
Itkhori	1,036	-	49.74	-	105,200	-
Gidhaur	962	-	45.73	-	30,775	-
Pathalgora	1,004	-	32.75	-	25,716	-
Simaria	963	-	47.09	-	84,572	-
Tandwa	962	-	43.14	-	81,170	-

LANGUAGES AND RELIGION

Main languages spoken in the district are Hindi and Urdu.

Religion-wise breakup of population of this district is not available separately, because it was the part of Hazaribagh district at the time of census taking. The combined figures in this regard are provided in case of its parent district.

GEOGRAPHY AND PHYSICAL FEATURES

Annual Rainfall : 1096 mm

Temperature : Max. 43°C and Min. 5°C

The Chatra district forms part of Chotanagpur plateau. It is the region of plateaus, residual hills and inter-mountain valleys, which occupy the southern half of the Jharkhand state. The district is covered with forests which is distributed almost uniformly throughout the district. The famous species of trees found in the jungles of this district are Sal, Khair, Salai, Simul, Mahua, Palas, Kusum, Kend, Asam, Piar, Bhelwa and Bamboo.

RIVERS, CANALS AND WATERWAYS

Garhi or Tandwa is the main river of this district. Another river called Lilajan run through a narrow gorge near the village Babaru, at a distance of 13 kms south-west of Chatra town. Goa waterfall is found in the village Jaled, 6 kms west of Chatra. The Damodar river rises in the Kharamput hill in Palamau joins the Garhi or Tandwa river near its entrance into the district where its bed is 1326 feet above sea level.

TOWNS, C.D. BLOCKS AND SUB-DIVISIONS

The district is comprised of one sub-division namely Chatra and ten Community Development Blocks namely Hunterganj, Pratappur, Kunda, Lawalaung, Chatra, Itkhori, Gidhaur, Pathalgora, Simaria, Tandwa. It has only one town.

COMMUNICATIONS

Chatra district is well connected by road transport. The Grand Trunk Road or National Highway No.2 forms some part of north-east boundary of the district of Itkhari Community Development Block. The State Highway is Simaria-Hazaribagh. The important Zila Parishad roads are Chatra-Katkamsandi-Hazaribagh and Tandwa-Hazaribagh.

The district headquarters, i.e. Chatra is not directly connected by rail.

AGRICULTURE AND IRRIGATION

Paddy is the main crop of the district. Bajra and maize are

the other important crops. Among the pulses, Arhar is grown in good quantity. The cash crop like sugarcane is grown in a small area.

In Chatra district, due to hilly area, there is not much scope for exploitation of surface water. Ground water exploitation has its limitation because deep boring was also not possible due to hard rocks. Tank irrigation is not very popular. The irrigational facilities have been extended in the district in the recent years through a number of medium and minor irrigation schemes, rahat, pumps, electric pumps, open boring, tube wells and hand-pumps. The possibility of implementing dug-well scheme has increased due to the subsidy being given under IRD scheme by the SFDA and financing by banks to the individual farmers. Likewise, the subsidy for pumping sets are also given by the SFDA and loans are being advanced on easy terms to the cultivators by the banks.

ANIMAL HUSBANDRY

The livestock population of the district includes cows, bulls, bullocks, buffaloes, sheep, goats and pigs. Bullocks and buffaloes are of small stature. They are not much suitable for hard ploughing. The bulls are also of inferior strain.

INDUSTRIES

The district is industrially backward, as there is no large or medium scale industry at present which is worth to be mentioned. This district is, however, rich in Mica, a mineral of economic importance. One of the rich Mica mines of the state is located in Chatra sub-division.

HANDICRAFTS

Cane and Bamboo

This area is generally noted for its bamboo work. The use of cut bamboo as a container, to drink water is an ancient practice, as also simple scoops for kitchen use. Large containers for storing grains are a common sight.

Textiles (embroidered)

In India embroidery has a hoary past and there is mention of needles for embroidery in very ancient books.

Woodwork

India has a luxuriant range in wood for each locale has its own particular properties of grain and strength. The discerning woodwork has evolved styles and items that particular types of wood lend themselves to, providing considerable range in wood work.

MINERALS AND ORES OCCURRENCES

Alkaline Earth

Occurrence of Alkaline Earth near MURPA (23.7, 84.9) and CHAMARGARA (23.8, 85.5) efflorescences occur on the eastern bank of the Khuri Nadi.

Antimony

Occurrence of Antimony near to Hisatu.

Coal

At Itkhuri (24.3, 85.2), after survey of the area, Mr. D.K. Chandra reports the occurrence of four coal seams in the Itkhuri coal field. The lowest seam (seam IV) is more shally than carbonaceous. Seam I and II are too thin to be taken into account, where as seam II, (1 ft. 4 inches to 2 ft. in thickness shows 37.84 to 40.58 per cent of fixed carbon. The poor thickness of this seam as well as its poor quality does not warrant its working. Coals seams are found in both the Barakar and Raniganj beds. A large number of seams are known to occur, some over 72 ft. thick.

During the re-survey of the North Karanpura coal field, Mr. Pijush Ghosh traced nine coal seams in the Barakars exposed in the *nala,* one mile east of Pindarkom. (23.8, 84.8) and four more coal outcrops in a *nala* 3 miles east of Pindarkom.

Coal seams of Barakar series, which are of economic value and vary in thickness from 6 to 25 ft. are exposed in the BARKI *nala* east of KISHUNPUR village (23.9, 85.1). The coal from these seams in non-cocking in character but is of high volatile nature.

Limestone

Limestone occurs in extensive deposits near the RAY (23.7; 85.1). HOSIR (23.7, 85.1) area and in the BABHANE (23.7, 85.1) area. KHALARI (23.6, 85) area. The lime stones are of cement grade and are at present being exploited for cement manufacture at Khalari. Impure portion of the'limestone bands are beneficiated here by froath flotation to reduce the content of insolubles in it.

TRADE. COMMERCE AND EXPORT

The following table provides information on most important commodities manufactured, exported from and imported in the town of this district. It also indicates number of banks available in Chatra town.

Name of the town	*Most important commodities*			*Banks*
	Manufactured	*Exported*	*Imported*	
Chatra	Katha, Bidi and Charcoal	Bidi, Timber and Gums	Rice, Wheat and Mustard oil	3

TOURISM

A brief account on the places of tourist interest in the district is given below:

Goa waterfall is situated near the village Jaled at a distance of about 6 kms west of Chatra. It is of a considerable scenic beauty and draws tourists/visitors.

Khaya Banaru. The river Lilajan passes through a narrow gorge at this place, near village Babaru, 13 kms south-west of Chatra town. It is a place of scenic beauty and tourist interest.

Kolhua hill. The hill, situated about 9 kms south-west of

Hunterganj, is noted for the annual fairs held on the occasions of Basant Panchmi and Ramnavami.

Kunda Fort. Remains of this historic fort lie in village Kunda, situated about 14 kms south of Pratappur. The village used to be the headquarters of the Kunda Zamindar family in the Muslim period. There is a Siva temple near the ruins, around which an annual fair is held on the occasion of Shivratri. It is situated amid forest and is noted for its production of catechu and lac.

FAIRS AND FESTIVALS

Important fairs and melas organised in various parts of the district are mentioned below:

Basant Panchmi mela, Shivratri mela, Dussehra mela, Makar Sankranti mela, Ramnavmi fair and Kartik Purnima mela.

EDUCATION

The following table gives details on types, categories of educational institutions including public libraries available in Chatra, town, As it may ,be seen from the table the district has no stadium:

Name of the town	*Educational institutions*	*Stadia*	*Public libraries, including reading rooms*
Chatra	Secnodary/Matriculation Schools (2), Junior Secondary and Middle Schools (8), Primary Schools (8)	—	PL : 1

COLLEGES (2000)

Chatra College Chatra, (Established 1962) Enrolment 2198 Teachers 20. (Constituent College)

R N M College, Hanterganj (Affiliated College)

(Above named colleges belong to Vinobabhave university)

MEDICAL

The table given below furnishes information regarding availability of medical facility in Chatra town of the district including that of beds facility.

Name of the towns	*Medical institutions*	*Number of Beds*
Chatra	Hospital (1)	21

ADMINISTRATION

(i) Administrative Divisions

Sub-division: Chatra.

Community development blocks : Itkhori, Chatra, Hunterganj, Pratappur, Simaria, Tandwa, Kunda, Lawalaung, Gidhaur, Pathalgora.

Towns and Urban Agglomerations with their Population, Sexratio, Decadal growth and Literacy rate (2001)

Town	Population	Percentage Decadal growth 1991-2001	Sex Ratio	Literacy Rate
Chatra (M)	41,990	34.81	880	78.53

(ii) Parliamentary Constituencies and Assembly Segments

No. and Name of Parliamentary Constituencies:
44–Chatra and 48–Hazaribagh

No. & Name of Assembly Segments **:**

Chatra

264. Chatra—Chatra, Pratappur and Hunterganj police stations in Chatra sub-division.

Hazaribagh

265. Simaria (SC)—Simaria Itkhori and Tandwa police stations in Chatra sub-divions.

The community wise breakup OBE in Chatra is Muslims (12 per cent), Scheduled Castes (32 per cent), Scheduled Tribes (9 per cent), Ahirs (13 per cent), and Koeris (5 per cent). Others with sizable presence are Rajputs, Brahmins, Telis and Kurmis. Of the Scheduled Castes, the most notable numbers come from Bhuiyas (13 per cent), Chamars (6 per cent) and Dosadhs (6 per cent). Oraons (4 per cent) and Kharwars (3 per cent) are the principal constituents of the Scheduled Tribes.

OBSERVATIONAL ORGANISATION

Seismological Organization

It is located at Chatra town. The data from this observatory is used for routine determination of epicentre of earthquakes, preparations of bulletins, special study and research. The headquarters of Seismological Organization located at New Delhi.

DISASTROUS WEATHER EVENTS

January 1981, Moderate.
29-30 November, 1982.
4-10 December 1982.
2-14 January, 1983 Moderate to severe.
December 3rd and 4th week severe.
2-3 January 1985, severe.
9-14 January 1985, severe.
2 January, 1986, severe.
22-25 January 1987, severe.
January 1st week 1988, severe.
13-16 January 1989, severe.
1-10 January 1990, severe coldwave.
January 1st and 2nd week 1992 severe coldwave.
11 January 1995, severe

Heatwave

June 1st 2nd and 3rd week 1981, moderate to severe.
1-7 July 1982, moderate to severe.
6 June 1983, severe.

7 June 1983, moderate.

2-3 June 1985 severe.

Floods and Heavy Rains

July 4th week to October 2nd week 1987, there was heavy rains and in some areas there was flood.

Thunderstorm

16 June 1993, severe, large number of trees, electric poles uprooted.

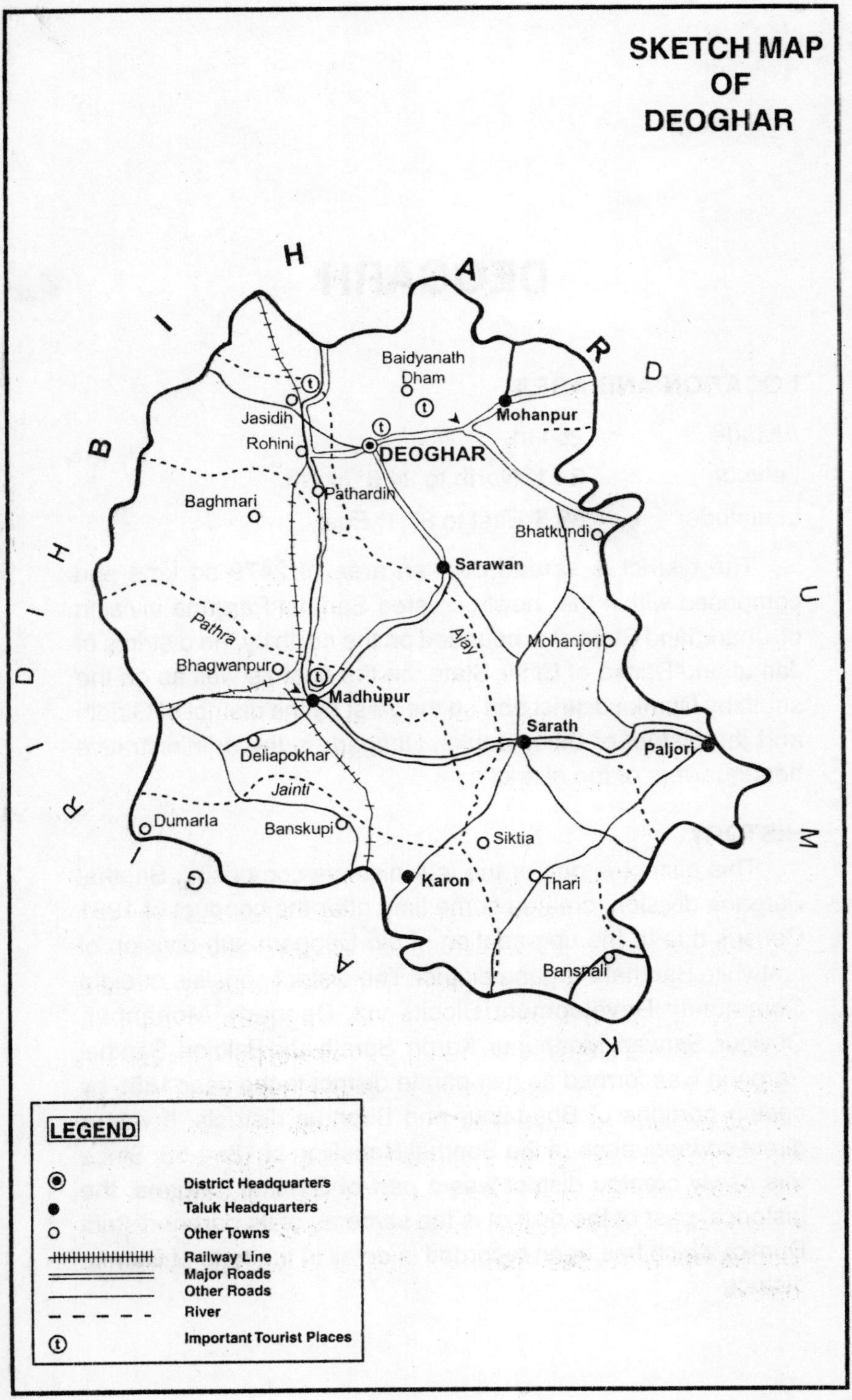

SKETCH MAP OF DEOGHAR
B I H A R
G I R I D I H
D U M K A
Baidyanath Dham
Jasidih
Rohini
DEOGHAR
Mohanpur
Pathardih
Baghmari
Bhatkundi
Sarawan
Pathra
Ajay
Mohanjori
Bhagwanpur
Madhupur
Sarath
Paljori
Deliapokhar
Jainti
Dumarla
Banskupi
Siktia
Karon
Thari
Bansnali
LEGEND
District Headquarters
Taluk Headquarters
Other Towns
Railway Line
Major Roads
Other Roads
River
Important Tourist Places

DEOGARH

LOCATION AND AREA

Altitude	:	264 m.
Latitude	:	24.1° North to 24.6° North.
Longitude	:	86.5°East to 87.1° East

The district is spread over an area of 2479 sq kms and comprised within the newly created Santhal Pargana division of Jharkhand State. It is bounded on the north by the districts of Jamui and Banka of Bihar State, on the east as well as on the south by Dumka district and on the west by the district of Giridih and the district of Bihar Banka. Deogarh is the administrative headquarters of the district.

HISTORY

This district is one of the four districts comprising Santhal Pargana division, created some time after the conduct of 1981 Census due to the upgradation of old Deogarh sub-division of erstwhile Santhal Pargana district. The district consists of eight Community Development Blocks viz. Deogarh, Mohanpur, Devipur, Sarwan, Madhupur, Karon, Sarath and Palojori. Santhal Pargana was formed as a separate district in the year 1855 by ceding portions of Bhagalpur and Birbhum districts. It was a direct consequence of the Santhal Rebellion of 1854-55. Since this newly created district was a part of Santhal Pargana, the historical past of the district is the same as of its parent district Dumka which has been recorded in detail in the note of Dumka district.

POPULATION (GENERAL, SC/ST)

Total population of the district according to 2001 Census is 1,161,370 persons, comprising of 606688 males and 554,682 females. Rural population of the district is 1,001,520 persons (520,048) males and 481,472 females) and urban population is 159,850 persons (86,640 males and 73,210 females).

The Community Development Block-wise population distribution with sex ratio and literacy rate of thus district is given below:

C.D. Block	Sex ratio		Literacy rate		Population	
	Rural	Urban	Rural	Urban	Rural	Urban
DEOGARH DISTRICT	**926**	**845**	**45.06**	**82.23**	**1001520**	**159850**
Deoghar	902	832	50.88	85.00	143,530	112,501
Mohanpur	926	-	43.47	-	140,449	-
Sarwan	932	-	43.91	-	128,872	-
Devipur	914	-	40.18	-	84,650	-
Madhupur	924	876	44.47	75.37	120,401	47,349
Karon	937	-	43.49	-	119,474	-
Sarath	920	-	48.04	-	136,880	-
Palojori	953	-	43.45	-	127,264	-

The Scheduled Castes and Scheduled Tribes population of the district as per 1991 census is 115,697 persons and 119085 persons respectively. The rural-urban breakup of this population is indicated below:

Rural	(i)	Scheduled Castes	:	105165
	(ii)	Scheduled Tribes	:	116368
Urban	(i)	Scheduled Castes	:	10532
	(ii)	Scheduled Tribes	:	2717

The decennial growth rate of population of the district as a whole in relation to the state between the period 1991 and 2001 is presented below:

State/ District	*Decenntal growth rate of population (per cent) 1991-2001*		
	Total	*Rural*	*Urban*
Jharkhand	23.49	21.62	28.99
Deogarh	24.46	23.96	27.72

LANGUAGES AND RELIGION

Hindi is the principal language spoken in the district.

Religion-wise breakup of population is indicated below as per 1991 census:

Hindus: 762990. Muslims: 167122. Christians: 2730. Sikhs: 76. Buddhists: 35, J ains: 121, Other religions and persuasions: 7. Religions not stated: 32.

GEOGRAPHY AND PHYSICAL FEATURES

Annual Rainfall : 1239 mm

Temperature : Max. 37.70°C and Min. 13.70°C

The area comprised in Deogarh district consists of uplands, undulations, long ridges and depressions. This area has plenty of fertile lands and is intensively cultivated. In the district, these are high hills with lofty peaks like Tieur (2505 ft) and Phuljore (2311 ft). The main line of the Eastern Railway traverses this plateau some 1000 ft high right from its entry into the district upto a little beyond Jasidih junction.

RIVERS, CANALS AND WATERWAYS

Mor and Ajai are the important rivers of Deogarh district. The river Mor, also known as Murakhi or Mayurakshi originates in the Tieur hills and flows through the central portion of Dumka in a south-easterly direction. Debouncing from the hills in south Munger, river Ajai journeys through Deogarh and Jamtara and joins the river Bhagirathi finally near Katwa in Murshidabad district of West Bengal. Other rivers in the district lying east of the Rajmahal hill ranges are Gumani, Bansloi, Palsi and Brahmani

TOWNS, VILLAGES AND AMENITIES

The district is at present comprises of 2 sub-divisions, 8 Community Development Blocks. It has 3 towns and 2704 villages (2327 inhabited villages and 377 uninhabited villages).

The urban population of the district as percentage of total

population in the census years 1991 and 2001 is indicated below. It also shows the sex ratio (females per 1000 males) and density (population per sq km) in the urban population of the dtstrict in relation to the state :

State/ District	*Urban population as percentage of total population*	*Sex ratio, 2001 (Females per 1000 males)*			*Density (Population per sq km)*
	2001	*Total*	*Rural*	*Urban*	
Jharkhand	22.25	941	963	870	338
Deogarh	13.76	914	926	845	468

Amenities

Number (With percentage) of villages having one or more amenities in the district as per 1991 census is given as follows:

Sl. No.	*Amenities*	*Number of inhabited villages*	*Percentage*
1.	Education	919	39.49
2.	Medical	213	9.15
3.	Drinking Water	2327	100.00
4.	Post and Telegraph	127	5.46
5.	Market/Hat	84	3.61
6.	Communications	348	14.95
7.	Approach by Pucca Road	236	10.14
8.	Power Supply	473	20.24

COMMUNICATIONS

The district is well connected by road transport from the neighbouring districts. All the block headquarters are also interlinked with pucca roads. However, as regards railway communication, this district is still deprived of the adequate facility. The main line of the Eastern Railway traverses close to the south-western boundary of the district, Baidyanath Dham station is the railway terminus. Jasidih which is on the main line of Eastern Railway is the changing junction from where a line branches off to

Baidyanath Dham at a distance of 2 kms only. No regular air transport services operate from the Deogarh though a small landing ground is located there. This landing ground is generally used for small planes belonging to the state government.

AGRICULTURE AND IRRIGATION

The district is predominantly agricultural in character. Kharif and Rabi are the main agricultural seasons in the district. Paddy is the main crop in recent years to utilise the river resources. the Mayurakshi Left Bank Canal Scheme being the important canal system commissioned. The most common source of irrigation is well at present in the district.

ANIMAL HUSBANDRY

Cows, buffaloes, sheep, goats and pigs are the main livestock of the district. Poultry is an important subsidiary occupation of the tribals residing in this district.

There are a number of veterinary hospitals and dispensaries spread over the entire district. Treatment, prevention and suppression of diseases of the livestock are the main functions of the veterinary institutions.

INDUSTRIES

The large industrial establishments set up in the districts are mentioned below:

1. Pharmaceutical Works of Dabur Pvt. Ltd. near Deogarh
2. Bihar Silicate Works, Madhupur.
3. Railway Wagon Factory, Jasidih.

Besides the above, a number of small-scale industries have also been set up in the district. With the establishment of an industrial estate at Jasidih, the district is expected to be industrialised faster.

MINERALS AND ORES OCCURRENCES

Asbestos

Tremolite asbestos have been reported to occur near the villages of Ghogh (24.5, 86.6) and DHAWANI (24.5, 86.6) close to Jasidih.

Coal

At Jainti (24.1, 86.8). It covers an area of about 8 sq. km. about 9 km. south of Madhupur Railway station. P.K. Chatterjee reports that coal seams occurring in the Jainti coalfield vary in thickness between 4 and 7 ft. and the coar ranges in quality from third grade to 'selected' grade. The coal is also of coking nature.

Near SAHARJURI (24.1, 86.9). This small outlier of Gondwana rocks totalling 12 sq. miles occur around Saharjuri. According to P.K. Chatterjee two coal seams are worked in the Saharjuri coalfield. Their thickness varies from 18 to 25 ft. and the coal ranges in quality from the lowest grade to second grade.

Copper

Near Bairukhi, the ore forms a red or silver coloured mass consisting of a mixture of cuprite, chalcopyrite and tetrahedrite with green carbonate of copper and galena. According to mallet, the ore occurs in a discontinuous band of termolite-schist, varying in width from a few inches to 6 or 8 ft. The veins had been followed to a depth of over 150 ft.

Lead and Silver

The copper-ores at this place were found associated with galena and cupro-plumbite. It obtained 154 grs of silver from 14 lb of the copper-ores. The deposit of lead-ore is distinct from that of copper and is situated mostly in the south portion.

TRADE, COMMERCE AND EXPORT

The chief imports of the district are fish, sugar, wheat, kendu leaves and tobacco, cloth and agricultural goods. The items of exports are jack fruits, pera, iron materials, dabar medicines, bidi, glass and phelspar stone. The chief centres of wholesale business in the district are Deogarh, Jasidih and Madhupur. The table given below lists the most important commodities manufactured, exported from and imported in the towns of this district.

Name of the town	Most important commodities		
	Manufactured	Exported	Imported
Deogarh	Pera, Hand-made Iron materials,	Jack Fruits, Pera, Iron Materials Rice	Fish, Sugar, Wheat
Jasidih	Dabar Medicines	Jack Fruits, Pattal, Dabar Medicines	—
Madhupur	Porcelain insulator, Glass, Hair Oil	Bidi, Glass, Phelspar stone	Kendu leaves and Cloth, Tobacco, Agricultural goods

Number of banks in the town of Deogarh district: Deogarh: 8, Jasidih: 1, Madhupur: 3.

TOURISM

Bakulia. It is a picnic spot situated about 10 kms west of Madhupur. It is famous for its waterfall.

Burhai. The village is located in Madhupur block and is situated about 13 kms from Jagdishpur railway station on the Madhupur-Giridih branch line. of Eastern Railway. It is famous for Burheshwari temple. There is a large congregation of pilgrims during the Newan mela held in the month of Agralaya (November-December). The place is also noted for its scenic beauty and finds of felspar and quartz.

Domohani. The village belongs to Sarat block. It is famous for the temple of Lord Shiva which is site of a big fair held during Paush Sankranti.

Karo. The village is located 8 kms north of Karmatanr railway station on the main line of the Eastern Railway between Madhupur and Jamtara. It is the headquarters of Karon block. There is an ancient temple of Lord Shiva, said to have been built by the Great almoner Karna of the Mahabharat fame. There is another old temple in a tank.

Deogarh. Deogarh is one of the important towns and administrative headquarters of the district. The town has a number of religious and historical places and health resorts of tourist interest. The prominent among them are detailed below:

Baidyanath Temple—Deogarh town is famous for the temple of Lord Baidyanath and is a well-known place of pilgrimage for Hindus since ancient times. Its sanctity is testified by the countless pilgrims who visit it every year, and its antiquity is traced back in some of the Puranas to the Treta Yuga or the second age of the world.

Within the precincts of the temple, there are the following 12 temples, dedicated to different Gods, including Lord Mahadeva.

They are (a) Baidyanath (b) Parvati (c) Lakshmi Narayan (d) Tara (e) Kali (f) Ganesha (g) Sun (h) Saraswati (i) Ramchandra U) Devi (k) Annapurna and (l) Anand Bhairava.

The Balanand Ashram—It was founded by Shri Balanand Brahmachari, a Yogi of Maharashtrian origin who died at Deogarh in 1937. The Ashram has temples of Baleshwar Mahadeva and Baleshwari Devi.

Jugal Mandir—It is also known as the Naulakha Mandir, implying a temple built at a cost of Rs 9 lakh. It is a beautiful, well-built temple dedicated to Lord Krishna and has a nice garden. Shrimati Charushila Devi met the entire cost of its construction.

Lila Mandir—It is located at a distance of 5 kms from Deogarh on Deogarh-Dumka road. The temple is a double storeyed building. It was established by Thakur Daya Nand Deo in 1921, who was also the founder of the Arunachal Mission. The Samadhi of the founder is in the temple hall where his disciples sing devotional songs and receive preachings.

Kundeshwari Temple—The temple has statues of Shakti and Navagrahas. The temple is located in a ditch (Kunda) 5 kms away from the town.

Trikutachal Ashram— The Ashram is located in the Trikut Hills. It is located about 18 kms east of Deogarh on the Dumka-Deogarh road. The Ashram is located in the caves and Acharya lives there. This Ashram is also managed by Arunachal Mission which stands for universal spiritual regeneration and for world peace and brotherhood.

Tapovan—This is a hillock about 10 kms south-east of Deogarh. It contains a temple of Lord Shiva. There are caves in the hill which have since been plastered. Balan and Brahmachari used to stay here.

Besides its having religious importance, Deogarh has also the reputation of being a health resort.

FAIRS AND FESTIVALS

Important fairs and melas organised in different parts of this district are mentioned below:

Gopastami mela, Dussehra mela, Makar Sankranti mela, Nawan mela, Shivratri mela and Durga Puja.

The most important seasonal fairs held at Deogarh are on the occasions of Shivaratri, Shravana Sombari and Shri Panchami.

EDUCATION

According to 2001 Census, total literates (excluding the population in the age group of 0-6 years) is 475,684 persons. Of these, 331,435 are males and 144,249 are females. In the rural areas of the district 361,803 persons (263,823 males and 97,980 females) are literates and in urban areas 113,881 persons (67,612 males and 46,269 females) are literates. The rate of literacy of this population to the total population, excluding 0-6 years age group according to 1991 census is shown below:

	Persons	*Males*	*Females*
Total	37.92	54.12	19.74
Rural	32.11	49.19	13.20
Urban	73.00	82.52	61.37

There are as many as 919 villages accounting for 39.49 per cent of the total number of inhabited villages in the district where educational facility is available. Primary and middle schools are available in the towns. The following table gives the details of various types of educational institutions available in towns of this district including the number of Stadia and Public libraries.

Name of the towns	*Educational institutions*	*Stadia*	*Public libraries including reading rooms*
Deogarh	Shorthand and Typing Training Institute, Higher Secondary/ Intermediate School, 5 Secondary/Matriculation Schools. 13 Junior Secondary and Middle Schools.	—	PL : 3
Jasidih	One Secondary/Matriculation School and four Junior Secondary and Middle Schools.	—	—
Madhupur	One Shorthand and Typing Training Institutes, 3 Secondary/ Matriculation and 4 Junior Secondary and Middle Schools.	—	PL : 5

UNIVERSITY AND COLLEGES

Amardyuti Satsang College, Deogarh (Established 1970) Enrolment 3468, Teachers 38. (Constituent College).

Deogarh College, Deogarh, (Established 1955), Enrolment 285, Teachers 55. (Constituent College)

Rama Devi Bajila Mahila College, Deogarh (Established 1970), Enrolment 1059. (Constituent College).

Madhupur College, Madhupur (Established 1970), Enrolment 881, Teachers 17.

Dr J.N. Mishra College, Jasidih (Established 1979), Enrolment 463, Teachers 35.

Teachers Training College. Deogarh.

(Above named colleges belong to Siddhu Kanhu University, Established 1992).

MEDICAL

The availability of medical facility in the villages is considerably low as only 9.15 per cent villages in the district have got it. The table given below furnishes information regarding various types of medical institutlons available in the towns of this district:

Name of the Towns	*Medical institutions*	*Number of Beds*
Deogarh	Hospital (1) :	80
	Dispensary (14) :	—
	T.B. Clinic (1) :	10
	Family Planning Centre (1) :	—
	Nursing Home (1) :	10
Jasidih	Hospital (1) :	8
	Dispensary (3) :	—
	Family Planning Centre (1) :	—
Madhupur	Hospital (3) :	50
	Dispensary (2) :	—

ADMINISTRATION

(i) Administrative Divisions :

Sub-divisions : Deogarh, Madhupur.

Community Development Blocks: Deogarh, Devipur, Mohanpur, Sarwan, Madhupur, Koran, Sarath, Palojori.

Towns and Urban Agglomerations with their Population, Sexratio, Decadal growth and Literacy rate (2001)

DEOGHAR UA

Deoghar (M)
Jasidih (NA)

Town	Population	Percentage Decadal growth 1991-2001	Sex Ratio	Literacy Rate
Deoghar (M)	98,372	28.79	830	86.26
Jasidih (NA)	14,129	48.38	848	76.02
Madhupur (M)	47,349	20.61	876	75.37

No. and Name of Parliamentary Constituencies:

27–Dumka (ST); 28–Godda; 29–Banka

No. and Name of Assembly Segments :

Dumka

156. Sarath—Sarath and Palojori police stations in Deoghar sub-division; and G.Ps. Karmatanr, Sahajpur, Pindari, Lakhanpur, Rataniya, Rampurbhitra and Kajra in Jamtara police station in Jamtara sub- division.

Godda

157. Madhupur—Madhupur and Karon police stations and G .Ps. Kusmil. Chanddih, Pathra and Basbariya in Jasidih police station in Deoghar sub-division.

Banka

158. Deoghar (SC) : Deoghar town Mohanpur police station in Deoghar subdivision Jasideh Police Station (Excluding Kushmel, Chanddih, Palhra and Baswaria Village Panchayat.)

OBSERVATIONAL ORGANIZATION

INSAT Data Collection Platform:

Latitude	:	24.5° North
Longitude	:	86.7° East
Altitude	:	285 m
Date of starting	:	June 1985

This instrument lies under Flood meteorological offices. Asansol and located in

Latitude	:	24.5° North
Longitude	:	86.7 East
Altitude	:	264 m
Date of starting	:	12.7.1964

DISASTROUS WEATHER EVENTS

Coldwave

1st January 1982, moderate.
29-30 November 1982, severe.
4-10 December 1982, severe.
2-14 January 1983, severe.
December 3rd and 4th week 1984 severe.
27-31 December 1989, severe, cattle heads period and people reported killed.
1-10 January 1990, severe, cattle heads perished and standing crop damaged.
January 1st and 2nd week 1992, severe, many people killed and cattle heads perished.
Jan. (1st and 2nd week) 1992, severe, crops damaged, cattleheads perished, people reported killed.

Heatwave:

On 6th June 1983, there was severe heatwave in this area, people reported killed, cattleheads perished.
On 7th June 1983, this area witnessed moderate type heatwave, resulted damage to the standing crops and cattleheads perished.

Squall:

On 28th April 1990, there was severe squall, surface wind speed was above 80 kms per hour, one boy died and 3 injured.

Thunderstorm:

On 22nd May 1988, severe thunderstorm reported in this area, several houses, trees and telephone pole reported damage.

ARCHAEOLOGICAL SITE

Deoghar	Dt Deoghar	Early Stone Age (Lower Palaeolithic (4.2) tools were found in thebed of the river Karnakolajore. IAR 1963-4.

DISTRIBUTION OF *SCHEDULED CASTE* POPULATION BY SEX DISTRICTWISE (1991)

	POPULATION		
	Total	Males	Females
DEOGHAR			
	1,15,697	60,254	55,443
Bantar	50	31	19
Bauri	3,511	1,749	1,762
Bhogta	364	197	167
Bhuiya	1,906	964	942
Chamar, Mochi	54,129	28,273	25,856
Chaupal	2	2	0
Dabgar	28	0	28
Dhobi	4,136	2,232	1,904
Dom, Dhangad	15,115	7,838	7,277
Dusadh, Dhari, Dharhi	5,827	3,052	2,775
Ghasi	73	45	28
Halalkhor	66	46	20
Hari, Mehtar, Bhangi	2,042	1,148	894
Kanjar	9	9	0
Kurariar	101	57	44
Lalbegi	4	4	0
Musahar	11,028	5,624	5,404
Nat	24	14	10
Pan, Sawasi	37	18	19
Pasi	6,507	3,416	3,091
Rajwar	5,916	3,176	2,740
Turi	4,807	2,354	2,453
Unclassified	15	5	10

DISTRIBUTION OF *SCHEDULED TRIBE* POPULATION BY SEX DISTRICTWISE (1991)

	POPULATION		
	Total	Males	Females
DEOGHAR			
	1,19,085	60,945	58,140
Baiga	31	6	25
Bedia	1	0	1
Bhumij	106	51	55
Birhor	20	10	10
Chick/Baraik	7	2	5
Gond	171	120	51
Gorait	25	23	2
Ho	13	13	0
Karmali	8	3	5
Kharia	141	67	74
Kharwar	654	301	353
Khond	1,051	631	420
Kisan	11	11	0
Kora	795	347	448
Korwa	142	51	91
Lohara, Lohra	2,842	1,371	1,471
Mahli	4,336	2,227	2,109
Mal Paharia	7,075	3,965	3,110
Munda	169	90	79
Oraon	224	135	89
Parhaiya	285	141	144
Santal	1,00,180	51,015	49,165
Sauria Paharia	588	286	302
Unclassified	210	79	131

SKETCH MAP OF DHANBAD

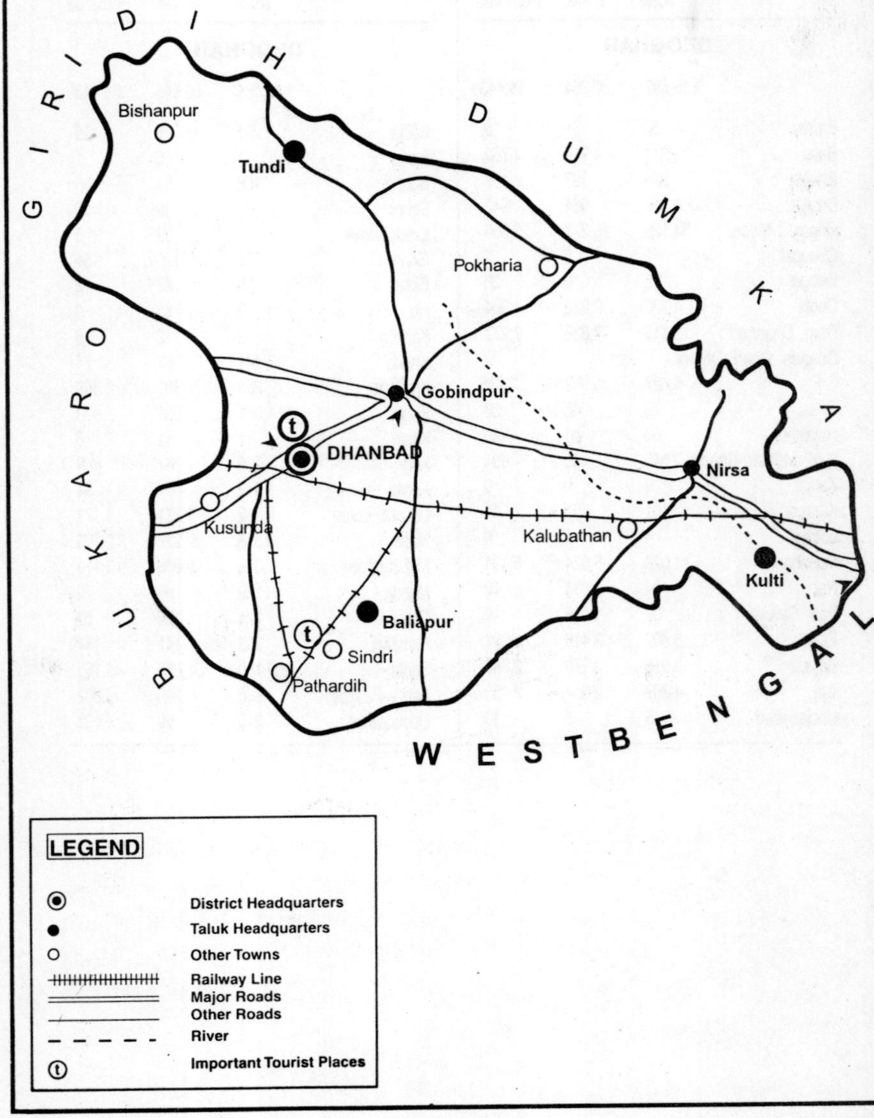

DHANBAD

LOCATION AND AREA

Altitude	:	258 m.
Latitude	:	23.6° North to 24.1° North.
Longitude	:	86.2° East to 86.8° East.

The district derives its name from Dhanbad the headquarters. There is, however, no authentic record to show how Dhanbad took its name. One of the theories popular among the public is that this area was famous for the growth of '*Baid Dham*' or *Bard* Paddy (Baid being a kind of paddy which ripens in October-November). Another far-fetched theory is that the name of Dhanbad is derived from Dhan, a Kolarian tribe that lived in this area. Baid has perhaps been taken from the Urdu word 'Abad' meaning occupied. The district was first known as Dhanbad (till 1st November 1956 Dhanbad was a sub-division of Manbhum district).The district is bounded on the west by Giridih and Bokaro, on the north by Giridih and Dumka and on the east and south by Purulia district of West Bengal.

HISTORY

Dhanbad district was constituted in 1956 by carving out the old Dhanbad subdivision and Chas and Chandankiyari police stations of the Sadar subdivision of the erstwhile Manbhum district. Its boundaries have remained virtually intact thereafter. The reorganisation of the districts in the state of Bihar which took place after 1971 did not affect the district of Dhanbad. Dhanbad Municipality is the chief town and the headquarters of the district.

The early history of the greater part of the Chotanagpur plateau is shrouded in mystery and that of Dhanbad district is particularly so. Details of even later periods are difficult to trace as the present district formed but a small and insignificant part of Manbhum. In the Settlement Report for Manbhum (1928), it has been stated that no rock inscriptions, copper plates or old coins were discovered and not a single document of copper plate or palm leaf was found in course of the Survey and Settlement operations. The oldest authentic documents produced were all on paper and barely even a hundred years old.

In view of these circumstances the District Gazetteer for Dhanbad (1964) merely reproduces the chapter on history in Settlement Report of 1928 which pertains to the entire district of Manbhum.

The earliest civilisation in the district was that of the Jains who are ascribed by Colonel Dalton to 500 or 600 B.C. The Saraks, who were the descendants of these Jains, were found in considerable number in the eastern part of the district as late as in 1928. The Jain civilisation was apparently superseded by the Brahmins before the seventh century A.D. The travel accounts of Hieun Tsang in the seventh century A.D. make mention of a powerful kingdom ruled by Sasanka, a persecutor of the Buddhists, which extended from Midnapur on the east to Surguja on the west. According to one view it is held that Mundari tribes occupied the area south of Bihar in Pliny's time. Brahmanical civilisation was at its prime in the tenth century. It was destroyed completely by the Bhumij, a Mundari tribe, although it is stated that the area occupied by the latter mainly extended to the south of the river Kasai in the area that is now largely contained in Purulia district of West Bengal.

During Akbar's reign in circa 1590, Raja Man Singh led his troops from Bhagalpur to Midnapur through Jharkhand and he might have passed through portions of Dhanbad. There are detailed accounts of the Panchet or Panchkote Estate which is now in Purulia district. Even when the district of Manbhum was acquired by the British in 1765, knowledge about the district scarcely extended beyond the Panchet Estate.

The history of the district during the early years of the British rule centred round a series of military operations to bring petty Zamindars or Chuars under control. In 1782-83 Major Crauford quelled the disturbances in Jharia. The Permanent Settlement was effected in 1796. By Regulation XVIII of 1805, the Jungle Mahals district was constituted into a separate magisterial charge with head- quarters at Bankura. The next 25 years were uneventful. In 1832 disturbances broke out on account of disputed succession in Barabhum in which only the southern parganas of Manbhum were involved. By Regulation XIII of 1833, the district of Jungle Mahals was broken up and a new district called Manbhum was constituted with headquarters at Manbazar which was transferred to Purulia in 1838.

In 1857, the Deputy Commissioner had to flee from Purulia on account of the insurrection of the garrison comprising sixty-four sepoys and twelve *sawars.* The garrison looted the treasury and released prisoners from the jail. They then marched off to Ranchi. The Court buildings and the Record Room at Purulia were burnt. The disturbances were, however, quelled eventually when the Deputy Commissioner returned with reinforcement from Raniganj about a month later.

Agrarian troubles between the Zamindar of Tundi and his Santal *raiyats* threatened the district in 1869 and 1870 but they were suitably warded off.

The people of Dhanbad did not lag behind in the struggle for freedom. The various movements under the leadership of Mahatma Gandhi were fully supported by the people of Dhanbad.

The district of Dhanbad bifurcated into two parts namely Dhanbad and Bokaro between the period 1991-96.

POPULATION (GENERAL, SC/ST)

Total population of district of Dhanbad according to 2001 census is 2,394,434 persons. Rural population of the district is 1,140,104 persons and urban population is 1,254,330 persons.

The Community Development Block-wise, population distribution with sex ratio and literacy rate of this district is given below:

	Sex ratio		Literacy rate		Population	
C.D. Block	Rural	Urban	Rural	Urban	Rural	Urban
DHANBAD DISTRICT	**909**	**844**	**58.71**	**75.20**	**1,140,104**	**1,254,330**
Tundi	959	-	45.77	-	123,824	-
Topchanchi	929	860	59.35	79.63	106,306	33,973
Baghmara-cum-katras	875	839	64.93	71.20	280,794	126,636
Gobindpur	925	858	54.00	76.25	193,168	8504
Dhanbad-cum-kenduadih-cum-Jagta	845	842	69.54	77.41	87,523	476,89
Jharia-cum-Jorapokhar-cum-Sindri	897	836	55.24	74.45	2292	472,687
Baliapur	926	-	60.70	-	105,551	-
Nirsa-cum-Chirkunda	921	873	56.43	72.55	240,646	136041

The Scheduled Castes and Scheduled Tribes population of the district as per 1991 census is 415614 persons and 225282 persons respectively. The rural-urban breakup of this population is indicated below:

Rural	(i) Scheduled Castes	:	220455
	(ii) Scheduled Tribes	:	174706
Urban	(i) Scheduled Castes	:	195159
	(ii) Scheduled Tribes	:	50576

The decennial growth rate of population of the district as a whole in relation to the state between the period 1991 and 2001 is presented below:

State/ District	Decennial growth rate of population (per cent) 1991-2001		
	Total	Rural	Urban
Jharkhand	23.19	21.62	28.99
Dhanbad	15.37	16.96	13.92

LANGUAGES AND RELIGION

Main languages spoken in the district are Hindi, Bengali, Puṇjabi and Urdu.

Religion wise breakup of population of the undivided district of Dhanbad is indicated below as per 1991 census:

Hindus: 2311881, Muslims: 328590, Christians: 12901, Sikhs: 13117, Buddhists: 265, Jains: 2890, Other religions and persuasions: 4963, Religions not stated: 44.

GEOGRAPHY AND PHYSICAL FEATURES

Annual Rainfall : 1636 mm
Temperature : Max. 44.40°C and Min. 7.60°C

The district can be divided into three broad natural divisions, *viz.* (i) the north and north-western portions consisting of the hilly region. (ii) the uplands containing coal mines and most of the industries and (iii) the remaining uplands and plains lying to the south of the Damodar river consisting of culturable flat lands and includes the Bokaro Steel Plant and the industrial-cum-mining complex surrounding it. The north and north-western division is separated for the entire length from the other two divisions by the Grand Trunk Road.

In the western middle part of the district are the Dhangi hills, situated in the strip falling between the Grand Trunk Road in the north and the Grand Chord Line of the Eastern Railway in the South. These hills extend from Pradhankhanta to Gobindpur, reaching a maximum altitude of 1256 feet at Dhangi. Further north, a branch of the Paraśnath hill runs through Topchanchi and Tundi, the highest point of 1500 feet being reached at Lalki. The southern part of the district is largely comprised of undulating land. The general slope is from west to east, the direction followed by the two major rivers, Damodar and Barakar.

Forests in the district are largely confined to the north, bordering on the districts of Giridih and Dumka. Some of the important trees in the forests are sal, sisoo, siris, palas, mahua, jamun, and simal. Bamboos are also common.

RIVERS, CANALS AND WATERWAYS

The Damodar is the most important river of the Chotanagpur plateau. It rises in Palamu and flows eastward between the plateaus of Ranchi and Hazaribagh. It is joined by the Bokaro, the Konar and the Barakar rivers. The Damodar enters Dhanbad district at its confluence with the Jamuria, a stream which marks the western boundary of Bokaro with Hazaribagh district. Further east, the Damodar is joined by the Katri river which rises in the foothills below Parasnath and traverses through the coalfield area. The Damodar flows for about 77 kms through the district being joined by the Barakar at its eastern border near Chirkunda. The Panchet Dam extending to roughly 6 kms is built on river Damodar. The hydal station there generates 40000 K.W. per hour.

The Barakar, which forms the northern boundary of the district, traverses about 77 kms in the district. It flows in south-westerly direction upto Durgapur and then south till it joins the Damodar near Chirkunda. The Maithan dam is located on this river about 13 kms off its confluence with the Damodar. Attached to it is the Maithan Power Station with a generating capacity of 60000 K.W.H.

TOWNS, VILLAGES AND AMENITIES

The district is at present comprised 1 sub-division. 8 Community Development Blocks. It has 35 towns and 1479 villages (1364 inhabited villages and 115 uninhabited villages).

The urban population of the district as percentage of total population in the census years 1991 and 2001 is indicated below. It also shows the sex ratio (females per 1000 males) and density (population per sq km) in the urban population of the district in relation to the state :

State/ District	Urban population as percentage of total population	Sex ratio, 2001 (Females per 1000 males)			Density (Population per sq km)
	2001	Total	Rural	Urban	
Jharkhand	22.25	941	963	870	338
Dhanbad	52.39	874	909	844	1168

Amenities

Number (with percentage) of villages having one or more amenities in undivided district of Dhanbad as per 1991 census is given below:

Sl. No.	Amenities	Number of inhabited villages	Percentage
1.	Education	997	72.77
2.	Medical	291	21.24
3.	Drinking Water	1370	21.24
4.	Post and Telegraph	166	12.12
5.	Market/Hat	78	5.69
6.	Communications	441	32.19
7.	Approach by Pucca Road	518	37.81
8.	Power Supply	543	39.64

COMMUNICATIONS

The district is well developed from the point of road communications. The Grand Trunk Road runs through the entire length of the district from west to east and divides it into two parts, i.e. one-third of the district to the north and two-thirds to the south. The area to the south is well served by roads as well as the railways whereas the northern portion, which consists of hills is deprived of adequate communication facility. The following are the roads maintained by the Public Works Department in the district.

Road	Length in kms
Grand Trunk Road (National Highway)	72
Gobindpur-Chas-Jamshedpur Road (upto Bengal border)	75
Gobindpur-Baliapur-Sindri road	24
Dhanbad-Pathardih-Sindri road	25.6
Raghunathpur-Chandankiyari-Chas road	31.6
Rajganj-Katras-Jamdiha road	19.6
Pathardih-Chandankiyari-Baramasia road	28.8
Giridih-Tundi-Gobindpur road	28
Jharia-Baltapur road	28

Most of the above roads are metalled. Besides the Public Works Department, a few roads in the district are also maintained by the Zila Parishad, the Dhanbad Municipality and the Forest Department.

The district is well served by railways. There is a network of railway lines running through colliery areas. Important among them being:

(i) *Kumardhubi-Gomoh Section*—It is a part of the Grand Chord section under the Eastern Railway. It connects Dhanbad with the Grand Chord mainline running from Howrah to Delhi via Assansol, Gomoh, Gaya and Mughal Sarai.

(ii) Pradhankhanta-Pathardih Section

(iii) Dhanbad-Phularitand Section

(iv) Dhanbad-Pathardih Section

(v) Sudamadih-Gomoh Section

Recently Dhanbad town has been connected with Patna, by two important rail connection, viz., the Patliputra Express and the Ganga Damodar Express.

Besides the above, there are other branch lines for carrying coal from one place of the district to another. The whole of the middle portion of the district is thus virtually infested with railways.

No river in the district is navigable as most of them are hill streams which remain *dry* except during the rains.

The district is not on the air route but there is a small landing ground about 3 kms. north of Dhanbad. There are several aerial ropeways used for transporting sand to different collieries.

AGRICULTURE AND IRRIGATION

Rice is the main crop of the district and covers the major portion of the gross areas own. Wheat is another important crop of the district. Among non-food crops sugarcane and oil seeds are most important although there is very small cultivation of them. The district's needs of vegetables and fruits are met from Ranchi, Gaya, Patna, Biharsharif, etc. The industrialisation of the district has resulted in non-agricultural use of even the cultivable lands.

The rivers and streams of the district are hilly in character and cannot be used for irrigation unless water is stored. The slope of the land is such that rain water quickly runs into the hill streams. The level of water in these streams subsides quickly after a spell of rain and most of streams *dry* almost completely after the rainy season. Wells are difficult and expensive to dig because of the presence of hard rock close to the surface. Bundhs and *Ahars* (artificial reservoirs) therefore, constitute the main source of the irrigation. Rain water is stored in *Ahars* or reservoirs and then led to the field by channels and subchannels. Uplands are not irrigated ordinarily.

Recently a number of medium and minor irrigation schemes have been taken up and executed in order to ensure a regular source of water supply. The schemes are intended more to supply assured irrigation to paddy crop.

ANIMAL HUSBANDRY

The livestock in this district is generally of a poor variety. Not much pasturage is available although there are strenches of jungles. There is no much popular response to improve the breed of the livestock. The development of the breed of cattle and buffaloes is essential for agriculutral activities and availability of adquate quality of milk. There has been a concerted effort on behalf of the state Government to tackle this problem by way of distribution of bulls of improved varieties. In order to improve the breed of cattle quickly and also at low cost, artificial insemination centres with sub-centres have been opened in the district. Distribution of frozen semen has also been introduced in the district.

There are a number of veterinary hospitals and dispensaries spread over the entire district. Treatment, prevention and suppression of diseases of the livestock are the main functions of veterinary institutions.

Cattle shows are sometimes organised and prizes in cash or kind are awarded with a view to encouraging the local breeders.

The aboriginals of the district keep poultry and derive a side-income. There is a great demand for good birds and eggs throughout the district. There is abundant scope for development of poultry farming.

The rivers, streams, low-lying fields where water accumulates in the rainy season, ponds and marshes, indicate a rich potentiality for fisheries in the district. A large number of tanks are kept reserved for rearing fish. The Fisheries Department of the state government has taken up a scheme for development of fisheries in the district.

In this district two types of boats, viz., (i) dug out canoes and (ii) plant built boats are used for catching fish in the Maithan and Panchet dams. Dug out canoes which ply in the rivers are stable and cheap. Plant built boats of various types are used in the strong current of large rivers like the Barakar and the Damodar. Small canoes are commonly used for catching hilsa, prawn, etc. Various types of nets and spears are used for catching fish.

The chief fish markets and trade centres in the district are at Jharia, Katras, Sindri, Chirkunda and Dhanbad. In Dhanbad town fish first goes to the wholesale fish market at Purana Bazar at Dhanbad and Jharia. From these markets fish is sent to retailers on auction basis.

INDUSTRIES

Dhanbad is the most industrialised district in the state of Jharkhand. The dominant industry of the district is coal mining and it is coal which has attracted and brought about a concentration of numerous other industries within its limits. The metallurgical coal of the Jharia coalfield within the district has given Dhanbad a very important place in tile industrial map of the nation.

Next in importance among the industries in this district is the Fertilisers and Chemicals Industry at Sindri and the Jharkhand State Superphosphate Factory, a govt. of Jharkhand undertaking. Another major industry in the district is the Refractory and Ceramic Industry. Among the few other large industrial establishments of the district, mention may be made of (i) Kumardhubi Fireclay and Silica Works Ltd., Kumardhubi (ii) Reliance Firebricks & Pottery Co. Ltd., Chanch, Chirkunda, (iii) The Bihar Firebricks and Potteries Ltd., Mugma. (iv) Hindustan General Electrical Corporation Ltd., Karampura, (v) Khandelwal Glass Works, Ambona, (vi) Loyabad Coking By-products Recovery Plant Bansjora (vii) M/s. Shalimar Tar Products Ltd., Jharia (viii) The A.C.C. Ltd. Sindri Cement Works. Sindri, and (ix) The Sijua (Jharia) Electric Supply Co. Ltd., Loyabad.

Apart from these heavy, medium and small industries, there are quite a number of small-scale units scattered all over the district. In Chas, there are a number of shellac factories, in Chandankiyari, quite a large number of weavers have been carrying on their trade from generation to generation. In Tundi and Gobindpur, there are weavers of silk yarn and a number of potters, carpenters and blacksmiths engaged in their family trade. Besides there are a number of flour mills, rice mills and small bidi manufacturing units.

MINERALS AND ORES OCCURRENCES

Coal

At Jharia (23.7°, 86.5°), specimens of coal from a thick and extensive seam near Jharia were sent to the Asiatic Society of Bengal by Haryngton in 1838. The field was surveyed by Hughes in 1865 when the total quantity of coal available was estimated at 465 million tons.

Drilling operation in the Kirkend (23.8°, 86.4°) area has proved the presence of seams V to XVIII below the Barren measures. In the borehole near Lohapiti (23.7, 86.2) the presence of twenty coal seams has been recorded, ranging in thickness from 3 incs. to 5 ft.6 incs within 2,500 ft. from the surface. The grade of the coal varies from inferior quality to second grade.

Mica

Several mica-bearing pegmatites occur to the North East of Maharaj Nagar (23.6, 86.2) near Kadori. The mica books range in size up to 5 by 5 ins. Mica is quarried at Kadori. Mica is also reported to occur in the area between Urma (23.7, 86.7) and Chirudih (23.7, 86.6).

Mineral Waters

Hot sulphurous springs are reported to occur at Charak (24.1, 86.4) and Jherbari (23.7, 86.8). The water contains the gases CO_2 and H_2S.

Quartz

Deposits quartz are found in the villages of Gopinathdih and Pilani near the Pradhan Khanta Railway station (23.6, 86.5). Veins of quartz also occur in the neighbour hood of Dharanipur, Lekhra Pahari and Jilingtan near Podardih (23.8, 86.7).

Steatite

An occurrence of steatite has been reported from the Pandra Kisment Estate (23.8, 86.7). Soapstone occurs near Sijua (23.9, 86.7).

Felspar

Pegmatites occurring near Dharampur and Madan Di village within 10 kms. of Poddardih (23.81; 86.73) contain workable deposits of felspar. Some pegmatites from south of the railway line near Pradhankhanta and Chhota Ambona (23.76, 86.55) near Dolabar (23.73, 86.56), Chhiru Dih (23.7, 86.61) Katral (23.7, 86.7) and Sanola Pur (23.71, 86.7).

Fire clay

Good fire clay occurs in the Barakar coal measures of the Jharia (23.73, 86.43) coal field at several localities which can be included in six areas, namely Chanderpura, Nadhkharki-Bahaldih, Sonardih- Tetulmari, East Kenduadih- Kusunda, Tisra-suranga and Chasnala-Pathardih areas.

Fire clays are also associates with the coal seeams of the Katrasgarh (23.76, 86.31) coal field. Near Nirsa Chatti (23.78, 86.71), Ramkanali (23.8, 86.7) Mugma (23.76, 86.76) Kumardhubi (23.73, 86.78).

Kaolin

An occurrence of Kaolin has been reported from Katras (23.8, 86.35)

Kayanite

Small blade of kayanite as also some massive variety of the mineral occur in mica-schist to the north of Birkham (23.56, 86.38)

TRADE, COMMERCE AND EXPORT

The development of means of communication has had a great impact on trade and commerce of the district. There are numerous passenger buses and carrier trucks running within the district and connecting the district with other parts of the state and the neighbouring states.

Trade in Dhanbad district consists mainly of exporting coal, hides and skins, marble and stone, oil, fuel, other mineral oils, gunnies, iron and steel, fireclay, firebricks, cement, sulphate of ammonia, etc. and of importing of cotton piece goods, salt, grains and pulses, kerosene oil, petrol, lime, vegetables, mustard oil, shoes, fish. sugar, tobacco and chillies.

The main retail centres in the district are at Dhanbad, Jharia. Kumardhubi. Chirkunda, Sindri, Pathardih, Gobindpur, Nirsa and Tundi. At all these places retail shops for almost all the commodities locally consumed are found.

TOURISM

Charak Pathar. The village is situated in Gobindpur Development Block. It has a very large ancient boulder of white stone. It derives its name from this stone.

Chati Gobindpur. The village, which also is located in Gobindpur Development Block contains two ancient pillars which are locally associated with Emperor Ashoka and the Afghan Chief Sher Shah.

Gopalpur. The village lies in Nirsa-cum-Chirkunda Development Block. It contains an ancient pillar said to date back to the time of Emperor Asoka. There is also a large stone image said to be of Ashoka himself.

Meva. The village is situated in Nirsa-cum-Chirkunda block. It contains an ancient pillar said to date back to the time of Emperor Ashoka. There is also a large stone image said to be of Ashoka himself.

Panrra. The village which also lies in Nirsa-cum-Chirkunda block, is said to have derived its name from the Pandavas. According to local legend the Pandavas spent some period of their exile in hiding at this place. The village contains an ancient temple of

Lord Shiva known as 'Pandaveshwar Mahdeo'. The temple is believed to have been constructed by a Hindu king at a much later date.

Chark-Khurd. The village, situated about 10 kms from Tundi on the Dhanbad-Gobindpur-Giridih road, is noted for its hot spring.

Maithan. It is a Census town situated about 48 kms from Dhanbad and 5 kms from Kumardhubi railway station. The Maithan Dam and Hydel Power Station are located in this town.

Panchet. This is also a Census town situated 9 kms south of Chirkunda and about 54 kms south-east of Dhanbad. The Panchet Dam, around which the township has developed, is located here.

HOTELS 2001

Hotel Black Rock (Government Approved) 3 star. Access: 5 km. from Airport, 2 kms. from Railway stations, 3 km. from Bus stand. No. of Rooms. 43, Double 43.

Hotel Skylark (Government Approved) 2 star. Access: 2 kms. from Railway station, 3 kms. from Bus stand. Rooms–26, single 8, double 18.

FAIRS AND FESTIVALS

Important fairs and melas organised in various parts of the district are mentioned as follows:

Dussehra mela, Kartik Purnima mela, Makar Sankranti mela, Divali mela, Basant Panchmi mela.

EDUCATION

According to 2001 census, total literates (excluding the population in the age group of 0-6 years) in undivided district of Dhanbad is 1,367,678 persons. Of these, 871,572 are males and 496106 are females. In the rural areas of the district 555,756 persons (374,403 males and 181,353 females) are literates and in urban areas 811922 persons (497,169 males and 314,753 females) are literates. The rate of literacy of this population to the total population, excluding the 0-6 years age group according to 2001 census is shown below:

	Persons	*Males*	*Females*
Total	67.49	80.03	52.93
Rural	58.71	75.07	40.48
Urban	75.20	84.22	64.31

There are as many as 997 villages in the district where educational facility of one type or other is available.

Facilities of primary and middle schools are generally available in all the towns. The following table gives details of the different categories of educational institutions per ten thousand population in different towns of the district:

Name of the towns	*Number per ten thousand population*			
	Higher Secondary/ Inter/PUC/ Junior College	*Secondary/ Matriculation*	*Junior Secondary Middle*	*Primary*
1	*2*	*3*	*4*	*5*
Angarpathar	—	1.85	1.85	5.55
Bhagatdih	—	0.44	1.33	3.55
Bhowrah	—	0.63	1.26	2.84
Bhuli	—	0.24	0.98	1.90
Chattudth	—	—	4.81	9.63
Chandaur	—	1.59	1.59	1.59
Chirkunda	—	1.93	3.86	2.57
Dhanbad	0.08	0.83	1.75	1.41
Dumarkunda	—	—	4.84	5.81
Jamadobar	—	0.40	0.79	2.78
Jharia	0.17	1.39	2.09	3.30
Jorapokha	—	0.15	0.92	1.23
Kenduadih	—	—	1.83	3.66
Kerkend	—	0.13	1.06	3.06
Kumardhubi	—	0.72	2.16	2.88

Lovabad	—	0.38	0.76	3.02
Maithon	—	0.74	3.70	2.22
Malkera	—	1.96	3.93	3.93
Nirsa	1.12	1.12	1.12	1.12
Panchet	—	1.37	1.37	2.74
Pathardih	—	0.44	2.20	3.52
Saraidhela	—	0.84	0.84	1.67
Sigua	—	0.49	0.97	4.37
Sindri	0.14	0.57	1.27	0.99
Tisra	—	0.21	0.43	1.92
Total	0.07	0.54	1.42	2.21

UNIVERSITY AND COLLEGES, 2000

B.S.K. College Maithon. (Established 1966) (Constituent College). Enrolment 3209, Teachers 40.

Katras College, Katrasgarh, (Established 1964) (Constituent College).

Enrolment 1701, Teachers 17.

P.K. Roy Memorial College, Dhanbad (Established 1960) (Constituent College).

Enrolment 3963, Teachers 45.

R.S. More College, Govindpur (Established 1967), Constituent College. Enrolment 2200.

Sindri College, Sindri (1964), (Established Constituent College) Enrolment 4502, Teachers 45.

SSLNTM College, Dhanbad (Established 1960) (Constituent College) Enrolment 4152 Teachers 60

B.B.M. College, Baliapur, (Established 1982). Teachers 32 (Affiliated College).

B.S.S. Mahila College, Dhanbad (Established 1977). Teachers 47 (Affiliated College).

Bihar Institute of Technology, Sindri (Established 1948) (Affiliated College).

Dhanbad Law College, Dhanbad (Established 1976), Teachers 13 (Affiliated College).

Gurunanak College, Dhanbad, (Established 1970), Teachers 25 (Affiliated College).

K.S. G.M. College, Nirsa (Established 1980), Teachers 35 (Affiliated College).

Patliputra Medical College, Dhanbad (Affiliated College)

(Above named colleges belong to Vinobabhave University, Established in 1992).

MEDICAL

The availability of medical facility in the villages of the district is quite low as only 291 villages have it.

The table below furnishes information regarding availability of beds in the medical institutions in the urban areas of the district:

Name of the town	*Number of beds in medical institutions per 1000 population*
Angarpathar	—
Bhagatdih	0.44
Bhowrah	2.21
Bhuli	2.22
Chaitudih	9.15
Chandaur	—
Chirkunda	0.77
Dhanbad	5.12
Dumlarkunda	0.77
Jamadobar	4.37
Jharia	1.67
Jorapokha	0.58
Kenduadih	—
Kerkend	0.64
Kumardhubi	2.23
Lovabad	2.64
Malthon	11.10
Malkera	3.73
NIrsa	0.90
Panchet	4.11
Pathardih	—
Saraidhela	69.00
Sijua	1.36
Sindri	2.51
Tisra	2.34
Total	3.01

The number of beds in medical institutions per 1000 population for urban areas of the district works out to 3.01. The availability of beds in the hospitals is the highest in Saraidhela town having 69.00 beds per 1000 population. The lowest number of beds is found to be in the case of Bhagatdih town only 0.44 beds per 1000 population. As many as 5 towns in the district viz., Angarpathar Bhojudih, Chandaur, Kenduadih and Pathardih do not have the facility of beds in medical institutions.

MEDIA

Awaj (Hindi)
Janmat, Daily, Hindi, circulation 41844
Bihar Observer, Daily, Hindi, circulation 62381
Chamakta Aina, Daily, Hindi
Antarkatha, Fortnightly, Hindi.

ADMINISTRATION

Sub-division: Dhanbad Sadar.

Community Development Blocks: Tundi, Topchanchi, Baghmara-cum-Katras, Gobindpur, Nirsa-cum-Chirkunda, Baliapur, Dhanbad-cum-Kenduadih-cum- Jagta, Jharia-cum-Jorapokhar-cum-Sindri.

Towns and Urban Agglomerations with their Population, Sexratio, Decadal growth and Literacy rate (2001)

DHANBAD UA

Dhanbad (M); Kailudih (CT); Katras (NA); Malkera (CT); Lakarka (CT); Angarpathar (CT); Sijua (CT); Chandaur (CT); Nagri Kalan (CT); Baua Kalan (CT); Loyabad (CT); Pandarkanali (CT); Kenduadih (CT); Baliari (CT); Chhotaputki (CT); Chhatatanr (NA); Basaria (CT); Bhuli (CT); Godhar (CT); Dhaunsar (CT); Kustai (CT): jamadoba (CT); Jharia (NA); Jharia Khas (CT); Bhagatdih (CT); Saraidhela (CT); Tisra (CT); Jorapokhar (CT); Bhowrah (CT); Pathardih (CT); Rohraband (CT); Sindri (NA)

CHIRKUNDA UA

Chrikunda (NA); Egarkunr (CT); Siuliban (CT); Mera (CT); Maithon (CT); Dumarkunda (CT); Gomoh (CT); Topchanchi (CT); Kharkhari (CT);

Sahnidih (CT); Gobindpur (CT); Nirsa (CT); Mugma (CT); Marma (CT); Panchet (CT)

Town	Population	Percentage Decadal growth 1991-2001	Sex Ratio	Literacy Rate
Angarpathar (CT)	8.179	30.36	768	64.02
Baliari (CT)	11,528	9.78	803	69.08
Basaria (CT)	3,966	-	886	62.00
Bhuli(CT)	89,584	57.79	867	74.78
Bhowrah (CT)	44,253	-2.58	847	75.03
Baua Kalan(CT)	8,829	21.90	833	59,95
Bhagatdih	33,263	10.24	819	68.56
Chirkunda (NA)	39,121	16.66	890	74.20
Chhatatanr (NA)	32,235	13.42	844	70.96
Chandaur (CT)	13,629	40.65	776	66.70
Chhotaputki (CT)	6,693	-	832	63.52
Dhanbad (M)	198,963	31.08	835	84.52
Dhaunsar (CT)	9,205	-	788	57.80
Dumarkunda (CT)	10,980	19.87	886	60.96
Egarkunr (CT)	10,212	-	868	62.82
Gobindpur (CT)	8,504	35.57	858	76.25
Godhar (CT)	9,544	32.56	848	61.77
Gomoh (CT)	28,576	29.40	856	82.13
Jamadoba (CT)	33,981	6.99	842	72.60
Jharia (NA)	81,979	17.72	848	78.83
Jaria Khas (CT)	19,808	-	821	65.32
Jorapokhar (CT)	85,218	16.87	852	75.87
Kharkhari (CT)	5,653	-	822	66.57
Kailudih (CT)	8,903	106.37	851	69.00
Kustai (CT)	12,268	3.70	801	72.83
Katras (NA)	51,182	36.41	857	76.66
Kenduadih (CT)	8,354	23.95	840	67.48

Lakarka (CT)	6,962	-	908	64.86
Loyabad (CT)	32,695	4.47	812	67.86
Marma (CT)	4,607	-	881	59.01
Maithon (CT)	19,728	18.97	875	83.29
Malkera (CT)	9,804	96.43	857	75.18
Mera (CT)	5,199	-	799	63.80
Mugma (CT)	2,978	-	790	62.18
Nagri Kalan (CT)	7,693	-	851	69.66
Nirsa (CT)	13,903	4.92	836	74.81
Panchet (CT)	8,353	-3.44	897	75.90
Pathardih (CT)	39,527	44.69	810	76.23
Pondarkanali (CT)	7,474	12.76	847	69.73
Rohraband (CT)	4,284	-	839	70.86
Sahnidih (CT)	5,802	-	833	70.20
Saraidhela (CT)	24,183	47.52	896	87.31
Sindri (CT)	76,827	6.21	848	77.22
Sijua (CT)	29,797	17.09	853	71.28
Siuliban (CT)	20,960	-	883	73.55
Tisra (CT)	53,547	-3.83	802	67.90
Topchanchi (CT)	5,397	-	884	66.38

(ii) Parliamentary Constituencies and assembly segments

No.* and *Name of Parliamentary Constituencies:
46-Giridih, 47-Dhanbad.

No.* and *Name of Assembly Segments:

Giridih

280. Tundi—Tundi police station in Dhanbad Sadar sub-division; Topchanchi police station and G.Ps. Dharkiro, Daludih, Rajganj, Bagdaha, Dhawachita, Nagri Kalan and Ramkanalichandur in Katras police station in Baghmara sub-division.

Dhanbad

282. Sindri—Sindri, Baliapur and Gobindpur police stations in Dhanbad Sadar sub-division.

283. Nirsa—Nirsa and Chirkunda police stations in Dhanbad Sadar sub-division..

284. Dhanbad—Dhanbad, Putki and Kenduadih police stations in Dhanbad Sadar sub-division.

285. Jharia—Jharia and Jorapokhar police stations in Dhanbad Sadar sub- division.

The communitywise break up (OBE) in Dhanbad is Muslims (13 per cent). Scheduled Castes (16 per cent) and Scheduled Tribes (11 per cent).This is one of those constituencies where demographic structure has changed quite a bit. However, the community that is found in large numbers is Kurmi Mahatos. Others like Brahmins, Rajputs, Ahirs and Telis are also there in substantial numbers. Chamars; Bauris and Bhuiyas, around 3 per cent each, dominate the Scheduled Castes. Amongst the Scheduled Tribes Santals 9 per cent are clearly dominant.

OBSERVATIONAL ORGANIZATION

Surface Observatories

It comes under Meterological centre Patna and Meteorological subdivision, Bihar Plateau.

Latitude	:	23.8° North
Longitude	:	86.4° East
Altitude	:	258 m
Date of starting	:	12-8-1956

Note: This Instrument is “Self Recording Raingauge”

Hydrometeorological Stations for Climatological Purposes:

This instrument located at: Chandankiari, Gansadih, Maithon, Nandadih, Panchet Hill, Putki, Rajdaha, Rajganj, Sindri.

DISASTROUS WEATHER EVENTS

Coldwave:

1st January 1982, Moderate.
29-30 December 1982, Severe.
4-10 December 1982, severe.
2-14 January 1983, severe,
December 3rd and 4th week 1984, severe,
9 December 1985, severe, people reported died.
27-31 December 1989, severe. Cattlehead perished and people reported died.
1-10 January 1990, severe, cattle heads perished and standing crop damaged.
January 1st and 2nd week 1992, severe, many people reported killed and cattle heads perished.
Jan (1st and 2nd week) 1992, severe, crops damaged, cattle heads perished, people reported killed.

Heatwave:

On 7th June 1983, this area witnessed moderate type heatwave, resulted damage to the standing crops and cattle heads reported perished.
On 6th June 1983, there was severe heatwave in this area, people reported killed.
On 3rd June 1995 this area witnessed severe heatwave 19 persons reported killed and several cattle heads perished.

Hailstorm:

On 13th April 1993, it was severe Hailstorm, Hail stone weighing 75 gms. reported. Several thatched houses damaged. Standing vegetables and mango fruits extensively damaged.

Lightning:

On 21st April 1994, this area witnessed disastrous lightning, 6 persons died at Gopalpur village under Topachanchi block.
On 10th July 1996, this area witnessed lightning, 3 persons reported died and several other injured.

ARCHAEOLOGICAL SITE

Ganja-Pahar Valley	Dt Dhanbad	Middle stone age (Middle Palaeolithic [4.3] site. IAR 1961-2.

DISTRIBUTION OF *SCHEDULED CASTE* POPULATION BY SEX DISTRICTWISE (1991)

	POPULATION		
	Total	Males	Females
DHANBAD	4,15,614	2,27,718	1,87,896
Bantar	200	96	104
Lauri	80,893	41,894	38,999
Bhogta	1,659	908	751
Bhuiya	45,855	25,954	19,901
Chamar, Mochi	80,094	45,194	34,900
Chaupal	378	169	209
Dabgar	219	149	70
Dhobi	28,888	15,731	13,157
Dom, Dhangad	16,480	8,773	7,707
Dusadh, Dhari, Dharhi	42,824	25,056	17,768
Ghasi	588	408	180
Halalkhor	160	72	88
Hari, Mehtar, Bhangi	20,181	11,064	9,117
Kanjar	790	403	387
Kurariar	614	269	345
Lalbegi	372	205	167
Musahar	12,674	7,080	5,594
Nat	119	74	45
Pan, Sawasi	826	425	401
Pasi	9,343	5,811	3,532
Rajwar	48,051	24,840	23,211
Turi	23,684	12,743	10,941
Unclassified	722	400	322

DISTRIBUTION OF *SCHEDULED TRIBE* POPULATION BY SEX DISTRICTWISE (1991)

	POPULATION		
	Total	Males	Females
DHANBAD	2,25,282	1,16,569	1,08,713
Asur	126	33	93
Baiga	235	110	125
Banjara	14	2	12
Bathudi	78	58	20
Bedia	515	237	278
Bhumij	505	184	321
Binjhia	3	3	0
Birhor	177	83	94
Birjia	118	43	75
Chero	55	28	27
Chick Baraik	162	93	69
Gond	1,909	1,076	833
Gorait	76	51	25
Ho	1,316	712	604
Karmali	104	57	47
Kharia	601	302	299
Kharwar	1,310	715	595
Khond	674	406	268
Kisan	103	39	64
Kora	8,264	4,460	3,804
Korwa	780	335	445
Lohara, Lohra	4,726	2,552	2,174
Mahli	8,523	4,478	4,045
Mal Paharia	298	194	104
Munda	10,599	6,014	4,585
Oraon	9,000	4,975	4,025
Parhaiya	85	33	52
Santal	1,74,020	88,871	85,149
Sauria Paharia	689	302	387
Savar	133	63	70
Unclassified	84	60	24

SKETCH MAP OF DUMKA

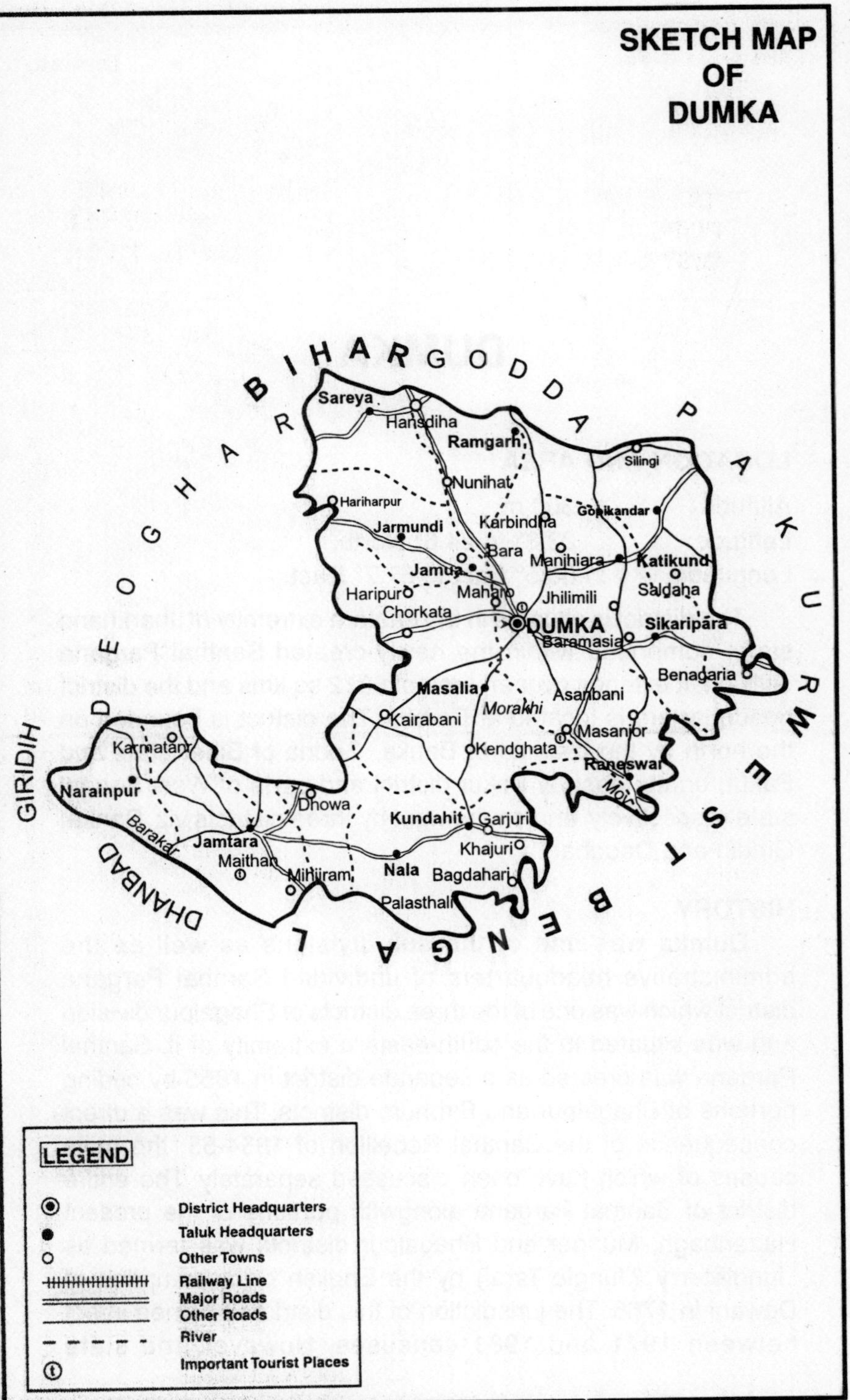

DUMKA

LOCATION AND AREA

Altitude : 300 m.
Latitude : 23.8° to 24.6° North.
Longitude : 86.5° East to 87.7° East.

The district is situated in the eastern extremity of Jharkhand state, comprised within the newly-created Santhal Pargana division. It extends over an area of 6212 sq kms and the district headquarters is located at Dumka. The district is bounded on the north by the districts of Banka, Godda of Bihar state and Pakur, on the east by Pakur district and parts of West Bengal state respectively, and on the west by three districts viz. Banka, Giridih and Deoghar .

HISTORY

Dumka was one of the sub-divisions as well as the administrative headquarters of undivided Santhal Pargana district which was one of the three districts of Bhagalpur division and was situated in the south-eastern extremity of it. Santhal Pargana was created as a separate district in 1855 by ceding portions of Bhagalpur and Birbhum districts. This was a direct consequence of the Santhal Rebellion of 1854-55, the main causes of which have been discussed separately. The entire district of Santhal Pargana alongwith portions of the present Hazaribagh, Munger and Bhagalpur districts was termed as 'Jungleterry' (Jungle Tarai) by the English on assumption of Dewani in 1765. The jurisdiction of this district remained intact between 1971 and 1981 censuses. However, the state government vide its notification recently upgraded Santhal Pargana as a division consisting of newly-created districts viz. Dumka, Deogarh, Godda, and Sahibganj. The present district of Dumka comprised of old Dumka and Jamtara sub-divisions of undivided Santhal Pargana district and at present divided into fourteen Community Development Blocks viz. Saraiyahat, Jarmundi, Jama, Ramgarh, Gopikandar, Kathikund, Dumka, Shikaripura, Ranishwar, Masalia, Kundahit, Nala, Jamtara and Narayanpur. The early history of old Santhal Pargana district has been described below in detail.

There is evidence of this area having been inhabited since very early times. Among the early settlers of this territory, of whom there is any record, 'are the Maler (Sauria Paharia) who still inhabit some areas of the Rajmahal hills. They have been identified with the Malli which find mentions in the notes of the Greek traveller Megasthenes, who visited Bihar in 302 B.C.

Little is known about the history of this area until the time of Hiuen Tsang, a Chinese pilgrim, who visited India 645 A.D. He probably referred to Teliagarhi Fort when he mentioned about "the lofty brick and stone tower, not far from the Ganges". From the description of the tower, Cunningham concludes that it must have been a Buddhist building. There is mention of the land and people of this tract and of the shrine of Lord Baidyanath at Deoghar in the Bhavishyat Purana which was compiled in the 15th or the 16th Century A.D. from ancient material.

A continuous history of the district is available from the 13th century when "Teliagarhipass" became the main gateway of Muslim armies marching to and from Bengal. During the rule of the Slave Dynasty at Delhi, Malim Jaduruddin Bin Bukhtiar Khilji marched to Bengal and Assam through Teliagarhi Pass. He captured Bihar and its king Lakshman Sen fled away to Cooch-Behar. He made Deoghar, which was then called "Deogarh" his capital in 1201 A.D.

In 1538 A.D. during his rebellion against Emperor Humayun, Sher Shah built his fortification near Teliagarhi. On 12th July,

1576 the battle of Rajmahal was fought and the foundation of the Mughal rule in Bengal laid. Man Singh, who was appointed the Viceroy of Bengal by Akbar, made Rajmahal the Capital of Bengal in 1592. Sher Shah had in fact selected the site as the seat of the government about half a century before, but it was left to Man Singh to carry out this measure. Man Singh did fortification and built a palace, and established himself there. But this honour to Rajmahal was shortlived because the capital shifted to Dhaka in 1608. Shortly after shifting, Teliagarhi became the site of a fierce battle between the rebellious Prince Shah Jahan and Ibrahim Khan, Viceroy of Bengal and brother-in-law of Empress Noor Jahan. Shah Jahan emerged victorious and became the master of Bengal for the time being, losing later in 1624 at Allahabad.

In 1639, Rajmahal regained its glory and was once more made the capital of Bengal by Shah Shuja, the second son of Emperor Shah Jahan, on his appointment as the Viceroy of Bengal. It continued to be the seat of the Mughal Viceroy upto 1660, and a mini-town till 1661. It was at Rajmahal that Dr Gobriel Boughton cured a lady of Shah Shuja's harem, and became the favourite of the Prince. According to another version the doctor is said to have cured the daughter of Emperor Shah Jahan. But the fact that Dr Boughton succeeded in securing a firman from Shah Shuja giving the English the liberty to trade in Bengal. The foundation of the British rule was, in a way, laid here. After the fall of Shah Shuja the English had to face a lot of trouble and they could regain their privileges only after paying Rs 45,000 to the Mughal Governor in 1709. In 1757, Siraj-ud-Daula was captured here during his fight from the Battle of Plassey.

The victory at Plassey gave the British control over the then Bengal which contained the present Santhal Pargana. They had yet to establish the foundations of their future empire. In Santhal Pargana they were up against a band of simple but determined opponents, the Paharias, who were great lovers of freedom and could not tolerate any intruders in their homeland'.

The English were very much concerned and Warren Hastings organised a special corps of 800 men in 1772 to curb the Paharias. Initially the corps was put under the command of Captain Brooke who partly succeeded in I774, found himself busy mostly in suppressing the rebellion of the Bhuiyas. He, however, prepared a scheme to win over the Paharias, which was left to be elaborated and put into action actually by Augustus Cleveland. He introduced the system of trial of cases by an assembly of Chiefs. This system received further sanction by Regulation I of 1796 which made it obligatory on the Magistrate to commit all important cases for trial by the assembly of Chiefs. The Magistrate was, of course, to attend the trial as superintending officer and had the power to confirm or modify a sentence. This show of self-rule continued till 1827 when hillmen were declared amenable to ordinary courts of law, though they still enjoyed the privilege to settle petty disputes.

Cleveland was followed by other administrators one of whom was Mr Sutherland, who in course of his tour in the district in 1818 suggested that the hill tracts inhabited by the tribals should be declared the direct property of government so that they could be looked after better. These recommendations were accepted by the government in 1823 and in 1837, Mr. Pontent was placed in charge of the revenue administration. The Santhals started pouring in and encouragement was given to them for clearing the jungle. One got the impression that all was well with the administration and that the Santhals were happy. But it was very deceptive appearance. The internal set-up of the administrative system could ensure proper justice to the common man and there was a deep underlying discontent among the simple-minded but excitable Santhals. The next event of importance was the Santhal Rebellion (Hul) of 1855.

The Santhals were a simple, hardy and industrious people. They, therefore, fell an easy prey to the unscrupulous hillmen and non-Santhal traders. It was a common, practice for the hillmen to apply for grant of land on the condition of cultivating it themselves but they frequently gave it up to the Santhals in the hope of collecting rent from them. Baniyas and Mahajans made heavy exaction from the innocent Santhals and there was no check on them. In the Damin area where Santhals had settled in large numbers, the Naib Sazawals, assistants of the English Superintendent, were very oppressive. The police was equally corrupt. The Santhal was ready to face justice at no cost. Besides, there was the Kamianti system. The idea behind it was repayment of a debt by physical labour. In practice, however, the debtor worked, in many cases for a generation or two and yet the loan, no matter how small, could not be repaid. The mahajans were crooked as a class and they took advantage of the Santhal's meekness.

Thus, the Santhals felt unhappy and insecure. Their discontent was all the more acute because others of their tribe who were outside the clutches of *mahajans* and *banias* earned handsome wages in the forests which were being cleared for the rail lines to be laid. All these facts and circumstances led to the Santhal Hul, better known as the Santhal Rebellion of 1855. The basic reason for this catastrophe was the economic privation of Santhals resulting from the permanent settlement.

Thousand of Santhals migrated in 1855 from the adjoining districts of Birbhum, Bankura and Hazaribagh and the swelling numbers encouraged the already discontented Santhals. They got leaders in Sidhu, Kanhu, Chand and Bhairab—four brothers of village Bhagnadihi, near Barhait. They declared themselves to be the messengers of Jaharera, the celebrated deity of the Santhals. Soon their home became a place of pilgrimage for the Santhals and thousands started pouring in from different parts of the district. On 7th July, 1855, the started killing the moneylenders and land lords. It came to the end after one year, with the assistance of military forces. Chandrai and Singrai were the main figures. Singrai was the son of Bijai Manjhi of Littipara, Kanhu was killed in action. Sidhu was arrested and hanged at Barhait.

The object of the Santhal insurrection was the economic emancipation of the Santhals. The first spark of the revolt was ignited at Littipara. Kena Ram Bhagat was a leading merchant and moneylender of Amrapara. The altercation which took place led to the arrest of Bijai Manjhi who was sent to Bhagalpur jail. There he died without any trial shortly after. His son Singrai raised the banner of revolt who also was hanged in Barhait bazar after summary trial. The Santhals got angry and the trouble started. The main victims were largely the oppressive mahajans and landlords.

The foreign rulers took this as a challenge to their authority and made no effort to understand and appreciate the reasons of Santhal discontent. They pounced upon the Santhals with mighty forces and engaged troops to quell the disturbances. As the English tried to arrest the Santhals and thereby protect the Bikus whom the Santhals had branded as their enemy, the trouble spread over a large area covering the present Santhal Pargana, Birbhum, Bankura and Hazaribagh districts. A large number of troops were put into action and all sorts of atrocities were resorted to as Martial Law was proclaimed on the 10th November, 1855 and with ruthless hands, the British government succeeded in suppressing the rebellion by December, 1855. The Santhals were beaten but the extraordinary courage and resolve exhibited by them during the rebellion left their impress on the British rulers. They realised that the Santhals had to be kept in good humour and their reasonable demands met if the government wanted to rule over the area. A separate district was created by Act XXXVII of 1855 and it was given the name of Santhal Pargana, perhaps to appease the Santhals. Steps were taken to remedy the grievances of the Santhals and to give them a homeland with a sense of security.

The 1857 movement touched the Santhal Pargana though the Santhals were too crippled to rise again and so shortly after the Hul (Rebellion). The sepoys of the 5th Irregular Cavalry stationed at Rohini revolted and Adjutant Sir Norman Leslie was killed, and Commandant Major Macdonald and Dr Grant were both wounded on the 8th of June, 1857. In June 1857, the

5th Irregular Regiment at Bhagalpur also revolted and marched on to Rohini where they were joined by the comrades of their regiment. From Rohini they proceeded to Bounsi, where the 32nd Native Infantry was stationed. But the untimely leakage and forewarning to the British Officers foiled the attempts of the sepoys and nothing noteworthy happened in the district.

Santhal Pargana was not immune from patriotic fervour, and played its role in the country's struggle for freedom from 1921 onwards. The decision of the Indian National Congress to boycott the Simon Commission and the commotion aroused by it had its repercussion all over India. Even in the hills and forests of Santhal Pargana, there was a patriot named Lambodar Mukherjee moving and rousing the people. He brought to the tribals glimpses of the outside world, so securely closed by the British, with the help of lantern slides. He became an eye-sore to the then Deputy Commissioner, E.S. Hoernle and the Commissioner, M. G. Hallet, both of whom pleaded strongly for his arrest even without evidence, on account of his 'seditious propaganda' against the government.

The district played its role in the Salt Satyagraha and the Civil Disobedience Movement of 1930 and in the boycott of foreign liquors and clothes. The Individual Satyagrah of 1940-41 spread to this district also and dozens of people offered Satyagrah and got arrested. The 1942 movement also spread to Santhal Pargana and on the 11th of August, 1942, on which day a procession was taken out at Deoghar and hartal was observed. On the 12th August a procession was taken out at Godda and soon the entire district was aflame. Thus, the district of Santhal Pargana marched hand-in-hand with other parts of the state in the struggle for country's freedom.

POPULATION (GENERAL, SC/ST)

Total population of the district according to 2001 census is 1,754,571 persons. comprising of 894,849 males and 859,722 females. Rural population of the district is 1,640,240 persons

(834,071 males and 806,169 females) and urban population is 114,331 persons (60,778 males and 53,553 females).

The Community Development Block-wise, population distribution with sex ratio and literacy rate of this district is given below:

C.D. Block	Sex ratio		Literacy rate		Population	
	Rural	Urban	Rural	Urban	Rural	Urban
DUMKA DISTRICT	**967**	**881**	**45.96**	**80.46**	**1640240**	**114331**
Saraiyahat	942	-	43.21	-	123,669	-
Jarmundi	974	923	41.33	65.49	137,367	14,119
Ramgarh	967	-	36.09	-	134,511	-
Gopikandar	966	-	36.61	-	35,511	-
Kathikund	974	-	43.28	-	59,516	-
Shikaripara	983	-	43.08	-	110,099	-
Ranishwar	967	-	48.12	-	89,007	-
Dumka	960	845	61.53	86.55	129,487	44,917
Jama	980	-	45.72	-	117,433	-
Masalia	971	-	43.66	-	106,705	-
Narayanpur	959	-	43.32	-	157,155	-
Jamtara	964	900	47.83	79.10	173,324	55295
Nala	965	-	47.77	-	153,763	-
Kundhit	972	-	53.92	-	112,817	-

The Scheduled Castes and Scheduled Tribes population of the district as per 1991 census is 104094 persons and 621484 persons respectively. The rural-urban breakup of these population is indicated below:

Rural	(i) Scheduled Castes	:	93892
	(ii) Scheduled Tribes	:	616449
Urban	(i) Scheduled Castes	:	10202
	(ii) Scheduled Tribes	:	5035

The decennial growth rate of population of the district as a whole in relation to the state between the period 1991 and 2001 is presented below:

State/ District	Decennial growth rate of population (per cent) 1991-2001		
	Total	Rural	Urban
Jharkhand	23.19	21.62	28.99
Dumka	17.31	16.76	25.76

LANGUAGES AND RELIGION

Hindi is the principal language spoken in the district. The religionwise breakup of population of erstwhile Santhal Pargana district, of which the present district (Dumka), has been carved out, is mentioned below as per 1991 census:

Hindus: 1306590, Muslims: 151068, Christians: 32359, Sikhs 266, Buddhists: 5, Jains : 602, Other religions and persuasions: 4783, Religion not stated: 36.

Details of some of the religions shown under other religions and persuasions are indicated below: Santhal (17336), Swarna (89813), Adivasi (7079), Bidin (1246) and Paharia (1746) .There are many other religions recorded under the category referred to above, though its numbers are not very significant.

GEOGRAPHY AND PHYSICAL FEATURES

Annual Rainfall : 1367 m.
Temperature : Max. 37.60°C and Min. 10.90°C

The area comprised in the district consists of the uplands, undulations, long ridges and depressions. This area has plenty of fertile lands and is intensively cultivated. The district once known for its thick and extensive forests is now bereft of much of its jungle wealth. There has been large scale destruction of forests in the past few years.

The most common tree of the district is sal. Some teak of inferior variety is also found. Other trees found are jack fruit, murga, simal, bamboo, asan and satsal. Sal and simal logs and jackfruit are exported in large quantities to the neighbouring districts and to places outside Jharkhand. Among the forest products of consequence are lac, sabai grass and tassar silk cocoons.

RIVERS, CANALS AND WATERWAYS

A dam across the river Mor or Mayurakshi is constructed within the village Massanjore. It has been used for many purposes viz. flood control, irrigation and to generate hydro-electric power. Apart from this dam, the district has two hot springs at Bara and Bhumka villages, one of the springs (at Bhumka village) is on the right bank of Mor river.

TOWNS, VILLAGES AND AMENITIES

The district at present comprises of 2 sub-divisions, 14 Community Development Blocks. It has 4 towns and 4090 villages (3712 inhabited villages and 378 uninhabited villages).

The urban population of the district as percentage of total population in the census year 2001 is indicated below. It also shows the sex ratio (females per 1000 males) and density (population per sq km) in the urban population of the district in relation to the state:

State/ District	*Urban population as percentage of total population*	*Sex ratio, 2001 (Females per 1000 males)*			*Density (Population per sq km)*
	2001	*Total*	*Rural*	*Urban*	
Jharkhand	22.25	941	963	870	338
Dumka	6.52	961	967	881	282

Amenities

Number (with percentage) of villages having one or more amenities in the district as per 1991 census is given below:

Sl. No.	Amenities	Number of inhabited villages	Percentage
1.	Education	1796	48.38
2.	Medical	520	14.01
3.	Drinking Water	3712	100.00
4.	Post and Telegraph	324	8.73
5.	Market/Hat	428	11.53
6.	Communications	755	20.34
7.	Approach by Pucca Road	445	11.99
8.	Power Supply	245	6.55

COMMUNICATIONS

Roads. Until 1857 there was only one proper road which existed in the district. It was the Bhagalpur-Suri road which passed through the district. But there is now a network of good roads in the district. All the Community Development Block headquarters are connected with the district headquarters by black topped all-weather roads. No important place in the district is left unconnected by a good metalled road. There are two roadlinks with through Jamtara and Suri. Patna, Kolkata is connected both via Bhagalpur and Chakai. The Jamtara Dumka-Sahibganj road provides a link with Assam after ferry across the Ganges and is quite busy.

A large number of buses ply on these roads.

Railways. The district is deprived of adequate railway communication. The district headquarters has no rail link.

Airways. There is a small landing ground at Dumka, the district headquarters. No regular air transport services operate from this landing ground. It is used by small planes belonging to the State Government.

AGRICULTURE AND IRRIGATION

Paddy is the main crop of the district especially the winter rice. Maize is an another important crop grown in the district. On account of non-availability of proper irrigational facilities, *rabi* crops are not grown very extensively. Vegetable growing is a late introduction in Dumka and is confined to the neighbourhoods of the towns only. Orchards are also maintained for the production of fruits such as mango, papaya, guava, jackfruit etc. Groundnuts, sweet potatoes and khesari are also widely grown. Sugarcane is raised in areas having assured irrigation.

Irrigation is generally provided to wheat and sugarcane crops. Maize grown in bari and homestead land is also irrigated. The most common source is the well and the popular device is latha. A major part of the district being rocky, it is difficult to dig wells. Rocks are generally found 10 to 15 ft below the surface except in the alluvial region. Slopes are steep and sub-soil water level in uplands falls as the summer approaches. Wells, therefore, are not a very dependable source of irrigation. The undulatory nature of the land makes it possible to store rain water by bunding. Seepage ponds are also found. Apart from being dependent upon rains, these are by no means adequate. The result is that failure of rains invariably involves failure of crops except in small pockets.

The district of Santhal Pargana abounds in rivers arid rivulets and it has immense water resources. If exploited, the rivers can supply water for irrigation and electricity for power generation. During the pre-independence days, no tangibe steps were taken for taming the rivers, But during the post-independence period the Government has taken various steps to utilise the river resources, the Mayurakshi Left Bank Canal, the Jaminikola Irrigation Scheme etc. being the important canal systems commissioned. The irrigation potential of the district has increased during the recent past through the adoption of various lift irrigation schemes and other minor, medium and major irrigational projects in all the subdivisions of the district.

ANIMAL HUSBANDRY

The district has one of the largest livestock population in the State. Stray cattle are a common sight in the district.

However, this cannot be taken as an index of the prosperity of cattle wealth. Despite the large population of cattle, the yield of milk in the district is very poor. Except in parts of Deoghar and Godda subdivisions, milk supply is extremely low. A typical cow or bullock of the district is a low, rickety cattle wearing a gloomy look. Milch-cows are limited in number even these that do give milk yield very little.

There has been a concerted effort on behalf of the State Government to improve the breed of the cattle by way of distribution of stud bulls of Haryana and Tharparkar varieties. In order to grade up the cattle quickly and also at low cost, artificial insemination centres with sub-centres have been opened at various places in the district.

There are a number of veterinary hospitals and dispensaries spread over the entire district. Treatment, prevention and suppression of diseases of the livestock are the main functions of the veterinary institutions.

INDUSTRIES

The district is mainly inhabited by the Santhals and the Paharias. The Santhals mostly use handloom fabrics, and this explains the existence of the large number of units in this category. The district of Santhal Pargana ranks first in the State in this group of industry. Poverty and backwardness of the people may be responsible for the largescale use of earthenware and earthen pottery. There are large jungle tracts where the manufacture of materials from bamboo cane leaves and other allied products is apart to flourish.

The traditional cottage and village industries practised by the Santhals and the Paharias constitute tassar rearing, village blacksmithy and carpentry, handloom weaving, rope making, carea flaying, stonewares, *bidi* making, earthenware and pot-making etc.

A number of small scale industries have also been set up

in the district. The availability of coal, copper, china clay, fire clay, *sabai* grass and bamboos underscores the industrial potentiality of the district. The district is close to Dhanbad and hydel power is available from Maithan and Masanjore. Quick transport, however, is the only problem. Rail communication is not adequate in the district. But there are good roads and industries can thrive.

MINERALS AND ORES OCCURRENCES

Coal

Near Brahmani (24.3, 87.5), at Panchbahini (24.3, 87.5), at Domanpur (24.3, 87.5), at Sarsabad (24.3, 87.5), Saldaha (24.3, 87.5), at Masania (24.2, 87.5) and Harising (24.2, 87.5). The coal is high volatile and long flame type.

Near Damin-i-koh., G.C. Chattrerjee reports about inferior coal in Damin-i-Koh, a Government Estate. At Dubrajpur (24.4, 87.5). Sherwill described seams from 1 ft. 2 ins. to 3 ft. in thickness, but according to McClelland none is of workable quality. At Kundit Karaia (23.9, 87.2). Area of Barakar Rocks is about 3 sq. km. Two seams occur one of 1 ft. 2 ins. containing fair quality coal. At Pachwara (24.5, 87.5) coal has been worked in a small way near Bargo (24.5, 87.4) and Ghilgo (24.5, 87.5). They are inferior high moisture coals Occurrence of inferior coal (carbonaceous shale) is reported from east of Manikbothen (24.4, 87.4) in Gullmari River valley. A large number of outcrops in the Bansoli River valley.

Lead

At Samkera Hills (24.3, 87.4). A deposit of lead ore is indicated here but the exact locality is not known. It was situated in the Chandrapahar (silver hill) to the S.W. of the main mass of the hills.

Limestone

Deposit of calcareous tufa occur at Mohwagarhi Hill (24.5, 87.45).

Mineral Waters

Near Nunbil (24.1, 87.2). There are several springs rising in a small marsh. Temperature of water is 48.6°C, discharge of water copious. Strong ebullition of sulphuretted gas was noted. Other springs are Bhumka (24.1, 87.4), Susampani (24.1, 87.3), Tapatpani (24.2, 87.3). Tantloi or Tapnai (24.4, 87.2) and Tanteshwari (24.1, 87.3)

Ochere

This pockets of red Ochre occur in Dubrajpur sand stones east of Kalkant (24.4, 87.4).

Quartz

Quartz crystals varying in length from fractions of an inch to a maximum of 8 inches occur near Majhitola (24.3, 87.4). The crystals are, however, imperfect, contain flaws and are clouded.

Handicrafts

Cane and Bamboo work; Folk paintings; Metalcraft; Stone work; Wood work.

Felspar

Main occurrences of pegmetites are located near the villages Dhammi, Kalajhor, Chihutia Durapahari, Ṣugapahari, Mohlitola, Makanpur, Jagtoba, and Amtita between 24.16 and 24.25 North and 86.56 and 86.65.

Fire-clay

Important localities are Bargo (24.51, 87.45) Bhulgora (24.95, 87.46) Khijaria (24.2, 87.31) Narganjo (24.41, 87.46), Surwa (24.45, 87.53) Umbapani (24.26, 87.58).

Kaolin:

At Dudhani (24.26, 87.45), Karanpura (24.31, 87.45), Katangi (24.46, 87.48), Bhurkunda (24.33, 87.4), Majhitola near Dumka town, Chilgo (24.55, 87.46), Karaikadar (24.15, 87.38), Ratanpur (24.31, 87.36), Waliganj (24.1, 87.45), Fazilpur (24.1, 87.43), Asanbani (24.3, 87.36), Gobindpur (24.53, 87.26).

TRADE, COMMERCE AND EXPORT

The table below lists the most important commodities manufactured, exported from and imported in the towns of the district.

Name of the town	Most important commodities: Manufactured	Exported	Imported	Banks
Basuklnath	Rice, M. Oil, Furniture	Rice, Bidi, Milk Cement	Cool, Wheat,	1
Dumka	Wooden furniture, Baskets, Bamboo Leather shoes	Goats, Fowls, Jack fruits	Cloth, Wheat, Patato	7
Jamtara	Mustard oil, Rice, Biscuits	Rice, M. oil, Biscuits	Wheat, Vegetable, Iron Rods	2
Mihijam	—	—	Wheat, M. oil, Cement	1

TOURISM

Bara. It is a village situated at the 9th milestone on the Dumka-Bhagalpur road. It is noted for a hot-water spring. A fair is also held during Magha Sankranti (January-February) .

Bhumka. It is a hot spring located about half a kilometre from village Ranibahal on the Dumka-Suri road. The spring is on the right bank of the river Mor or Mayurakshi.

Choto. The village Gadi Choto contained in Jama block has a temple of 'Choto Baba'. It is situated in the valley of what is known as the Choto Nath hill. It is the site of a big annual fair held during the Chaitra Sankranti. The place is also known for its scenic beauty.

Gardo. The village lies in Dumka block. In the early days it was the seat of the Paharia Zamindars of the Sankara estate and the descendants of the family still live in the village Sankara where the family lived once upon a time. It is said that the family deity Singha-bahini used to be offered human sacrifice. There is a temple of Singhababahini at Gando and puja is offered here every year with great pomp and ceremony.

Massanjore. It is a dam across the river Mor or Mayurakshi. It was constructed by the West Bengal government with foreign assistance from Canada. It is a multipurpose project, controls flood in West Bengal, supplies water for irrigation to parts of Santhal Pargana and to the western districts of West Bengal and also generates hydro-electric power for parts of Bihar and West Bengal. The dam connects two high hills and is rich in scenic beauty. It can be reached from Dumka by a macadamised road.

Basukinath. The town is situated on the Dumka-Deoghar road. It is famous for the temple of Lord Shiva which is considered to be very holy and powerful by the Hindus. The temple is about 150 years old and is said to have been built by Basaki Tatme, a Harijan. It is visited by thousands pilgrims every year especially during Shivaratri.

Dumka. Dumka is the headquarters of this district, and has developed in recent years though slowly. Situated against the backdrop of hills, Dumka is located at a picturesque site. The town is important only as the administrative headquarters of the district and now also as the new division.

FAIRS AND FESTIVALS

Important fairs and melas organised in the various parts of this district are indicated below:

Hijala mela, Dussehra mela, Basant Panchami mela, Shivaratri mela. Divali mela, Makar Sankranti (Nunbil) mela, Shravana Sombari and Shri Panchami.

EDUCATION

According to 2001 census, total literates (excluding the population in the age group of 0-6 age years) is 699682 persons. Of these, 468188 are males and 231,494 are females. In the rural areas of the district 620,312 persons (421,472 males and 198570 females) are literates and in urban areas 79,370 persons (46,446 males and 32,924 females) are literates. The rate of literacy of this population to the total population, excluding 0-6 years age group according to 2001 census is shown below:

	Persons	*Males*	*Females*
Total	48.31	63.28	32.68
Rural	45.96	61.37	29.98
Urban	80.46	88.25	71.55

There are as many as 1796 villages accounting for 48.96 per cent of the total number of inhabited villages in the district where educational facility is available. Primary and Middle schools are available in the towns. The following table gives the details of various types of educational institutions available in towns of this district including the number of stadia and public libraries :

Name of the town	*Educational institutions*	*Stadia*	*Public libraries, including reading rooms*
Basukinath	3 Junior Secondary and Middle Schools.	—	PL : 2
Dumka	One Shorthand and Typewriting trainings, institute, 3 Secondary/ Matriculation Schools and 12 Junior Secondary and Middle Schools.	—	—
Jamtara	Two each Secondary/ Matriculation Schools and Junior-Secondary and Middle schools.		
Mihijam	One Shorhand and Typewriting training institute, 2 Secondary/ Matriculation Schools and 6 Junior Secondary and Middle Schools.		

UNIVERSITY AND COLLEGES, 2001

Jamtara College Jamtara, (Established 1967), (Constituent College). Enrolment 1854. Teachers 18.

S.P. College, Dumka (Established 1955), (Constituent College). Enrolment 3187, Teachers 76. (Constituent College)

S.P. Mahila College Dumka (Established 1973) (Constituent College). Enrolment 732. Teachers 15.

A.N. College, Dumka (Established 1979), Enrolment 1146, Teachers 58. (Affiliated College)

Bhagwat Jha College, Kundhit (Established 1981). Enrolment 404, Teachers 22.(Affiliated College)

J.J.S. College, Mihijam (Established 1983), Enrolment 372. Teachers 31. (Affiliated College)

M.G. College Ranishwar (Established 1985), Enrolment 250. Teachers 13. (Affiliated College)

Nala College, Nala (Established 1988), Enrolment 150, Teachers 24. (Affiliated College)

Shikaripara College, Shikaripara (Established 1982). Enrolment 235, Teachers 32. (Affiliated College)

(Above mentioned Colleges belong to Siddhu Kanhu University, Established 1992.)

MEDICAL

The availability of medical facility in the village is considerably low as only 520 per cent villages in the district have got it. The table given below furnishes information regarding various types of medical institutions available in the towns of this district:

Name of the towns	*Medical Institutions*	*With number of beds*
Basukinath	Hospital (1) :	4
	Dispensary (1) :	
	Health Centre (1) :	
Dumka	Hospital (2) :	89
	T.B. Clinics (1) :	10
	Family Planning Centre (1) :	10
Jamtara	Hospital (1) :	30
Mihijam	Hospital (Homeopathic) (1) :	10
	Dispensary (5) :	—

ADMINISTRATION

(i) Administrative Divisions :

Sub-divisions: Dumka, Jamtara.

Community development blocks: Saraiyahat, Jarmundi, Jama, Ramgarh, Gopikandar , Kathikund, Dumka, Shikaripara, Ranishwar, Masalia, Kundahit, Nala, Jamtara, Narayanpur.

Towns and Urban Agglomerations with their Population, Sexratio, Decadal growth and Literacy rate (2001)

Town	Population	Percentage Decadal growth 1991-2001	Sex Ratio	Literacy Rate
Basukinath (NA)	14,119	21.29	923	65.49
Dumka (M)	44,917	17.90	845	86.55
Jamtara (NA)	22,426	25.91	932	75.90
Mihijam (NA)	32869	40.66	879	81.74

(ii) Parliamentary Constituencies and assembly segments

No.* and *Name of Parliamentary Constituencies:

27-Dumka (ST), 28-Godda.

***No.* and *Name of Assembly Segments* :**

Dumka

153. Sikaripara (ST)—Sikaripara, Ranishwar and Kathikund police stations in Dumka Sadar sub-division.

154. Nala—Nala and Kundahit police stations in Jamtara sub-division.

155. Jamtara—Jamtara police station (excluding G.Ps. Karmatanr, Sahajpur, Pindari, Lakhanpur, Rataniya, Rampurbhitra and Kajra) and Narayanpur police station in Jamtara sub-division.

160. Dumka (ST)—Dumka Town, Dumka Muffassil and Masalia police stations in Dumka Sadar sub-division.

161. Jama (ST)—Jama and Ramgarh police stations in Dumka Sadar sub-division.

Godda

159. Jarmundi—Jarmundt police station in Dumka Sadar sub-division; and Sar,awan police station in Deoghar sub-division.

The communitywise break up (OBE) in Dumka is Muslims (12 per cent), Scheduled Castes (8 per cent) and Scheduled Tribes (48 per cent). Others with some presence are Ahirs, Kahars, Brahmins, Telis and Rajputs. Of the Scheduled Tribes, the most dominant group is that of Santals (38 per cent). Kharwars are also found in small numbers.

OBSERVATIONAL ORGANIZATIONS

Surface Observatories

It lies under meteorological subdivision, Bihar Plateau.

Latitude	:	24.3° North
Longitude	:	87.2° East
Altitude	:	149 m.
Date of starting	:	5-7-1983.

Note: It is a climate measuring station for which monthly matological means of surface elements are transmitted.

Hydrometeorological Stations for Climatological Purposes:

This instrument is located in Ramgarh lies in

Latitude	:	24.5
Longitude	:	87.2
Altitude	:	300 m
Date of starting	:	15-3-1961

DISASTROUS WEATHER EVENTS

Coldwave:

1st January 1982, moderate.
29-30 November 1982, severe.

4-10 December 1982, severe.
2-14 January 1983, severe.
December 3rd and 4th week 1984, severe.
27-31 December 1989, severe.
1-10 January 1990, severe.
January 1st and 2nd week 1992.

Heatwave:
1-7 July, 1982, moderate to severe.
28 May to 2 June 1983, Moderate to severe.
6 June 1983, severe.
7 June 1983, moderate.

Drought:
August and First week of September 1982. The drought was of moderate categories and the transplantation of paddy crop badly affected.

Flood and Heavy Rains:
In August 3rd and 4th week 1983, this area witnessed heavy rains and flood.
July 4th week to October 2nd week 1987, this area witnessed heavy rains. Standing crops damaged.

Thunderstorm:
22 May 1988, this area witnessed a severe thunderstorm, the wind speed was more than 75 km per hour, thatched houses collapsed. Several trees uprooted and number of Telephones poles tilted.

ARCHAEOLOGICAL SITE

Amjani	Dt . Dumka	Lower Palaeolithic (4.2) tools, scrap ers of Series II (Mesolithic (4.3) and microliths. IAR 1960-1
Amrapara	Dt . Dumka	Tools of Series III (Mesolithic (4.5) from the bed of the Bansloi IAR 1960-1
Amuar	Dt. Dumka	Microliths (4.5) on the bank of a small river called Chir IAR 1961-2

Baljor nullah	Dt Dumka	Microliths (4.5). IAR 1961-2
Bandarkola	Dt Dumka	Palaeoliths (4.2), scrapers of Series II (Middle Palaeolithic [4.3]) and microliths (4.5). IAR 1960-1.
Bheladih	Dt Dumka	Microliths and black-and-red ware (11.6.4). IAR 1963-4.
Buddudih	Dt Dumka	Microliths (4.5). IAR 1963-4.
Chandsai	Dt Dumka	Two Shouldered celts of copper (4.11) were found. Patna museum collection.
Chawdhridih	Dt Dumka	Microliths (4.5). IAR 1963-4.
Suraj Bera Hill	Dt Dumka	Tools of Series II (Middle Palaeolithic (4.3) were found at the foot of the hill; 80 km e. of Dumka. IAR 1960-1.
Chorda-dih	Dt Dumka	Microilithic (4.5) site. IAR 1963-4.
Dabur	Dt Dumka	Microliths (4.5) and black-and-red ware. IAR 1963-4.
Dubar-Kunda	Dt Dumka	Microliths and black-and-red were (4.14.3). IAR 1963-4.
Dumar	Dt Dumka	Microliths (4.5). IAR 1963-4.
Gholajuri	Dt Dumka	Microliths (4.5) IAR 1963-4
Ghoralash	Dt Dumka	Microliths (4.5) IAR 1963-4
Harhar Valley	Dt Dumka	Microliths (4.5) were found about 17 km off Deoghar-Chakia road. IAR 1961-2.
Indapahari	Dt Dumka	Microliths (Mesolithic (4.5). IAR 1963-4.
Jasikir	Dt Dumka	Middle Stone Age (Middle Palaeolithic [4.3] tools were found at the mouth of the river Kotania. IAR 1963-4.
Kankershola	Dt Dumka	Microlithis (of unspecified nature). IAR 1963-4.
Karnakolajore	Dt Dumka	Microliths (of unspecified nature). IAR 1963-4.
Kathi-Kunda	Dt Dumka	Tools of Series III (Mesolithic [4.5] were collected from the bed of the Gumra. IAR 1960-1.
Khutiya	Dt Dumka	Microliths and black-and-red ware (both of unspecified nature). IAR 1963-4.
Lidapisa hills	Dt Dumka	Microliths (of unspecified nature) were found about 10 km to the right of the Jamtara-Dumka road from Jhorjukha. IAR 1961-2.
Madhuban	Dt Dumka	Microliths (of an unspecified nature). IAR 1963-4.

Parekola	Dt Dumka	Tools of Series II (Middle Palaeolithic (4.3) were collected from the bed of the Sankhurgara IAR 1960-1.
Phuljhari Hill	Dt Dumka	Microliths of unspecified nature were found at the site about 10 km. to the left bank of the Jamtara-Dumka road from Dubrajpur IAR 1961-2.
Mohantada	Dt Dumka	Stone age site IAR 1960-1.
Paharpur	Dt Dumka	On the South Bank of the Gomai river were discovered Lower Palaeolithic (4.2) flakes tools on quartzite, scrapers of series II (Middle Palaeolithic 4.3)

DISTRIBUTION OF *SCHEDULED CASTE* POPULATION BY SEX DISTRICTWISE (1991)

	POPULATION		
	Total	Males	Females
DUMKA	1,04,094	53,577	50,517
Bantar	171	86	85
Bauri	24,692	12,770	11,922
Bhogta	151	83	68
Bhuiya	6,174	3,050	3,124
Chamar, Mochi	28,851	15,042	13,809
Chaupal	149	71	78
Dabgar	48	27	21
Dhobi	6,898	3,358	3,540
Dom, Dhangad	25,219	12,912	12,307
Dusadh, Dhari, Dharhi	2,121	1,213	908
Ghasi	77	31	46
Halalkhor	7	1	6
Hari, Mehtar, Bhangi	2,035	1,080	955
Kanjar	2	2	0
Kurariar	289	170	119
Lalbegi	14	12	2
Musahar	1,242	558	684
Nat	20	19	1
Pan, Sawasi	32	12	20
Pasi	916	556	360
Rajwar	2,814	1,503	1,311
Turi	1,539	704	835
Unclassified	633	317	316

DISTRIBUTION OF *SCHEDULED TRIBE* POPULATION BY SEX DISTRICTWISE (1991)

	POPULATION		
	Total	Males	Females
DUMKA	6,21,484	3,14,616	3,06,868
Asur	31	10	21
Baiga	137	92	45
Banjara	22	12	10
Bathudi	285	164	121
Bedia	106	45	61
Bhumij	5	1	4
Binjhia	567	201	366
Birhor	2,150	1,187	963
Chero	92	40	52
Chick Baraik	12	1	11
Gond	101	76	25
Gorait	78	33	45
Ho	18	17	1
Karmali	237	87	150
Kharia	196	75	121
Kharwar	132	65	67
Khond	331	175	156
Kisan	13	0	13
Kora	3,326	1,592	1,734
Korwa	97	67	30
Lohara, Lohra	8,108	3,464	4,644
Mahli	14,685	7,620	7,065
Mal Paharia	21,821	11,654	10,167
Munda	897	440	457
Oraon	1,029	593	436
Parhaiya	3,519	1,736	1,783
Santal	5,55,192	2,80,834	2,74,358
Sauria Paharia	8,266	4,315	3,951
Savar	10	10	0
Unclassified	21	10	11

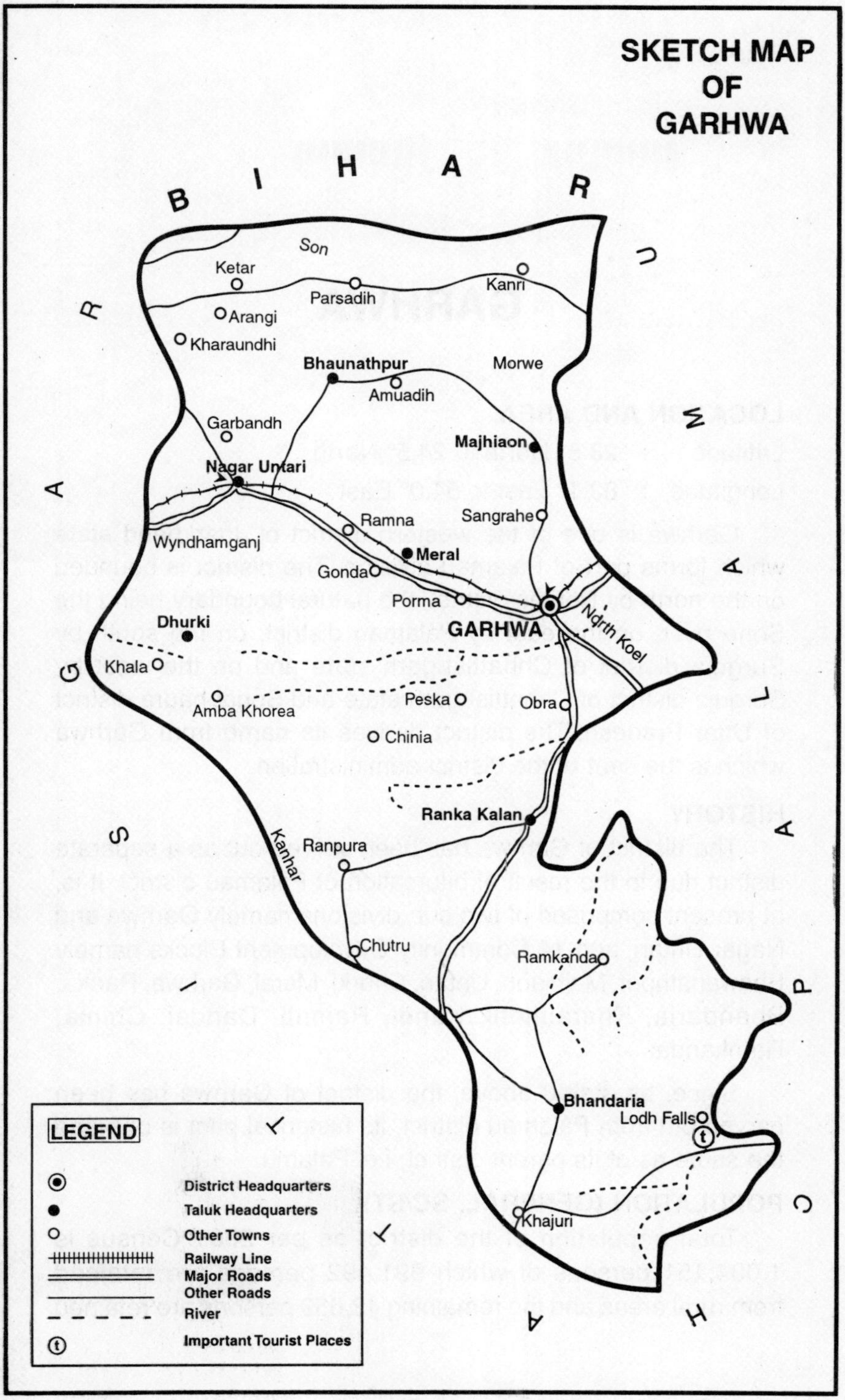
SKETCH MAP
OF
GARHWA
BIHAR
UTTAR PRADESH
MADHYA PRADESH
SARGUJA
Son
Ketar
Parsadih
Kanri
Arangi
Kharaundhi
Bhaunathpur
Amuadih
Morwe
Garbandh
Majhiaon
Nagar Untari
Ramna
Sangrahe
Wyndhamganj
Meral
Gonda
Porma
GARHWA
North Koel
Dhurki
Khala
Peska
Obra
Amba Khorea
Chinia
Ranka Kalan
Kanhar
Ranpura
Chutru
Ramkanda
Bhandaria
Lodh Falls
Khajuri
LEGEND
District Headquarters
Taluk Headquarters
Other Towns
Railway Line
Major Roads
Other Roads
River
Important Tourist Places

GARHWA

LOCATION AND AREA

Latitude : 23.6° North to 24.5° North

Longitude : 83.1° East to 84.0° East

Garhwa is one of the western district of Jharkhand state which forms part of Palamau division. The district is bounded on the north by Rohtas district, the natural boundary being the Sone river, on the east by Palamau district, on the south by Surguja district of Chhattishgarh state and on the west by Surguja district of Chhattishgarh state and Sonabhadra district of Uttar Pradesh. The district derives its name from Garhwa which is the seat of the district administration.

HISTORY

The district of Garhwa has been carved out as a separate district due to the result of bifurcation of Palamau district. It is, at present comprised of two sub-divisions namely Garhwa and Nagar Untari; and 14 Community Development Blocks namely Bhawanathpur, Majhiaon, Untari, Dhurki, Meral, Garhwa, Ranka, Bhandaria, Kharaundhi, Kandi, Ramna, Dandai, Chinia, Ramkanda.

Since, as stated above, the district of Garhwa has been carved out from Palamau district, its historical past is one and the same as of its parent district, i.e. Palamu.

POPULATION (GENERAL, SC/ST)

Total population of the district as per 2001 Census is 1,034,151 persons of which 991,492 persons are retained from rural areas and the remaining 42,659 persons are retained from urban areas. The Scheduled Castes and Scheduled Tribes population of this district as per 1991 census, are 221303 persons and 150667 persons respectively.

The Community Development Blockwise population distribution of this district is given below :

The Community Development Block-wise, population distribution with sex ratio and literacy rate of this district is given below:

C.D. Block	Sex ratio		Literacy rate		Population	
	Rural	Urban	Rural	Urban	Rural	Urban
GARHWA DISTRICT	**938**	**864**	**37.88**	**72.57**	**991492**	**42659**
Kharaundhi	917	-	34.62	-	40,802	-
Bhawanathpur	939	866	39.74	71.12	101,891	5951
Kandi	934	-	49.74	-	64646	-
Majhiaon	936	-	37.77	-	87,635	-
Ramna	930	-	35.79	-	80,751	-
Nagar-Untari	926	-	46.07	-	80,775	-
Dhurki	936	-	29.92	-	66,199	-
Dandai	945	-	29.09	-	49,001	-
Chinia	946	-	25.04	-	30,754	-
Meral (Pipra Kalan)	946	-	37.42	-	100,232	-
Garhwa	939	864	45.07	72.81	131,013	36708
Ranka	944	-	33.70	-	72,613	-
Ramkanda	943	-	36.81	-	33761	-
Bhandaria	957	-	34.04	-	51419	-

LANGUAGES AND RELIGION

Main language spoken in the district are Hindi and Urdu.

Religionwise breakup of population is not available, because it was the part of Palamau district at the time of census taking. The combined figures in this regard are provided in case of its parent district.

GEOGRAPHY AND PHYSICAL FEATURES

Annual Rainfall : 941.0 mm

Temperature : Max. 40.10°C and Min. 3.00 °C

In shape, Garhwa district is vertically located in the map. The length between north and south being greater than that of east to west. The erstwhile Belaunja Pargana forms a long strip of broken hills occasionally forming 1618 kms in breadth on the southern bank of the Sone, and extending from Sonabhadra district of UP on the west and Koel to the east. The hills in the district are widely scattered.

RIVERS, CANALS AND WATERWAYS

Sone and Koel are the main rivers of this district. The line of drainage of Sone river is from west to east, which forms the northern boundary of the district.

Auranga and Amant are the main tributaries of Koel river. Apart from these two rivers, there are many smaller streams, most of which are mere mountain torrents with rock strewn beds. Among other rivers of note in the district is Kanhar which forms a part of the south-western boundary of the district for above 80 kms separating it from Surguja in Madhya Pradesh.

TOWNS, VILLAGES AND AMENITIES

The district is at present comprised of two sub-divisions and 14 Community Development Blocks. It has only one town.

COMMUNICATIONS

Roads: Although no National Highway runs through the district but has a good number of state roads. The main road is the Rehla-Godarmana road passes through Garhwa and Ranka and runs for 57 kilometres in the district up to the Chhattishgarh border.

Besides, there are a number of District Board roads, the most important of which is Garhwa-Daltonganj Road.

Railways: A branch of the Eastern Railway runs from Dehri-on-Sone to Gomoh via Garhwa Road. A branch-line has been taken from Garhwa Road to Sonabhadra in Uttar Pradesh.

Rivers: There is hardly any traffic by boat.

AGRICULTURE AND IRRIGATION

Main crop of the district is paddy. Other important crops are wheat and maize. Sugarcane is the cash crop which is grown mostly in the valley, in the northern part of the district.

Canal, minor bandh, ahar, pyne, wells etc. are the main source of irrigation.

ANIMAL HUSBANDRY

The livestock population of the district consists of cows, buffaloes, bulls and bullocks, sheep, goats and pigs. Bullocks of Shahabadi breed are gradually replacing the local breeds.

The district has veterinary hospital and a number of dispensaries manned by the district Animal Husbandry Department. Various schemes for the cattle improvement are undertaken in the district.

INDUSTRIES

The cultivation of lac is widely spread in the district and lac industry is a valued subsidiary occupation of the cultivators. Biri making industry is also found throughout the district. There are a number of small units for crushing stone and preparation of stone chips.

MINERALS AND ORES OCCURRENCES

Limestone

Muktinath records occurrences of crystaline limestone near Banpahar, Harhi Pahar and Gore.

Graphite

At Sikar (23.93, 83.76), Bhalauni (23.95, 83.11)

TRADE, COMMERCE AND EXPORT

The following table provides information on the most important commodities manufactured, exported from and imported in the Garhwa town of this district alongwith the bank facility :

Name of the town	Most important commodities			
	Manufactured	Exported	Imported	
Garhwa	Biscuits, Ice-cream, and Shellac.	Lac, Oil-seeds and Wood charcoal	Food stuff, Clothes and Cement	4

TOURISM

A brief note on places of tourist interest available in the district is given below:

Vanshidhar Temple. It is situated at the Nagar Untari, which is the headquarter of Nagar Untari Tehsil.

Sukhạdari. The village is situated on the river Kinhar about 35 kms south of Nagar Untari. It is noted for a beautiful waterfall. A fair is held annually on the eve of Makar Sankranti.

Kanjia. The village lies about 8 kms from Bhandaria and is noted for its Catholic *Ashram* which was started in 1937.

FAIRS AND FESTIVALS

Important fairs and melas organised in various parts of the district are Makar Sankranti, Kartik Purnima and Ram Navami mela.

EDUCATION

The following table gives details of different categories of educational institutions including stadia and public library available in the Garhwa town of this district.

Name of the town	*Educational institutions*	*Stadia*	*Public libraries, including reading rooms*
Garhwa	Higher Secondary/ Intermediate School (1), Secondary Matrtculation Schools (3), Junior Secondary and Middle Schools (6), Primary Schools (4)	—	PL : 1

COLLEGES (2000)

S.S.J.S. Namdhari College, Garhwa. (Constituent College)

S.J.G. Singh Namdhari College - Garhwa (Established 1980) Affiliated College.

(Above named colleges belong to Ranchi University)

MEDICAL

The table given below furnishes information regarding availability of medical facility available in Garhwa town of this district including that of beds facility.

Name of the towns	*Medical institutions*	*Number of Beds*
Garhwa	Hospital (1) :	36
	Dispensaries (12, A-3, Hom-5) :	—
	T.B. Clinic (1) :	10
	Family Planning Centre (1) :	6
	N. H. (1) :	6

ADMINISTRATION

(i) Administrative Divisions:

Sub-divisions: Garhwa, Nagar Untari

Community Development Blocks: Bhawanathpur, Majhiaon, Untari, Dhurki, Meral, Garhwa, Ranka, Bhandaria, Kharaundhi, Kandi, Ramna, Dandai, Chinia, Ramkanda.

Towns and Urban Agglomerations with their Population, Sexratio, Decadal growth and Literacy rate (2001)

Town	Population	Percentage Decdal growth 1991-2001	Sex Ratio	Literacy Rate
Garhwa (M)	36,708	32.28	864	72.81
Sinduria (CT)	5,951	-	866	71.12

(ii) Parliamentary Constituencies and assembly segments

No.* and *Name of Parliamentary Constituencies:

54-Palamau (SC)

No.* and *Name of Assembly Segments:

320. Garhwa—Garhwa police station (excluding G.Ps. Jarhi Balekhar, Raro, Sonehara and Dandai) and Ranka police station in Garhwa sub-division.

321. Bhawanathpur—Bhawanathpur and Nagar Untari police stations and G.Ps. Jarhi, Balekhar, Raro, Sonehara and Dandai in Garhwa police station in Garhwa sub- division.

DISASTROUS WEATHER EVENTS

Coldwave:

1st January 1982, moderate.
29-30 November 1982, severe.
4-10 December 1982, severe.
2-14 January 1983, severe.
December 3rd and 4th week 1984, severe.
27-31 December 1989, severe.
1-10 January 1990, severe.
January 1st and 2nd week 1992.

Heatwave:

1-7 July 1982, moderate to severe.
28 May to 2 June, 1983, moderate to severe.
6 June 1983, severe.
7 June 1983, moderate.

Heavy Rains:

July 4th week to October 2nd week 1987, there was heavy rainfall, it caused damage to crops.

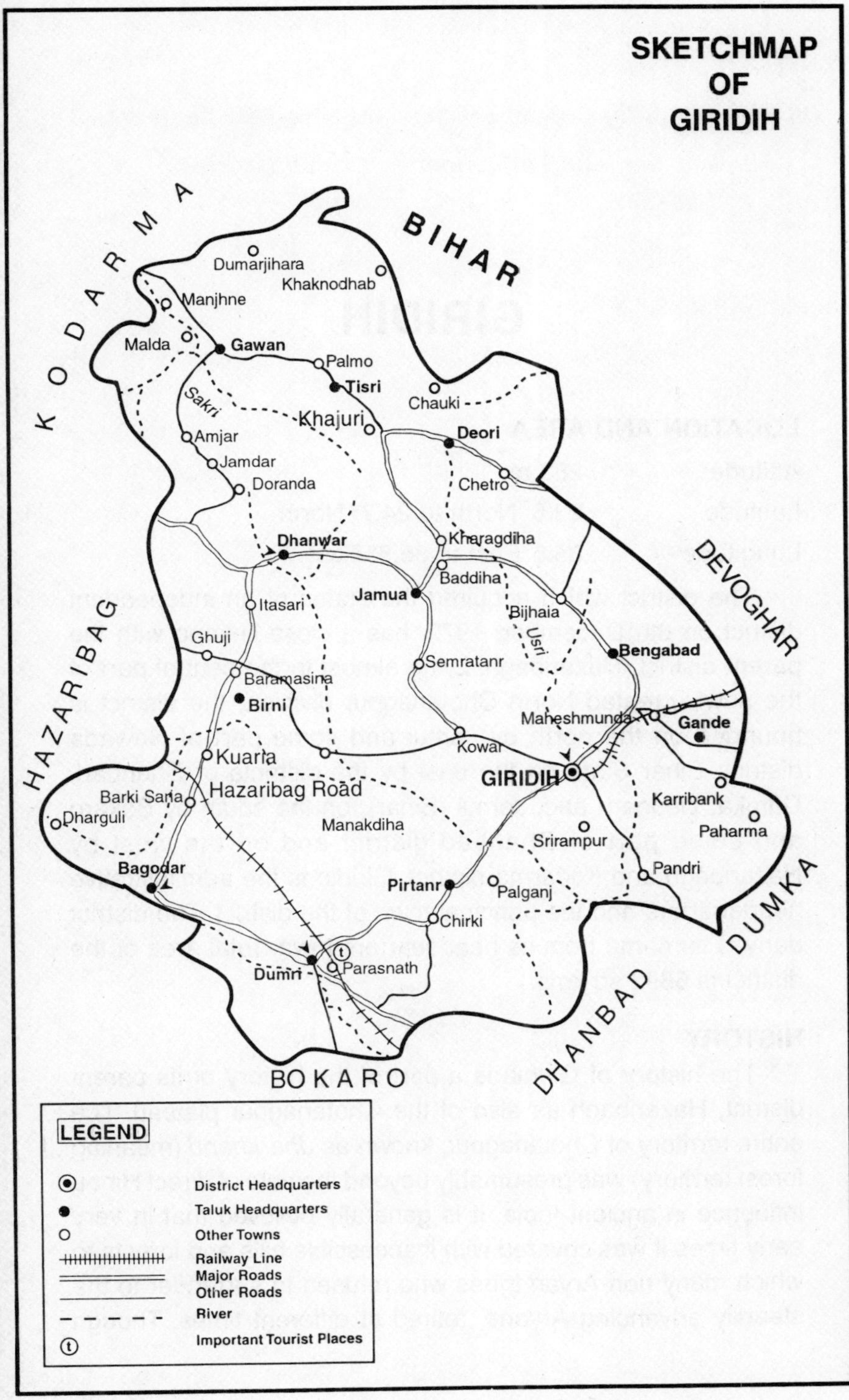
SKETCHMAP OF GIRIDIH
BIHAR
KODARMA
HAZARIBAG
DEVOGHAR
DUMKA
DHANBAD
BOKARO
Dumarjihara
Khaknodhab
Manjhne
Malda
Gawan
Palmo
Tisri
Chauki
Sakri
Khajuri
Amjar
Deori
Jamdar
Chetro
Doranda
Kharagdiha
Dhanwar
Baddiha
Jamua
Itasari
Bijhaia
Usri
Ghuji
Semratanr
Bengabad
Baramasina
Birni
Maheshmunda
Gande
Kowar
Kuarla
GIRIDIH
Barki Sana
Hazaribag Road
Karribank
Dharguli
Manakdiha
Srirampur
Paharma
Bagodar
Pandri
Pirtanr
Palganj
Chirki
Dumri
Parasnath
LEGEND
District Headquarters
Taluk Headquarters
Other Towns
Railway Line
Major Roads
Other Roads
River
Important Tourist Places

GIRIDIH

LOCATION AND AREA

Altitude : 283 m

Latitude : 23.5° North to 24.7° North

Longitude : 85.6°East to 86.5° East

The district which acquired the status of an independent district on 6th December, 1972, has a close linkage with the parent district, Hazaribagh. Lying almost in the central part of the newly-created North Chotanagpur division, the district is bounded on the north by Jamui and some part of Nawada district, Bihar State on the east by the districts of Dhanbad, Dumka, Deogarh and, Jamui (Bihar), on the south by Bokaro and some part of Dhanbad district and on the west by Hazaribagh and Kodarma district. Giridih is the administrative headquarters and the principal town of the district. The district derives its name from its headquarters town. Total area of the district is 6892 sq kms.

HISTORY

The history of Giridih is a part of the history of its parent district, Hazaribagh as also of the Chotanagpur plateau. The entire territory of Chotanagpur, known as *Jharkhand* (meaning forest territory) was presumably beyond the pale of direct Hindu influence in ancient India. It is generally believed that in very early times it was covered with inaccessible hills and forests to which many non-Aryan tribes who refused to surrender to the steadily advancing Aryans, retired at different times. Though this tract was in touch with many parts of India, yet these non-Aryan tribes had no king. All through the long centuries of Hindu rule in India, Chotanagpur including the district of Giridih appears to have remained unmolested, though foreign invaders on rare occasions might have succeeded in exercising nominal overlordship over it. Mr Chapman was practically the first civilian administrator of Chotanagpur. The conquered provinces as they were then called, were formed into a British district which comprised *parganas* Ramgarh, Kendi, Kunda and Kharagdiha (which together constituted the old district of Hazaribagh comprising Giridih), the whole of Palamau, Chakai Panchet and the area around Sherghati.

Subsequent to the Kol rising in 1931 which, however, did not seriously affect Giridih, the administrative structure of the territory was, however, changed. The *parganas* Ramgarh, Kharag-diha, Kendi and Kunda became part of the South-west Frontier Agency and were formed into a division named Hazaribagh, with Hazaribagh as the administrative headquarters. In 1854 the designation of the South-west Froniter Agency was changed to Chutia Nagpur and it began to be administered as a Non-regulation Province under the Lieutenant Governor of Bihar. In 1855-56 there was the great uprising of Santhals against the British but it was brutally suppressed.

POPULATION (GENERAL, SC/ST)

Total population of the district according to 2001 census is 1,901,564 persons, comprising of 958,904 males and 942,660 females. Rural population of the district is 1,779,621 persons (895,007 males and 884,614 females) and urban population is 121,943 persons (63,897 males and 58,046 females).

The Community Development Block-wise, population distribution with sex ratio and literacy rate of this district is given below:

C.D. Block	Sex ratio Rural	Urban	Literacy rate Rural	Urban	Population Rural	Urban
GIRIDIH DISTRICT	**988**	**908**	**42.67**	**78.87**	**1779621**	**121943**
Gawan	1,028	-	36.71	-	88,594	-
Tisri	1,019	-	33.36	-	73,604	-
Deori	981	-	40.47	-	140,486	-
Dhanwar	1,025	950	43.81	77.06	190,210	7935
Jamua	1,005	-	46.79	-	210,107	-
Bengabad	969	-	43.27	-	118,951	-
Gande	949	-	39.48	-	136,112	-
Giridih	931	908	48.33	79.08	193,178	105,212
Birni	1,010	-	42.55	-	134,425	-
Bagodar	1,009	-	44.87	-	236,482	-
Dumri	984	882	39.06	77.97	170,318	8796
Pirtanr	957	-	40.21	-	87,204	-

The Scheduled Castes and Scheduled Tribes population of the district as per 1991 census is 296302 persons and 271924 persons respectively. The rural-urban breakup of these population is indicated below:

Rural	(i) Scheduled Castes	:	251971
	(ii) Scheduled Tribes	:	257347
Urban	(i) Scheduled Castes	:	44331
	(ii) Scheduled Tribes	:	14577

The decennial growth rate of population of the district as a whole in relation to the state between the period 1991 and 2001 is presented below:

State/ District	*Decennial growth rate of population (per cent) 1991-2001*		
	Total	*Rural*	*Urban*
Jharkhand	23.19	21.62	28.99
Giridih	27.09	28.16	13.31

LANGUAGES AND RELIGION

Main languages spoken in the district are Hindi and Urdu.

Religion-wise breakup of population is indicated below as per 1991 census:

Hindus: 1850332, Muslims: 358679, Christians: 10640, Sikhs: 3216, Buddhists: 162, Jains: 2053, Other religions and persuasions: 362, Religions not stated: 36.

GEOGRAPHY AND PHYSICAL FEATURES

Annual Rain Fall : 1220 mm

Temperature : Max. 43.40°C and Min. 6.20°C

The district may be divided broadly into three natural divisions, viz.

1. The central plateau
2. The lower plateaus
3. The Damodar valley

The central plateau touches the western portion of the district near Bagodar block. Around the central plateau are the lower plateaus on all sides except the west on which side a ridge connects the central plateau to the Palamau district. The lower plateaus average 1300 feet in height, their surface being undulating. In the north and north-west, the lower plateaus form fairly level tablelands until they reach the *ghats* when they drop to about 700 feet. In the east, the general elevation is lower and the descent gradual. Along the southern part of the district is the Damodar valley.

The district contains the famous Parasnath Hill which has the distinction of having the highest peak in the state, with an altitude of 4479 feet above the mean sea level.

The district contains a large portion of forested area which is distributed almost uniformly all over. *Sal* is the most famous and predominant species of trees in the jungles of the district. Among other common species are bamboo, *khair* (catechu), *salai,* simul, *mahua, palas, kusum, kend, asan piar* and *bhelwa.*

RIVERS, CANALS AND WATERWAYS

The district is divided into three main waterheads, viz, the Damodar, the Barakar and the Sakri rivers. The Damodar and Barakar rivers drain the major portion of the district. The river Damodar covers Peterbar and Bermo blocks whereas the Barakar enters the district near Birni block and also flows through certain portions of Pirtanar block. The Sakri river touches the areas of Deori and Gawan blocks.

TOWNS, VILLAGES AND AMENITIES

The district is at present comprised of 1 sub-division, 12 Community Development Blocks. It has 4 towns and 3149 villages (2865 inhabited villages and 284 uninhabited villages).

The urban population of the district as percentage of total population in the census years 2001 is indicated below. It also shows the sex ratio (females per 1000 males) and density (population per sq km) in the urban population of the district in relation to the state:

State/ District	*Urban population as percentage of total population*	*Sex ratio, 2001 (Females per 1000 males)*			*Density (Population per sq km)*
	2001	*Total*	*Rural*	*Urban*	
Jharkhand	22.25	941	963	870	497
Giridih	27.09	983	988	908	323

Amenities

Number (with percentage) of villages having one or more amenities in the district as per 1991 census is given below:

Sl. No.	Amenities	Number of inhabited villages	Percentage
1.	Education	1601	55.88
2.	Medical	362	12.64
3.	Drinking Water	2865	100.00
4.	Post and Telegraph	266	9.28
5.	Market/Hat	238	8.17
6.	Communications	550	19.20
7.	Approach by Pucca Road	438	15.29
8.	Power Supply	670	23.21

COMMUNICATIONS

Roads. The district is well served by a network of good roads. Besides the Grand Trunk Road and the National Highway (N.H. 2 and N.H. 23), there are a number of State Highway and R.E.O. roads connecting one place of the district with other places within and outside the district.

All the block headquarters of the district are connected with district headquarters by metalled roads. The following are the important State Highways:

	Name of Road	Length in kms
(1)	Giridih-Dumri	45
(2)	Giridih-Madhupur	31
(3)	Giridih-Jamua	26
(4)	Giridih-Gobindpur	23
(5)	G1rtd1h-Jamua Sarawan	49
(6)	Parasnath Hill	6
(7)	Dhanwar Saraiya	46
(8)	Pataldih Satganwa	64
(9)	Dumri Bermo	50
(10)	Bokaro-Bermo	20
(11)	Narki-Bokaro	25
(12)	Jaridih Link Road	12

Railways. The district headquarters of Giridih is connected by Madhupur Giridih branch of Eastern Railway. Only Mahesmunda and Giridih stations on this route fall within the district.

Airways. There is a landing airstrip for small planes at the district headquarters of Giridih.

Riverways. All the rivers in the distrjct are shallow. Mostly they dry up in summer. For these reasons, there is not much of river traffic in the district.

AGRICULTURE AND IRRIGATION

The main agricultural seasons in the district are *Kharif* and *Rabi.* The Kharif season starts from the third week of May and lasts till the end of October followed by the *Rabi* season. The main crop of the district is rice which covers more than 50 per cent of the gross area sown. Among other important crops are maize, wheat, sugarcane, pulses etc. Vegetables are also grown in the winter and rainy seasons. There is a great scope for growing more vegetables in this district.

Irrigation plays an important role in the agricultural economy of the district. However, in Giridih district, due to the hilly topography of the area, there is not much scope for the exploitation of surface water. The other means of irrigation are exploitation of ground water and taking recourse to lift irrigation. Tank irrigation is quite popular in the district. Groundwater exploitation has also its limitations. The water surface sometimes goes down considerably due to failure of rains and deep boring is also not possible due to hard rocks.

However, after independence, considerable attention has been paid to the provision of irrigational facilities in the district. Several schemes have been taken up by the Damodar Valley Corporation. Besides, irrigation facilities have been extended in the district through a number of medium and minor irrigation schemes, open boring tube-wells and hand-pumps.

ANIMAL HUSBANDRY

The livestock population of the district include cows, buffaloes, bulls and bullocks, sheep, goats and pigs.

The Animal Husbandry Department has distributed a number of pedigree bulls in the rural areas of the district. An Artificial Insemination Centre has been functioning at Giridih. The Animal Husbandry Department is discouraging the use of inferior bulls for breeding purposes by encourging mass castration of bull calves.

Dairying has not been taken up in the organised sector as an occupation and means of livelihood. Similar is the case with poultry. The district, however, offers an excellent potential for growth of dairy and poultry farms being close to the industrial towns such as Bokaro, Hazaribagh, Ranchi, etc.

INDUSTRIES

The main occupation of people of Giridih is cultivation but industries in the district are coming up fast and absorbing a large number of people. There are rich mineral deposits in the district. Mica and coal are the two most important minerals found in abundance. The Damodar Valley Corporation, a multi-purpose project has made power available in certain areas at moderate rates.

Giridih district abounds in forest and mineral resources and among the large industrial establishments of the district mention may be made of :

C.M. Rajgarhia Giridih Factory No.1, Giridih

The Indian Mica Supply Co.Ltd. Giridih Factory. Giridih

Inderchand Rajgarhia & Sons Ltd. Giridih

C.M. Rajgarhia Giridih Factory No.3. Giridih

Bharat Mica Industries Private Ltd., Giridih

Giridih Factory of C.M.I. Ltd. Giridih

Besides the above. there has been considerable increase in the number of small industrial units engaged in manufacture of materials from bamboo, cane, leaves, etc making of earthenware and pottery etc.

MINERALS AND ORES OCCURRENCE

Coal

At Giridih (24.2, 86.4), Karharbari (24.2, 86.3). A report on this field was published in 1850 by McClelland. Twenty seams of coal were counted with an aggregate thickness of 92 ft. A seam of excellent coal 11 ft. thick was being worked in 1851. The area of the field is about 11 sq. miles of which 7 sq. miles occupied by Barakar rocks. The principal seams are:

(i) Karabari lower seam. Area 11 Sq. Km. average thickness 15 ft. 4 ins.

(ii) Karabari upper seam. Area 150 Acres average thickness 6 ft.

(iii) Bhadolah seam. Area 913 Acres, average thickness 6 ft.

The remaining seams have an aggregate thickness of 66 ft. but much of the coal in them is of inferior quality. The field is greatly dislocated by faults and traversed by numerous dykes of basalt and mica-peridotite, which have destroyed many thousand tons of coal.

Gemstone (Apetite)

Baragunda (24.08, 86.05).

TRADE, COMMERCE AND EXPORT

Giridih is mainly important for mica. Next to mica, this market is also important for exporting forest fruits such as *amla, bahera* and *harreh.* Most of the important items are exported to Kolkata. Livestock products such as hides. etc. are also exported from Giridih market. So far as foodgrains are concerned, Giridih exports paddy to other places including West Bengal. The main commodities imported in this district consist of sugar, potato, onion, wheat, pulses, gram, green vegetables, etc.

Within the district the main markets are Giridih, Bagodar and Peterbar. Fairs are also important centres for agricultural marketing,

TOURISM

Baidadih. It is a small village situated near Maheshmunda railway station on the Madhupur-Giridih section of the Eastern Railway. It is noted for its large well, Whole water contains important minerals and is transported to Kolkata and other places for medicinal use. A large annual fair is held in the village on the occasion of *Lakshmi Puja*.

Dalgando. The village is situated about 6 kms north-west of the block headquarters at Bengabad. A mica belt was discovered here. The village has a Shiva temple where an annual fair is held on the occasion of *Shivaratri.*

Khandoli. It is also a small village situated on the foot of the hills about 8 kms north of Giridih railway station. The village is noted as a picnic spot.

Madhuban. The village, which lies in Pirtanr block, has a famous temple believed to be more than 2000 years old. It is a place of considerable religious importance for the Jains. The Samosharan temple and Bhomiyaji Asthan are very beautiful places of attraction. The 'Dharm Mangal Vidyaplth' temple is under construction.

Parasnath. The Parasnath hill, which is the highest in Chotanagpur plateau, constitutes an important place of pilgrimage for the Jains. It draws a large number of pilgrims every year. The hill is situated about 11 kms east of Isri railway station on the Grand Chord Line of Eastern Railway.

Usri Fall. It is a famous waterfall over the river Usri, situated about 13 kms. east of Giridih town. It is a favourite picnic spot.

FAIRS AND FESTIVALS

Important fairs and melas organised in various parts of the district are mentioned below:

Dussehra mela and Paush Purnima mela.

EDUCATION

According to 2001 census, total literates (excluding the population in the age group of 0-6 years) is 679,053 persons. Of these, 476,833 are males and 202,220 are females. In the rural areas of the district 597,514 persons (430,233 males and 167,281 females) are literates and in urban areas 81,539 persons (46,600 males and 34,939 females) are literates. The rate of literacy of this population to the total population, excluding 0-6 years age group according to 2001 census is shown in the table.

	Persons	*Males*	*Females*
Total	45.16	63.07	27.05
Rural	42.67	61.32	23.94
Urban	78.87	85.75	71:26

There are as many as 1601 villages in the district where educational facility of one type or other is found within the village itself. Primary and middle school education facilities are generally available in all towns.

UNIVERSITY AND COLLEGES, 2000

Giridih College, Giridih (Established 1955) (Constituent College), Enrolment 3134, Teachers 42.

R.K. Mahila College, Giridih (Established 1978) (Constituent College), Enrolment 1517, Teachers 16.

Jhabbu Singh Memorial College, Phusro (Established 1980), Teachers 21. Affiliated College.

KRMV College, Girdih, Teachers 35. Affiliated College.

Langta Baba College, Mirzaganj, Giridih (Established 1985), Teachers 18. Affiliated College.

Suriya College Suriya, Giridih (Established 1984), Teachers 14. Affiliated College.

Above mentioned colleges belong to Vinoba Bhave University (Established 1992)

MEDICAL

Medical facility in the villages of this district is not very satisfactory as only 362 villages have it.

ADMINISTRATION

(i) Administrative Divisions:

Sub-divisions: Giridih.

Community Development Blocks: Gawan, Isri, Deori, Dhanwar, Jamua, Bengabad, Gande, Giridih, Birni, Bagodar, Dumri, Pirtanr.

Towns and Urban Agglomerations with their Population, Sexratio, Decadal growth and Literacy rate (2001)

GIRIDIH UA
Giridih (M)
Paratdih (CT)

Town	Population	Percentage Decadal growth 1991-2001	Sex Ratio	Literacy Rate
Dhanwar (CT)	7,935	-	950	77.06
Giridih (M)	98,569	26.21	904	80.64
Isri (CT)	8,796	46.38	882	77.97
Paratdih (CT)	6,643	-	965	53.87

(ii) Parliamentary Constituencies and Assembly Segments:

No.* and *Name of Parliamentary Constituencies:

45-Kodarma, 46-Giridih.

No.* and *Name of Assembly Segments:

Giridih

271. Dhanwar—Dhanwar and Gawan police stations in Giridih Sadar sub-division.

272. Bagodar—Bagodar and Birni police stations in Giridih Sadar sub-division.

273. Jamua (SC)—Jamua and Deori police stations in Giridih Sadar sub-division.

274. Gandey—Gandey and Bengabad police stations and G.Ps. Leda, Semaria, Badgunda, Palmo, Sathibad, Senadoni, Dhanaidih, Guro, Jitpur, Telodih, Ranidih and Karharbari in Giridih Mufassil police station in Giridih Sadar sub-division.

Giridih

275. Giridih—Giridih Town police station and Giridih Mufassil police station (excluding, G.Ps, Leda, Semaria, Badgunda, Palmo, Sathibad Senadoni, Dhanaidih, Guro, Jitpur, Telodih, Ranidih and Karharbari) and Pirtanr police station in Giridih Sadar sub- division.

276. Dumri—Dumri police station in Giridih Sadar sub-division; and Nawadih police station in Bermo sub-division.

The communitywise breakup (OBE) in Giridih is Muslims (14 per cent), Scheduled Castes (15 per cent), Scheduled Tribes (18 per cent), and Kurmis and Ahirs, around 10 per cent each. Others in some strength are Telis, Koeris, Brahmins and Rajputs. Chamars (7 per cent) are the dominant Scheduled Caste. Santals (16 per cent) are clearly dominant among the Scheduled Tribes.

OBSERVATIONAL ORGANIZATIONS

Hydrometeorological Stations for Climatological Purposes:

Latitude	:	23.8° North
Longitude	:	81.0° East
Altitude	:	283 m
Date of starting	:	16-4-1948

DISASTROUS WEATHER EVENTS

Coldwave:

1st January 1982, moderate.
29-30 November 1982, severe.

4-10 December 1982, severe.

2-14 January 1983, severe.

December 3rd and 4th week 1984, severe.

27-31 December 1989, severe.

1-10 January 1990, severe.

January 1st and 2nd week 1992.

Heatwave:

1-7 July 1982, moderate to severe

28 May to 2 June, moderate to severe.

6 June 1983, severe.

7 June 1983, moderate.

Heavy Rains:

July 4th week to October 2nd week 1987, this area witnessed moderate to heavy rains. Standing crops and sowing badly affected.

DISTRIBUTION OF *SCHEDULED CASTE* POPULATION BY SEX DISTRICTWISE (1991)

	POPULATION		
	Total	Males	Females
GIRIDIH	2,96,302	1,50,970	1,45,332
Bantar	222	139	83
Bauri	2,741	1,506	1,235
Bhogta	13,498	7,009	6,489
Bhuiya	11,428	5,870	5,558
Chamar, Mochi	1,20,585	60,221	60,364
Chaupal	133	79	54
Dabgar	487	248	239
Dhobi	22,041	11,565	10,476
Dom, Dhangad	4,325	2,260	2,065
Dusadh, Dhari, Dharhi	30,115	15,387	14,728
Ghasi	6,058	3,184	2,874
Halalkhor	154	82	72
Hari, Mehtar, Bhangi	4,156	2,230	1,926
Kanjar	83	25	58
Kurariar	170	97	73
Lalbegi	133	48	85
Musahar	5,328	2,801	2,527
Nat	19	16	3
Pan, Sawasi	67	47	20
Pasi	8,728	4,499	4,229
Rajwar	12,297	6,560	5,737
Turi	53,191	26,932	26,259
Unclassified	343	165	178

DISTRIBUTION OF *SCHEDULED TRIBE* POPULATION BY SEX DISTRICTWISE (1991)

	POPULATION		
	Total	Males	Females
GIRIDIH	2,71,924	1,39,560	1,32,364
Asur	87	64	23
Baiga	6	2	4
Banjara	13	13	0
Bathudi	11	11	0
Bedia	1,385	699	686
Bhumij	62	32	30
Binjhia	10	10	0
Birhor	544	243	301
Birjia	58	48	10
Chero	33	25	8
Chick Baraik	39	17	22
Gond	2,470	1,421	1,049
Gorait	79	40	39
Ho	106	77	29
Karmali	8,335	4,655	3,680
Kharia	381	113	268
Kharwar	4,457	2,383	2,074
Khond	421	202	219
Kisan	374	146	228
Kora	1,520	696	824
Korwa	149	68	81
Lohara, Lohra	1,231	621	610
Mahli	5,881	3,009	2,872
Mal Paharia	861	487	374
Munda	10,780	5,585	5,195
Oraon	3,564	1,985	1,579
Parhaiya	216	43	173
Santal	2,28,433	1,16,712	1,11,721
Sauria Paharia	315	120	195
Savar	63	26	37
Unclassified	40	7	33

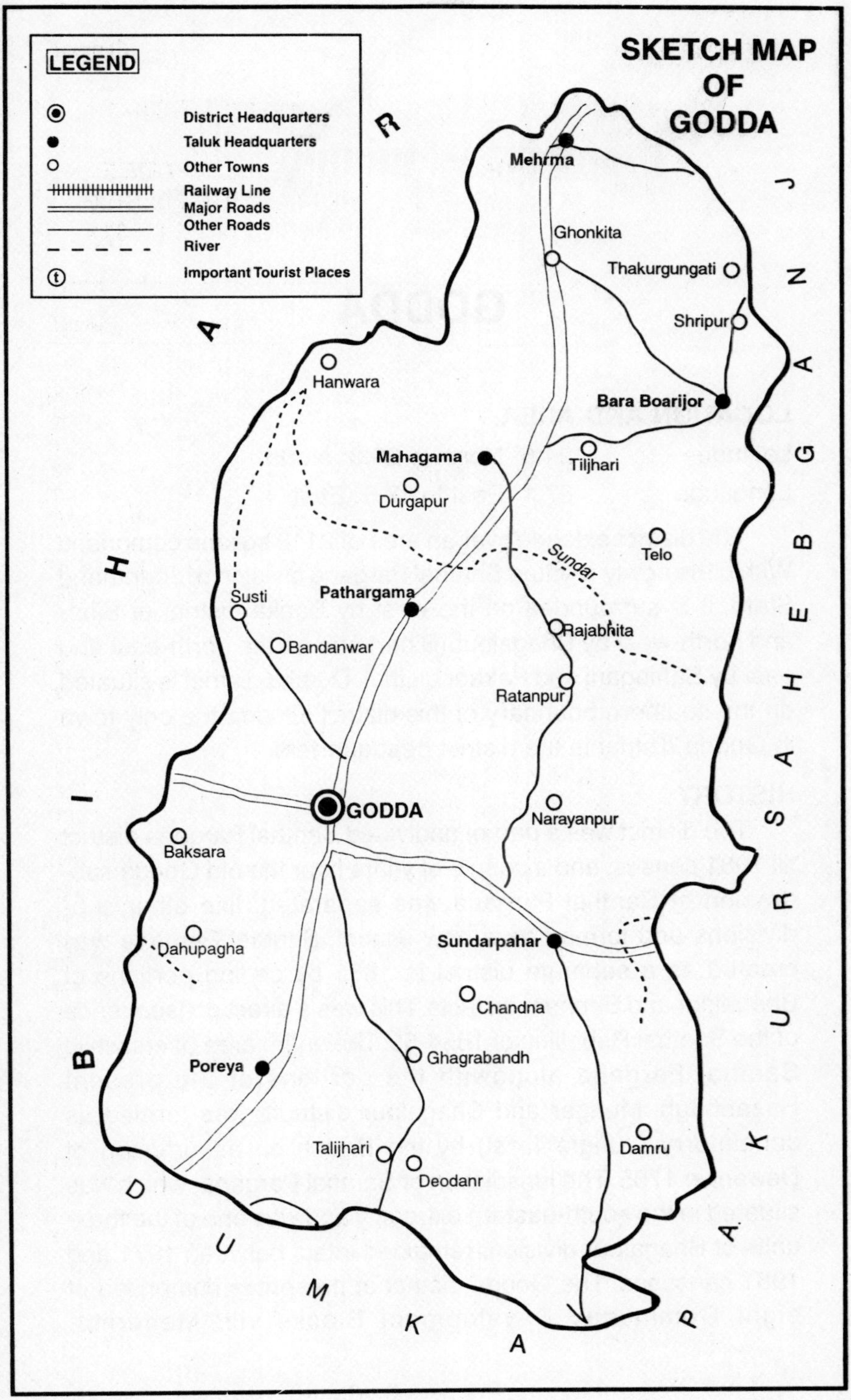

SKETCH MAP
OF
GODDA
LEGEND
District Headquarters
Taluk Headquarters
Other Towns
Railway Line
Major Roads
Other Roads
River
Important Tourist Places
Mehrma
Ghonkita
Thakurgungati
Shripur
Bara Boarijor
Hanwara
Mahagama
Tiljhari
Durgapur
Telo
Sundar
Pathargama
Susti
Rajabhita
Bandanwar
Ratanpur
GODDA
Narayanpur
Baksara
Sundarpahar
Dahupagha
Chandna
Ghagrabandh
Poreya
Damru
Talijhari
Deodanr
B I H A R
S A H E B G A N J
P A K U R
D U M K A

GODDA

LOCATION AND AREA

Latitude : 24.5° North to 25.3° North

Longitude : 87.1° East to 87.5° East

The district extends over an area of 2110 sq kms comprised Within the newly created Santhal Pargana division of Jharkhand State. It is surrounded on the west by Banka district of Bihar and north-west by Bhagalpur (Bihar) and on the north-east and east by Sahibganj and Pakaur district. Dumka district is situated on the southern boundary of this district. Godda the only town in Godda district is the district headquarters.

HISTORY

The district was a part of undivided Santhal Pargana district till 1981 census, and a couple of years later the old Godda sub-division of Santhal Pargana was separated, like other sub-divisions and formed as a new district. Santhal Pargana was created as a separate district in 1855 by ceding portions of Bhagalpur and Birbhum districts. This was a direct consequence of the Santhal Rebellion of 1854-55. The entire area of erstwhile Santhal Pargana alongwith the portions of the present Hazaribagh. Munger and Bhagalpur districts was termed as Jungleterry (Jungle Tarai) by the British on assumption of Dewani in 1765. The jurisdiction of Santhal Pargana, which was situated in the south-eastern extremity and was one of the three units of Bhagalpur division, remained intact between 1971 and 1981 censuses. The Godda district at present is comprised of eight Community Development Blocks viz. Meherma,

Mahagama, Boarijor, Pathargama, Godda, Sundaryahari, Pareyahat and Thakur Gangati. As stated above, this newly created district of Godda was a part of Santhal Pargana, obviously the historical past of the district is the same as of its parent district, which has been explained in details in the note of Dumka district.

POPULATION (GENERAL, SC/ST)

Total population of the district according to 2001 census is 1,047,264 persons, comprising of 543,784 males and 503,480 females. Rural population of the district is 1,010,257 persons (523,799 males and 486,458 females) and urban population is 37,007 persons (19,985 males and 17,022 females).

The Community Development Block-wise, population distribution with sex ratio and literacy rate of this district is given below:

	Sex ratio		Literacy rate		Population	
C.D. Block	Rural	Urban	Rural	Urban	Rural	Urban
GODDA DISTRICT	**929**	**852**	**42.22**	**82.94**	**1010257**	**37007**
Meherma	887	-	45.80	-	115,820	-
Thakur Gangti	925	-	43.37	.-	77,457	-
Boarijor	947	-	33.56	-	113,129	-
Mahagama	927	-	44.43	-	150,638	-
Pathargama	931	-	44.85	-	166,985	-
Godda	918	852	46.50	82.94	178,692	37,007
Poreyahat	953	-	40.66	-	154,262	-
Sundarpahari	953	-	27.55	-	53,274	-

The Scheduled Castes and Scheduled Tribes population of the district as per 1991 census is 72893 persons and 216047 persons respectively. The rural-urban breakup of this population is indicated below:

Rural	(i) Scheduled Castes	:	71661
	(ii) Scheduled Tribes	:	2149361
Urban	(i) Scheduled Castes	:	1232
	(ii) Scheduled Tribes	:	1111

The decennial growth rate of population of the district as a whole in relation to the state between the period 1991 and 2001 is presented below:

State/ District	*Decennial growth rate of population (per cent) 1991-2001*		
	Total	*Rural*	*Urban*
Jharkhand	23.19	21.62	28.99
Godda	21.61	20.62	56.56

LANGUAGES AND RELIGION

Hindi is the principal languge spoken in this district.

Religionwise breakup of population is indicated below as per 1991 census:

Hindus: 699250, Muslims: 152556, Christians: 6583, Sikhs:—, Buddhists: —, Jains: 2, Other religions and persuasions: 2791, Religions not stated:—.

GEOGRAPHY AND PHYSICAL FEATURES

Annual Rainfall : 1128.0 mm

Temperature : Max. 47.00°C and Min. 6.60°C

Godda district consists of the uplands, undulations, long ridges and depressions. There are high hills here and there with lofty peaks like Masanjore in the adjoining Dumka district and Rajmahal Hills and other hill ranges found in Damin-i-Koh area. The western range of Rajmahal hills passes through Godda and Dumka and its eastern range runs parallel to the loop line of the Eastern Railway upto Patna, where it bends westward to join the western range. These hill ranges enclose between them about 5120 sq kms of hilly tract, 3471 sq kms. of which are known as Damin-i-Koh. The district once known for its thick and extensive forest is now bereft of much of its jungle wealth. There has been large scale destruction of forests in the past few years. The most common tree of the district is sal. Some teak of inferior variety is also found. Other trees found are jack fruits. simal and bamboo. Among the forest products of consequences are lac, sabai grass and tassar silk cocoons. The erstwhile Santhal Pargana was a sanctuary of wild animals upto the 19th century. However, large scale destruction of forests and wanton killings has reduced their number considerably.

RIVERS, CANALS AND WATERWAYS

The Ganges is the largest and the most important river of the district. A big tank spread over in an area of 20 hectares is situated in Basanthai village, which is considered sacred and a holy dip is taken every year on the occasion of Sankranti (March-April) by the; people of this district as well as of the adjoining districts.

TOWNS, VILLAGES AND AMENITIES

The district is at present comprised of one sub-division and 8 Community Development Blocks. It has 1 town and 2304 villages (1599 inhabited villages and 705 uninhabited villages).

The urban population of the district as percentage of total population in the census year 2001 is indicated below. It also shows the sex ratio (females per 1000 males) and density (populapon per sq km) in the urban area of the district in relation to the state:

State/ District	*Urban population as percentage of total population*	*Sex ratio, 2001 (Females per 1000 males)*			*Density (Population per sq km)*
	2001	*Total*	*Rural*	*Urban*	
Jharkhand	22.25	941	963	870	338
Godda	3.58	926	929	852	496

Amenities

Number (with percentage) of villages having one or more amenities in the district as per 1991 census is given below:

Sl. No.	Amenities	Number of inhabited villages	Percentage
1.	Education	988	61.79
2.	Medical	208	13.01
3.	Drinking Water	1599	100.00
4.	Post and Telegraph	166	10.38
5.	Market/Hat	147	9.19
6.	Communications	154	9.63
7.	Approach by Pucca Road	272	17.01
8.	Power Supply	287	17.89

COMMUNICATIONS

The district has no rail link with the rest of the country even today. This indicates that the people of this district are deprived of such an essential mode of transport even in this modern age. However, there is a network of good roads in the district and all the neighbouring districts viz Bhagalpur, Sahibganj, Dumka, Deoghar are connected with Godda by black topped all weather roads. All the Community Development Block headquarters are also interlinked with Godda, the district headquarter by all weather good roads.

AGRICULTURE AND IRRIGATION

The main occupation of the people of Godda district is cultivation. Kharif and rabi are the main agricultural seasons. Paddy and maize are the main crops grown in the district. Due to inadequate irrigational facilities, rabi crops are not grown very extensively. Vegetables, linseed, khesari are other crops grown in the different parts of Godda. Linseed usually forms the second crop to rice. Well is the common source of irrigation. A major part of the district being rocky, it is difficult to dig wells. Sugarcane is raised in areas having assured irrigation.

ANIMAL HUSBANDRY

Cattle found in this district are generally poor in quality. There has been a concerted effort on behalf of the State Government to improve the breed of the cattle by way of distribution of stud bulls of Haryana and Tharparkar variety. In order to grade up the cattle quickly and also at low cost, artificial insemination centres with sub-centres have been opened at various places in the district. Cows, buffaloes, bulls and bullocks, goats, sheep and pigs are the common livestock found in this district as well. Poultry is subsidiary occupation of the local people. A number of poultry development centres and extension centres have been opened in the district.

INDUSTRIES

Godda district is inhabited by tribals, particularly by Santhals and Paharia. The Santhals mostly use handloom fabrics and this can be substantiated with the existence, of a large number of units in this category. Because of poverty and backwardness of the local inhabitants, large scale use of earthenware and earthen pottery are seen. There are large jungle tracts where the manufacture of materials from bamboo, cane, leaves and other allied products is apt to flourish. The traditional cottage and village industries practised by the Santhal and Paharia tribes constitute earthenware pot making, *bidi* making etc. There is no large scale industry in this district.

MINERALS AND ORES OCCURRENCES

Coal

Coal at Domin-i-koh G.C. Chatterjee reports occurencess of inferior coal in Damin-i-Koh, a Government Estate comprised within the later subdivision of Dumka Pakaur Godda and Rajmahal in then Santal Parganes the coal seams are less than 4ft. in thickness.

Lead

Near Akasi or Panch Pahar (24.6, 87.2). A vein of lead-ore occurs in small crystels in a decomposing bed of quartz and actinalite, consisting about 2 per cent of the mass. The ore is sulphide of antimony. A vein 1/4 inch in width was met with specimens are stated to yield 60 per cent of lead.

Fire-clay

Gilhuria (24.85, 87.46).

TRADE, COMMERCE AND EXPORT

The chief imports of the district are medicines, clothes and coal whereas the chief exports are paddy, vegetable and gur. The table below lists three most important commodities manufactured, exported from and imported in the only town of this district:

Name of the town	*Most important commodities*		
	Manufactured	*Exported*	*Imported*
Godda	Hume pipe, Bakery, Earthen pot	Paddy, Vegetables Gur	Medicines, Clothes, Coal

Number of Bank in the town of Godda *district* : Godda: 3.

TOURISM

The district does not have many places of religious, historical archaeological importance or of the places of tourist interest. Brief description of the only village of the district which has some significance is mentioned below:

Basantrai—It is an old village in Pathargama block named after an ancient king Basantrai who was known for his generosity. There is a big sacred tank of about 20 hectares in existence since time immemorial. A fair is held during Sankranti in Chaitra (March-April) when people take a holy dip in the tank.

FAIRS AND FESTIVALS

Important fairs and melas organised in different parts of Godda district are indicated below:

Shivaratri mela, Chaitra Sankranti mela, Divali mela, Muharram mela, Dussehra mela, Makar Sankranti mela, Basant Panchmi. Goshala mela. Kaliya Banba mela, Thakur mela, Rathyatra and Charak puja mela.

EDUCATION

According to 2001 census. total literates (excluding the population in the age group of 0-6 years) is 371,184 persons. Of these. 258,025 are males and 113,159 are females. In the rural areas of the district 345,121 persons (242,699 males and 102,422 females) are literates and in urban areas 26,063 persons (15,326 males and 10,737 females) are literates. The rate of literacy of this population to the total population, excluding 0-6 years age group according to 2001 census is shown below:

	Persons	*Males*	*Females*
Total	43.73	58.07	27.98
Rural	42.22	56.81	26.25
Urban	82.94	89.65	71.39

There are as many as 988 villages accounting for 61.79 per cent of the total number of inhabited villages in the district where educational facility is available. Primary and Middle schools are available in the town. The following table gives the details of various types of educational institutions available in the only town of this district including the number of stadia and public libraries.

Name of the town	*Educational institutions*	*Stadia*	*Public libraries, including reading rooms*
Godda	2 Secondary/ Matriculation Schools and 4 Junior Secondary/ Middle Schools.	—	PL : 2

COLLEGES (2000)

Godda College Godda (Established 1955) Constituent College. Enrolment 1784, Teachers 48.

Mellat College, Parsa (Established Godda) 1982. Constituent College. Enrolment 73, Teachers 16.

Mahila College Godda (Established 1983). Enrolment 453, Teachers 32. Affiliated College

(Above named colleges belong to Siddhu Kanhu University, Established 1992).

MEDICAL

The availability of medical facility in the villages is considerably low as only 13.01 per cent villages in the district have got it. The table given below furnishes inrormation regarding various types of medical institutions available in the town of this district:

Name of the towns	*Medical institutions*	*Number of Beds*
Godda	Hospital (1)	34
	Family Planntng Centre (1)	—

ADMINISTRATION

(i) Administrative Divisions:

Sub-division: Godda.

Community Development Blocks: Meherma, Mahagama, Boarijor, Pathargama, Godda, Sundarpahari. Poreyahat. Thakur Gangati.

Towns and Urban Agglomerations with their Population, Sexratio, Decadal growth and Literacy rate (2001)

Town	Population	Percentage Decadal growth 1991-2001	Sex Ratio	Literacy Rate
Godda (M)	37,007	56.56	852	82.94

(ii) Parliamentary Constituencies and assembly segments

No.* and *Name of Parliamentary Constituencies:

28-Godda, 30-Bhagalpur.

No.* and *Name of Assembly Segments:

Godda

162. Poreyahat—Poreyahat police station and G.Ps. Burhikura, Dammajhilua, Sandmara. Nonbatta, Makhni. Pathra and Punsiya in Godda police station in Godda sub-division; and Saraiyahat police station in Durrika Sadarsub-division.

163. Godda—Godda police station (excluding G.Ps. Burhikura, Dammajhilua, Sandmara, Nonbatta, Makhni, Pathra and Punsiya) and Pathargama police station in Godda sub-division.

Bhagalpur

164. Mahgama— Mahgama and Mahrama Police Circle in Godda subdivision.

Godda was in Dumka Parliamentary constituency in 1957. The communitywise breakup (OBE) in Godda is Muslims (15 per cent), Scheduled Castes (13 per cent), Scheduled Tribes (19 per cent), Ahirs (8 per cent). Others in sizable numbers are Telis, Brahmins and Kahars. Among the Scheduled Tribes, the most numerous are the Santals (14 per cent) .

DISASTROUS WEATHER EVENTS

Coldwave:

1st January 1982, moderate.
29-30 November 1982, severe.
4-10 December 1982, severe.
2-14 January 1983, severe.
December 3rd and 4th week 1984, severe.
27-31 December 1989, severe.
1-10 January 1990, severe.
January 1st and 2nd week 1992.

Heatwave:

1-7 July 1982, moderate to severe.
28 May to 2 June 1983, moderate to severe.
6 June 1983, severe.
7 June 1983, moderate.

Drought:

August and First week of September 1982. The drought was of moderate category. Transplantation of paddy crop badly affected.

Flood and Heavy Rains:

In August 3rd and 4th week 1983 this area witnessed heavy rains and flood.

July 4th week to October 2nd week 1987, this area witnessed heavy rains, damaged to property reported.

Thunderstorm:

On 22nd May 1988, this area witnessed a severe thunder storm, the wind speed was more than 75 km per hour which caused damage to the trees, thatched houses and the telephone poles.

DISTRIBUTION OF *SCHEDULED CASTE* POPULATION BY SEX DISTRICTWISE (1991)

	POPULATION		
	Total	Males	Females
GODDA			
	72,893	37,921	34,972
Bantar	45	29	16
Bauri	734	397	337
Bhogta	1	0	1
Bhuiya	6,977	3,533	3,444
Chamar, Mochi	28,426	14,729	13,697
Chaupal	1,001	588	413
Dabgar	1	0	1
Dhobi	3,682	2,096	1,586
Dom, Dhangad	7,780	4,072	3,708
Dusadh, Dhari, Dharhi	11,147	5,583	5,564
Ghasi	261	146	115
Halalkhor	60	51	9
Hari, Mehtar, Bhangi	699	397	302
Kanjar	81	61	20
Kurariar	94	43	51
Lalbegi	8	7	1
Musahar	7,205	3,616	3,589
Nat	60	31	29
Pan, Sawasi	11	1	10
Pasi	1,160	650	510
Rajwar	1,724	1,020	704
Turi	1,485	738	747
Unclassified	251	133	118

DISTRIBUTION OF *SCHEDULED TRIBE* POPULATION BY SEX DISTRICTWISE (1991)

	POPULATION		
	Total	Males	Females
GODDA			
	2,16,047	1,09,314	1,06,733
Asur	10	0	10
Baiga	356	138	218
Banjara	36	24	12
Bathudi	10	10	0
Bedia	38	11	27
Binjhia	19	10	9
Birjia	10	10	0
Gond	308	132	176
Gorait	65	20	45
Karmali	71	33	38
Kharia	86	69	17
Kharwar	179	106	73
Khond	30	30	0
Kisan	23	11	12
Kora	1,288	628	660
Korwa	91	29	62
Lohara, Lohra	7,855	3,841	4,014
Mahli	2,043	1,146	897
Mal Paharia	8,631	4,657	3,974
Munda	432	258	174
Oraon	5,615	2,774	2,841
Parhaiya	4,536	2,297	2,239
Santal	1,77,806	89,808	87,998
Sauria Paharia	6,440	3,232	3,208
Unclassified	69	40	29

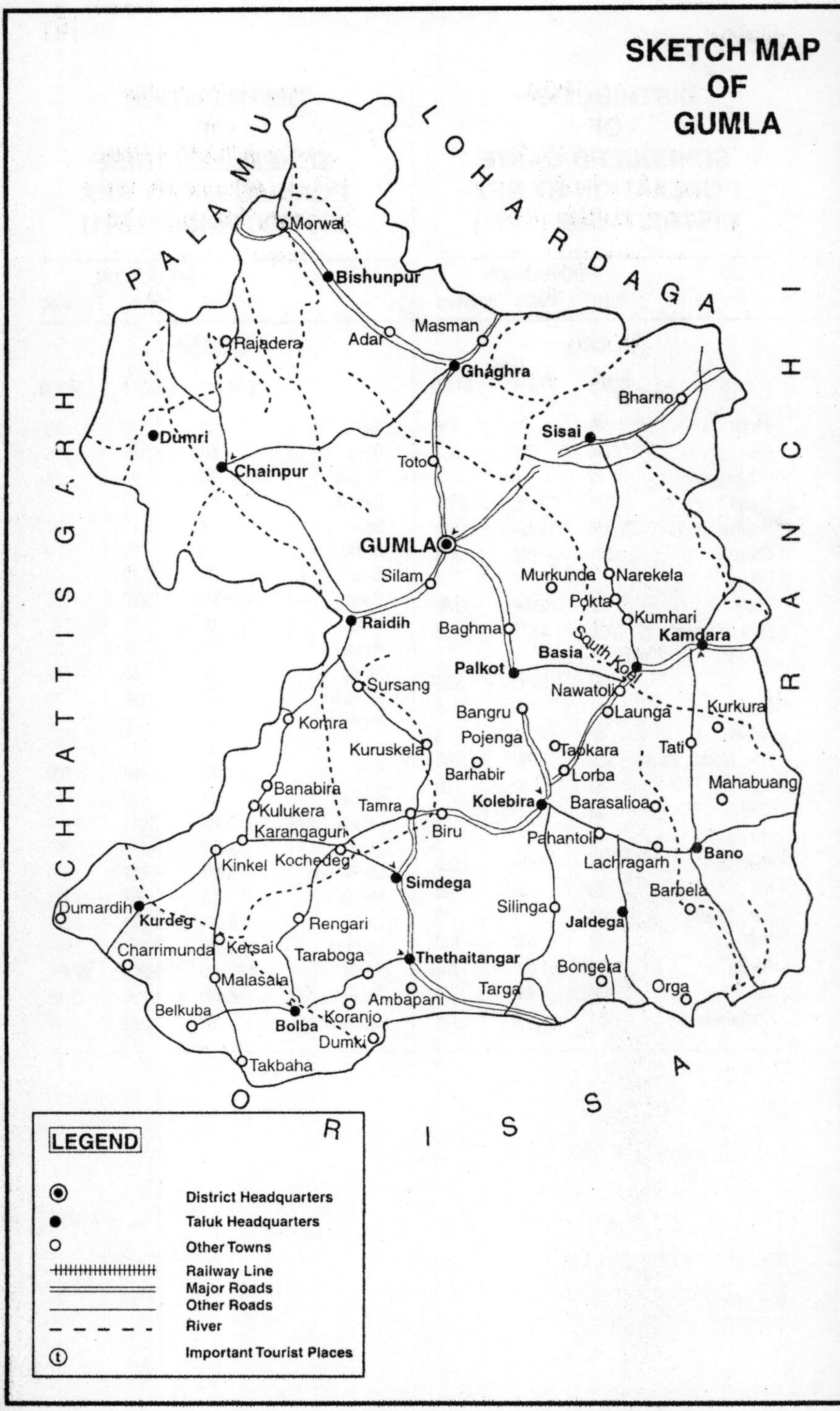
SKETCH MAP OF GUMLA
PALAMU
LOHARDAGA
RANCHI
CHHATTISGARH
ORISSA
Morwal
Bishunpur
Masman
Adar
Rajadera
Ghaghra
Bharno
Sisai
Dumri
Chainpur
Toto
GUMLA
Silam
Murkunda
Narekela
Pokta
Kumhari
Kamdara
Raidih
Baghma
Basia
South Koel
Palkot
Nawatoli
Sursang
Bangru
Launga
Kurkura
Kohra
Pojenga
Tapkara
Tati
Kuruskela
Barhabir
Lorba
Banabira
Mahabuang
Kulukera
Tamra
Kolebira
Barasalioa
Karangaguri
Biru
Pahantoli
Kinkel
Kochedeg
Lachragarh
Bano
Simdega
Barbela
Dumardih
Kurdeg
Silinga
Jaldega
Rengari
Kersai
Charrimunda
Taraboga
Thethaitangar
Bongera
Malasala
Targa
Orga
Ambapani
Belkuba
Bolba
Koranjo
Dumki
Takbaha
LEGEND
District Headquarters
Taluk Headquarters
Other Towns
Railway Line
Major Roads
Other Roads
River
Important Tourist Places

GUMLA

LOCATION AND AREA

Altitude : 646 m.

Latitude : 22.4° North to 23.6° North.

Longitude : 84.0° East to 85.1° East.

The district lies in the south-western corner of Jharkhand state, comprised within South Chotanagpur division. It is bounded on the north by the districts of Palamu and Lohardaga, on the east by the district of Ranchi and part of Pashchimi Singhbhum, on the south by Sundargarh district (in Orissa) and on the west by the district of Raigarh (in Chhattishgarh).Total area of the district is 9077 sq kms and Gumla is the district headquarters.

HISTORY

The district was a part of undivided Ranchi district at the time of 1981 census. It was carved out as a separate district only in the recent past as a result of the upgradation of old Gumla and Simdega subdivision of erstwhile Ranchi district. Since this newly-created district was a part of Ranchi, the historical past of this district is the same as of its parent district, i.e. Ranchi.

POPULATION (GENERAL, SC/ST)

Total population of the district according to 2001 census is 1,345,520 persons, comprising of 674,555 males and 671,065 females. Rural population of the district is 1,271,768 persons 636,314 males and 635,454 females) and urban population is 73,752 persons (38,141 males and 35,611 females).

The Community Development Block-wise, population distribution with sex ratio and literacy rate of this district is given below:

	Sex ratio		Literacy rate		Population	
C.D. Block	Rural	Urban	Rural	Urban	Rural	Urban
GUMLA DISTRICT	**999**	**934**	**50.43**	**84.27**	**1271768**	**73,752**
Bishunpur	988	-	38.90	-	49895	-
Ghaghra	973	-	41.86	-	87398	-
Sisai	989	-	47.98	-	91629	-
Verno	983	-	43.06	-	62,048	-
Kamdara	1,035	-	55.40	-	53,935	-
Basia	1,009	-	54.78	-	68,968	-
Gumla	982	929	49.89	87.85	125,574	39,962
Chainpur	999	-	59.19	-	50,833	-
Dumri	980	-	57.14	-	68,686	-
Raidih	1,011	-	54.48	-	62,120	-
Palkot	1,008	-	46.15	-	70,637	-
Simdega	1,001	939	52.65	80.07	92,871	33,962
Kurdeg	1.012	-	52.89	-	77,019	-
Bolba	1,008	-	47.80	-	26,759	-
Thethaitangar	1,015	-	54.15	-	76,893	-
Kolebira	1,000	-	56.24	-	60,041	-
Jaldega	1,004	-	47.31	-	74,388	-
Bano	1,009	-	48.63	-	72,074	-

The Scheduled Castes and Scheduled Tribes population of the district as per 1991 census is 61299 persons and 816988 persons respectively. The rural-urban breakup of this population is indicated below:

Rural	(i) Scheduled Castes	:	58342
	(ii) Scheduled Tribes	:	797668
Urban	(i) Scheduled Castes	:	2957
	(ii) Scheduled Tribes	:	19320

The decennial growth rate of population of the district as a whole in relation to the state between the period 1991 and 2001 is presented below:

State/ District	Decennial growth rate of population (per cent) 1981-91		
	Total	Rural	Urban
Jharkhand	23.19	21.62	28.99
Gumla	16.60	15.44	41.05

LANGUAGES AND RELIGION

Main languge spoken in the district is Hindi.

Religionwise breakup of population is indicated below as per 1991 census:

Hindus: 495097, Muslims: 34697, Christians: 375459, Sikhs: 76, Buddhists: 5, Jains: 125. Other religions and persuasions: 248390, Religions not stated: 37.

GEOGRAPHY AND PHYSICAL FEATURES

Annual Rainfall : 1430.6 mm

Temperature : Max. 41.00°C and Min. 6.40°C

In the northern portion (and the south of Palamau district) there are a number of lofty flat topped hills, called *Pats* which are capped by great masses of laterite. The *Pat* area extends over the blocks of Bishunpur, Chainpur and Ghaghra, and has an altitude of 2500 to 3000 feet above the sea level. In the *Pat* region the highest areas are Netarhat Pat (3356 feet), Lamiti Pat (3777 feet), and Galgal Pat (3823 feet). The crest of the Neharhat Pat is an undulating tableland about 6 kms long and 4 kms broad. It has a cooler climate than Ranchi.

RIVERS, CANALS AND WATERWAYS

The South Koel and the Sankh are the main rivers of the district. The South Koel rises near Mandar (from the same ridge as the Subarnarekha) and flows in a north-westerly direction for some distance. It turns towards the south near Lohardaga and enters the Ranchi district. Its main tributaries are the Kara and the Paras. The Sankh rises in the north-western part of the district near the Rajadera plateau. It flows in a southerly direction along the western part of the district.

TOWNS, VILLAGES AND AMENITIES

The district, at persent comprises of 2 sub-divisions, 18 Community Development Blocks. It has 2 towns and 1398 villages (1393 inhabited villages and 5 uninhabited villages).

The urban populations of the district as percentage of total population in the census year 2001 is indicated below. It also shows the sex ratio (females per 1000 males) and density (population per sq km) in the urban population of the district in relation to the state.

State/ District	*Urban population as percentage of total population*	*Sex ratio, 2001 (Females per 1000 males)*			*Density (Population per sq km)*
	2001	*Total*	*Rural*	*Urban*	
Jharkhand	22.25	941	963	870	338
Gumla	5.48	995	999	934	148

Amenities

Number (with percentage) of villages having one or more amenities in the district as per 1991 census is given below:

Sl. No.	*Amenities*	*Number of inhabited villages*	*Percentage*
1.	Education	1072	76.96
2.	Medical	346	24.84
3.	Drinking Water	1393	100.00
4.	Post and Telegraph	209	15.00
5.	Market/Hat	368	26.42
6.	Communications	196	14.07
7.	Approach by Pucca Road	206	14.79
8.	Power Supply	133	9.55

COMMUNICATIONS

The district is well-served by a network of good roads.

Ranchi-Gumla-Simdega-Rourkela is the chief road which runs for about 270 kms and connects both the towns of this district with Ranchi as well as with Rourkela. The other important roads are: Gumla-Chainpur, Gumla-Sisai and Simdega-Kurdeg. Municipal roads are maintained by Gumla municipalities. The district has a good number of metalled roads and all the block headquarters are connected by such roads. Nearest airport is at Ranchi.

AGRICULTURE AND IRRIGATION

As a result of gradual deforestation of the district, more and more land is being brought under cultivation. Two types of cultivable lands are found in the district. These are *don* and *tanr.* The *don* land are the terraced low lands on which mainly paddy is grown, and the *tanr* are the uplands useful to produce a course form of rice, pulses and oilseeds. The cultivators of this district traditionally depend on a good rainfall for paddy crops. The wells, springs and ahars are other sources of irrigation in the district.

ANIMAL HUSBANDRY

Cows, buffaloes, bulls and bullocks, sheep, goats and pigs are the main livestock of this district. The cattle found in the district are small and under-sized which is largely due to lack of good pasturage and good fodder. There has been a concerted effort on behalf of the state government to improve the breed of the cattle by way of distribution of stud bulls of Hariana and Tharparkar varieties. There are a number of veterinary hospitals and dispensaries spread over the entire district. Treatment, prevention and suppression of diseases of the livestock are the main functions of the veterinary institutions. The population of poultry birds has been steadily increasing in recent days. Poultry farms have been opened at a number of places in the district.

INDUSTRIES

A number of small scale industries have been set up in the district. Candles, *bidi,* soap and steel materials are manufactured there. There is no large scale industry within the district.

MINERALS AND ORES OCCURRENCES

Bauxite

The bauxite enrichments in the laterite cappings on the western side of the then Ranchi district, now Gumla district, constitute at present the most important deposit in India. The important occurrences are:- Barkadih (23.0, 84.2) Baglatoli (23.2, 84.3) Bijapat (23.2, 84.2), Chandipat Area (23.2, 84.1) and several other places.

Clay

Important occurrences of lithomargic clay are recorded at different places in the district.

Lead

Small pieces of crocite have been found about a mile S.E. of Nawatoli located at (22.5, 84.1) in mica-schists. Sporadic occurrences of galena in a quartz vein have also been recorded to the south of Lathakamhan (22.5, 84.4).

Limestone

Occurrences of calcareous tufa have been reported from Dhibadihtoli (23.2, 84.4) and Balato (23.3, 84.4°).

Mica

Books of ruby mica occur in pegmetites near Kanjoga (22.8, 84.7). The maximum size of the books seen at surface is 5 inches across. Mica has also been recorded at Sikriadaur (22.7, 84.5).

Gemstone (Rock crystal)

Occurrences of small clear crystals of quartz derived from the disintegration of a quartz vein are reported from about two furlongs south of Konjona (22.75, 84.76).

Iron

At Sikorda (22.68, 84.95), Bagdam (22.51, 84.55), Mahautole (22.5, 84.25)

Kayanite

Kayanite occurs in mica-schist associated with vein quartz Khijurbahar (22.5, 84.96) and Chhapartoli (22.51, 84.96).

TRADE, COMMERCE AND EXPORT

Gumla and Simdega are the main centres of trade in this district. The chief articles of export of this district are rice, vegetables, mahua, dori, kusum and hens. Tobacco, kerosene oil and sugar are imported in Gumla whereas rice, mineral oil and wheat are imported in Simdega. The table given below lists the most important commodities manufactured, exported and imported in two towns of this district :

Name of the town	*Most important commodities*			
	Manufactured	*Exported*	*Imported*	
Gumla	J. oil, Candles, Bidi.	Rice, Vegetables, Hens	Tabacco, K.oil, Sugar	5
Simdega	Soap, Steel matrials	Mahua, Dori,	Rice, M.Oil,	4
	Kusum	Wheat		

TOURISM

Following are the places of tourist interest:

Basudeokora. It is a tola of village Nawagarh, situated about 3 kms south-east of the block headquarters at Raidih. It is noted as a religious centre. There are several stone images in the village similar to those of Ajanta. The image of Basudeva (from which the village derives its name) is greatly venerated. There is a very old Shiva temple which is traditionally believed to have been constructed in one day.

Chingri. It is a small village situated about 3 kms north-west of the block headquarters at Bishunpur. It is noted as the birth place of Tara Bhagat. An annual fair is held on the 5th of Pausa (December) every year to commemorate Tara Bhagat's death. There is a tomb in the village with structure of mud walls and tiles. It is believed that a large building will replace the kutcha structure by supernatural means.

Deogaon. The village lies about 11 kms south of the block headquarters at Palkot. It has a Shiva temple located on the top of a hill. An image of Goddess Durga was found in a cave in the same hill.

Bagdega. It is a village situated about 16 kms from the block headquarters at Kurdeg and about 32 kms. 'from Simdega. A large annual fair is held on the occasion of Rath-Yatra in June.

Nagar. The village is situated about 10 kms away from the block headquarters at Sisai and about 72 kms south-west of Ranchi. The remains of the historic Navratan Garh are located here. The fortress with nine storeys is said to have been built about 250 years ago.

Nagpheni. The village falling in Sisai block is situated about 18 kms east of Gumla. There is a legend about its name according to which Maharaj Mutuk Nath Sah Deo was saved by a cobra when, as a child, he was left near a tank. The boy later founded the Nagbansi dynasty. There is a dilapidated temple on the hillock in the village and a small waterfall. The Rath-Yatra festival in the month of Asadh (June-July) is an important event in the village.

Palkot. The village is the headquarters of the development block bearing the same name. The village is said to have derived its name from the ancient Pampapur where the mythological Banar Raja Bali and Sugreeva had their capital. The place has many caves. A tank named Pampasar is located near Palkot hill.

Rajadera. The village lies in Chainpur block situated about 26 kms south of Netarhat. Situated in a saucer like depression with hills on all sides. it has a great scenic value. The famous Sadani fall is located nearby.

Ramrekha. It is a tola of village Kairbera, situated about 29 kms west of Simdega. It is treated as a centre of pilgrimage.

A large annual fair is held on the occasion of Kartik Purnima (October-November) which draws a huge crowd. The pilgrims who come here first bathe in the Ganga Shrot (tank) on the day of Kartik Purnima and then offer prayers at the temple of Lord Rama situated on a hillock. It is said that Lord Rama had stayed at this place in the course of his wanderings during the period of exile.

Taisar. It is a village in Kurdeg block, situated about 48 kms west of Simdega. It is noted for the large fair held annually on the occasion of Rath-Yatra in July. Visitors to the fair bathe in the nearby tank and worship Goddess Kali enshrined in a magnificent temple.

Taraloya. It is a small village in Raidih block situated about 48 kms south of Gumla town. It is noted for its waterfall known as Permaghagh.

FAIRS AND FESTIVALS

Important fairs and melas organised in various parts of the district are mentioned below:

Karabari mela, Palish Yatra mela, Bishu mela, Makar Sankranti, Rath Yatra and Basant Panchmi melas, Ram Navami mela, Dharma Yatra mela, Dussehra mela, Ashivin Purnima and Agrahyana Purnima melas.

EDUCATION

According to 2001 census, total literates (excluding the population in the age group of 0-6 years) is 578,182 persons. Of these, 354,358 are males and 223,824 are females. In the rural areas of the district 525,325 persons (325,154 males and 200,171 females) are literates and in urban areas 52,857 persons (29,204 males and 23,653 females) are literates. The rate of literacy of this population to the total population, excluding 0-6 years age group according to 2001 census is shown below:

	Persons	Males	Females
Total	52.35	64.14	40.56
Rural	50.43	62.53	38.37
Urban	84.27	89.84	78:27

There are as many as 1072 villages accounting for 76.96 per cent of the total number of inhabited villages in the district where educational facility is available. Primary and Middle Schools are generally available in both the towns of this district. The following table gives the details of various types of educational institutions available in the towns of this district, including the number of stadia and public libraries:

Name of the town	*Educational institutions*	*Stadia*	*Public libraries, including reading rooms*
Gumla	Shorthand typewriting training institute (1), Secondary/Matriculation Schools (5), Junior Secondary and Middle Schools (4)	—	PL : 2
Simdega	Shorthand Typewriting Training Institute (1), Secondary/Matriculation Schools (4), Junior Secondary and Middle Schools (4)		PL : 2

COLLEGES (2000)

K.O. Gumla College, Gumla (Established 1960) Constituent college.

Simdega College, Simdega (Established 1960). Affiliated College.

S.K. Bage College, Kolebira, (Established 1985).Affiliated College.

(Above named colleges belong to Ranchi university, Established1960)

MEDICAL

The availability of medical amenities in the villages is considerably low as only 24.84 per cent villages in the district have got it. The table given below furnishes information regarding various types of medical institutions available in both the towns of this district.

Name of the towns	*Medical institutions*	*Number of Beds*
Gumla	Hospital (1) :	20
	Dispensaries (3) :	—
	Family Planning Centre (1) :	—
Simdega	Hospitals (2) :	44
	Dispensaries (2) :	—
	Health Centres (2) :	—
	Family Planning Centres (2) :	—

ADMINISTRATION

(i) Administrative Divisions:

Sub-divisions: Gumla and Simdega.

Community Development Blocks: Bishunpur, Ghaghra, Chainpur, Dumri, Raidih, Gumla, Sisai, Verno, Karndara, Basia, Palkot, Simdega, Kolebira, Bano, Jaldega, Thethaitangar . Kurdeg, Bolba.

Towns and Urban Agglomerations with their Population, Sexratio, Decadal growth and Literacy rate (2001)

Town	Population	Percentage Decadal growth 1991-2001	Sex Ratio	Literacy Rate
Gumla (M)	39,790	39.42	929	87.85
Simdega (NA)	33,962	43.00	939	80.07

(ii) Parliamentary Constituencies and Assembly Segments

No. and Name of Parliamentary Constituencies:
53–Lohardaga (ST), 54–Khunti (ST)

No. and Name of Assembly Segments:

Lohardaga (ST)

310. Sisai (ST)—Sisai, Kamdara and Basia police stations in Gumla sub-division.

313. Gumla (ST)—Gumla municipality, G.Ps. Hurhuria, Ghatagaon, Asani, Chanciali, Telgaon, Pugu, Bangaru, Karaundi, Dumardih and Murkunda in Gumla police .stations and Raidih, Chainpur and Dumri police stations in Gumla sub-division.

314. Bishunpur (ST)—Bishunpur and Ghaghra police stations and Gumla police station (excluding Gumla municipality and G.Ps. Hurhuria, Ghatagaon, Asani, Chandali, Telgaon, Pugu, Bangaru, Karaundi, Dumar dih and Murkunda) in Gumla sub-division; and Senha police station in Lohardaga sub-division.

Kunti (ST)

311. Kolebira (ST)—Kolebira, Thethaitangar and Bolba police stations in Simdega sub-division.

312. Simdega (ST)—Simdega and Kurdeg police stations in Simdega sub-division; and Palkot police station in Gumla sub-division.

OBSERVATIONAL ORGANISATION

Hydrometeorological Stations for Climatological Purposes

This instrument work under "Flood Meteorological Offices" Bhubaneswar. The instrument lies in

Latitude	:	22.9° North
Longitude	:	89.5° East
Altitude	:	646 m.
Date of starting	:	18-2-1980

DISASTROUS WEATHER EVENTS

Coldwave:

1st January 1982, moderate.

29-30 November 1982, severe.

4-10 December 1982, severe.

2-14 January 1983, severe.

December 3rd and 4th week 1984, severe.

27-31 December 1989, severe.

1-10 January 1990, severe.

January 1st and 2nd week, 1992.

Heatwave:

1-7 July 1982, moderate to severe.

28 May to 2 June, 1983, moderate to severe.

6 June 1983, severe.

7 June 1983, moderate.

Heavy Rains:

July 4th week to October 2nd week 1987, this area witnessed moderate to heavy rains, caused damaged to property and crops.

Lightning:

On 13th September 1996, this area witnessed lightning, caused damage to crops and many people reported killed.

DISTRIBUTION OF *SCHEDULED CASTE* POPULATION BY SEX DISTRICTWISE (1991)

	POPULATION		
	Total	Males	Females
GUMLA			
	61,299	31,091	30,208
Bantar	77	76	1
Bauri	209	104	105
Bhogta	12,903	6,773	6,130
Bhuiya	13,002	6,538	6,464
Chamar, Mochi	3,251	1,665	1,586
Chaupal	74	62	12
Dabgar	43	20	23
Dhobi	3,505	1,708	1,797
Dom, Dhangad	1,913	1,001	917
Dusadh, Dhari, Dharhi	1,157	553	604
Ghasi	13,727	6,812	6,915
Halalkhor	67	23	44
Hari, Mehtar, Bhangi	515	219	296
Kanjar	19	2	17
Kurariar	38	38	0
Lalbegi	9	5	4
Musahar	909	319	590
Nat	83	59	24
Pan, Sawasi	378	209	169
Pasi	903	593	310
Rajwar	215	129	86
Turi	8,229	4,128	4,101
Unclassified	68	55	13

DISTRIBUTION OF *SCHEDULED TRIBE* POPULATION BY SEX DISTRICTWISE (1991)

	POPULATION		
	Total	Males	Females
GUMLA			
	8,16,988	4,08,004	4,08,984
Asur	7,400	3,755	3,645
Baiga	421	145	276
Banjara	90	75	15
Bathudi	324	134	190
Bedia	812	404	408
Bhumij	268	148	120
Binjhia	9,797	5,220	4,577
Birhor	321	149	172
Birjia	772	335	437
Chero	117	34	83
Chick Baraik	27,935	14,226	13,709
Gond	19,158	9,461	9,697
Gorait	425	250	175
Ho	283	163	120
Karmali	291	132	159
Kharia	1,22,812	60,659	62,153
Kharwar	6,342	3,068	3,274
Khond	82	60	22
Kisan	6,460	3,150	3,310
Kora	486	332	154
Korwa	2,629	1,311	1,318
Lohara, Lohra	42,875	21,933	20,942
Mahli	10,777	5,185	5,592
Mal Paharia	4,120	2,090	2,030
Munda	1,56,995	77,382	79,613
Oraon	3,87,940	1,95,104	1,92,836
Parhaiya	339	182	157
Santal	5,171	2,141	3,030
Sauria Paharia	1,318	655	663
Savar	89	40	49
Unclassified	139	81	58

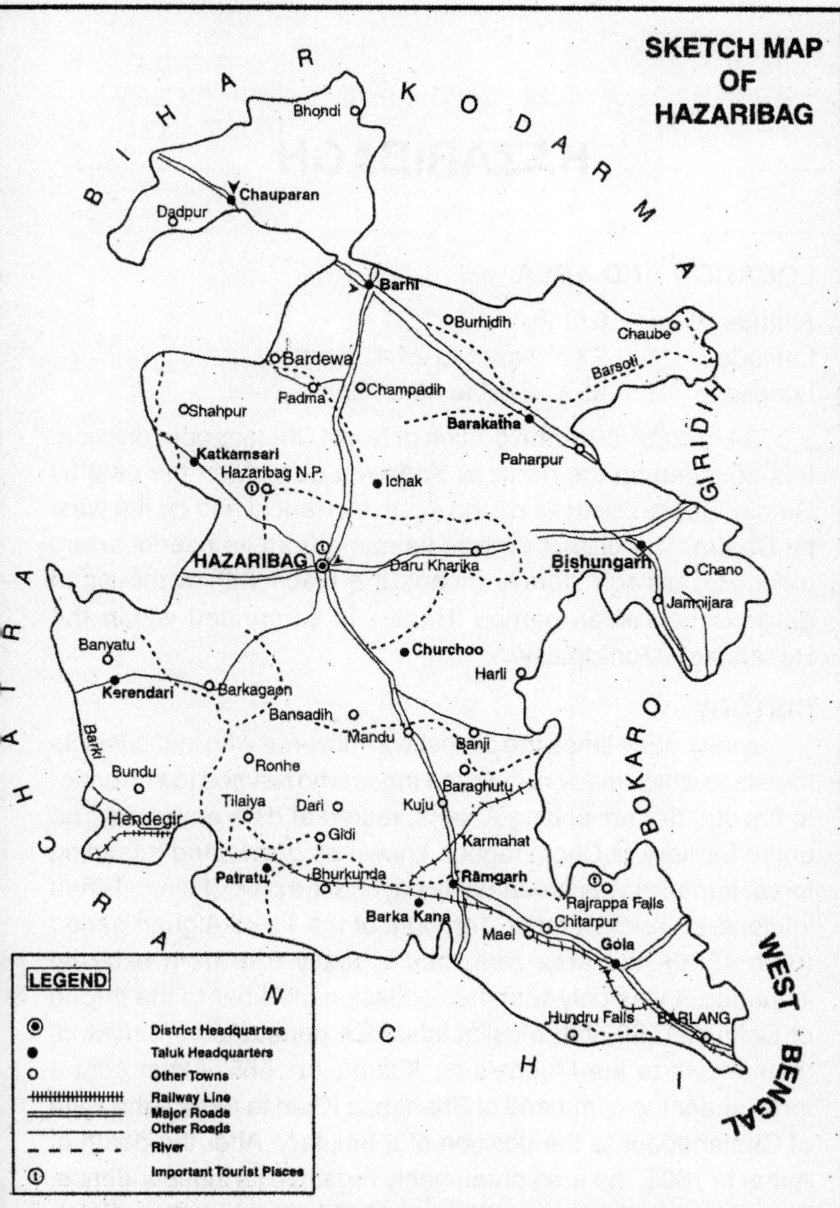

SKETCH MAP OF HAZARIBAG

HAZARIBAGH

LOCATION AND AREA

Altitude	:	611 m
Latitude	:	23.5° North to 24.4° North.
Longitude	:	85.1° East to 85.9° East.

The district forms the portion of North Chotanagpur division. It is bounded on the north by Kodarma district, on the east by Giridih, Bokaro districts on the south by Ranchi and on the west by Chatra. The district derives its name from its headquarters town. Hazaribagh literally means the place with 'a thousand gardens'. A village named 'Hazari' is comprised within the Hazaribagh Municipality.

HISTORY

In very early times the district was covered with inaccessible forests to which many non-Aryan tribes who refused to surrender to the steadily advancing Aryans, retired at different times. The entire territory of Chotanagpur, known as *Jharkhand* (meaning forest territory) was presumably beyond the pale of direct Hindu influence in ancient India. Throughout the Turko-Afghan period (upto 1526), the area remained virtually free from external influence. It was only with the accession of Akbar to the throne of Delhi in 1556, that Muslim influence penetrated *Jharkhand,* then known to the Mughals as *Kokrah.* In 1585, Akbar sent a force under the command of Shahabaz Khan to reduce the Raja of Chotanagpur to the position of a tributary. After the death of Akbar in 1605, the area presumably regained its independence. This necessitated an expedition in 1616 by Ibrahim Khan Fateh

Jang, the Governor of Bihar and brother of Queen Noorjehan. Ibrahim Khan defeated and captured Durjan Sal, the 46th Raja of Chotanagpur. He was imprisoned for 12 years but was later released and reinstated on the throne after he had shown his ability in distinguishing a real diamond from a fake one. In 1632 Chotanagpur was given as Jagir to the Governor at Patna for an annual payment of Rs 1,36,000. This was raised to Rs. 1,61,000 in 1636 A.D. During the reign of Muhammad Shah (1719-1748). Sarballand Khan, the Governor of the then Bihar, marched against the Raja of Chotanagpur and obtained his submission. Another expedition was led by Fakhruddoula, the Governor of Bihar in 1731. He came to terms with the Raja of Ramgarh who owed all egiance to the Raja of Chotanagpur. In 1735 Alivardi Khan had some difficulty in enforcing the payment of the annual tribute of Rs 12000 from the Raja of Ramgarh, as agreed to by the latter according to the terms settled with Fakhruddoula. This situation continued until the occupation of the country by the British. During the Muslim period, the main estates in the district were Ramgarh, Kunda, Kendi, Chai and Kharagdiha. Subsequent to the Kol rising in 1831 which, however, did not seriously affect Hazaribagh, the administrative structure of the territory was changed. The parganas Ramgarh, Kharagdiha, Kendi and Kunda became parts of the South-West Frontier Agency and were formed into a division named Hazaribagh as the administrative headquarters. In 1854 the designatlon of the South-West Frontier Agency was changed to Chutia Nagpur and it began to be administered as a Non-regulation province under the Lieutenant Governor of the then Bihar. In 1855-56 there was the great uprising of the Santals against the British but it was brutally suppressed.

After 1991 census, the district of Hazaribagh has been divided into three separate districts viz. Hazaribagh. Chatra and Kodarma. The two sub-divisions namely Chatra and Kodarma were upgraded to the status of independent districts.

POPULATION (GENERAL, SC/ST)

Total population of the district according to 2001 census is 2,227,108 persons. Rural population is 174,093 persons and urban population is 529,015persons.

The Community Development Block-wise, population distribution with sex ratio and literacy rate of this district is given below:

	Sex ratio		Literacy rate		Population	
C.D. Block	Rural	Urban	Rural	Urban	Rural	Urban
HAZARIBAG DISTRICT	**989**	**833**	**51.26**	**79.05**	**1748093**	**529015**
Chauparan	1,044	-	49.01	-	167,206	-
Barhi	1,047	887	49.08	72.23	88,798	99,33
Padma	1,006	-	52.67	-	43,403	-
Ichak	1,032	-	53.64	-	115,800	-
Barkatha	1,130	-	38.92	-	125,852	-
Bishungarh	1,065	-	42.99	-	142,856	-
Hazaribag	913	847	63.19	86.98	126,620	143,993
Katkamsandi	967	903	54.16	73.49	137,990	9,757
Keredari	978	-	44.70	-	91,295	-
Barkagaon	958	-	49.43	-	110,907	-
Patratu	928	830	48.65	76.48	82,147	152,624
Churchu	946	860	52.24	75.49	94,917	28,511
Mandu	921	847	54.33	73.73	143,080	81,788
Ramgarh	938	790	60.64	77.92	151,744	102,409
Gola	974	-	50.89	-	125,475	-

The Scheduled Castes and Scheduled Tribes population of the district as per 1991 census is 302854 persons and 32465 persons respectively. The rural-urban breakup of this population is indicated below:

Rural	(i) Scheduled Castes	:	180958
	(ii) Scheduled Tribes	:	173754
Urban	(i) Scheduled Castes	:	53345
	(ii) Scheduled Tribes	:	44367

The decennial growth rate of population of the district as a whole in relation to the state between the period 1991 and 2001 is presented below:

State/ District	Decennial growth rate of population (per cent) 1991-2001		
	Total	Rural	Urban
Jharkhand	23.19	21.62	28.99
Hazaribagh	24.02	23.10	27.15

LANGUAGES AND RELIGION

Main languages spoken in the district are Hindi and Urdu.

Religionwise breakup of population of undivided district of Hazaribagh is indicated below as per 1991 census:

Hindus: 2434245, Muslims: 374493, Christians: 20767. Sikhs: 8595, Buddhists: 67, Jains: 2907, Other religions and persuasions: 2398, Religions not stated: 72.

GEOGRAPHY AND PHYSICAL FEATURES

Annual Rainfall : 1234.5 m
Temperature : Max. 42.20 and Min. 4.00

The district forms part of Chotangpur plateau. It is a region of plateaus, residual hills and valleys, which occupy the southern half of the state of Jharkhand.

The district may be divided into the following broad natural divisions:

(i) the central plateau

(ii) the lower plateaus, and

(iii) the Damodar Valley.

The central plateau, averaging 2000 feet high, is situated in the centre of the district and contains the town of Hazaribagh: Around the central plateau are the lower plateaus on all sides except the west on which side a high ridge connects the central plateau to the Palamau district. The lower plateaus average 1300 feet in height, their surface being undulating. In the north and northwest, the lower plateaus form fairly level tablelands until they reach the ghats when they drop to about 700 feet. On the east, the general elevation is lower and the descent gradual. Along the southern part of the district is the Damodar valley in which the town of Ramgarh is situated at a level of 1000 feet lower than Hazaribagh.

The chief hills in central Hazaribagh are Chandwara and Jillinga which rise above the central plateau to 2816 and 3057 feet respectively above the mean sea level. To the south of the central plateau lies the Sugu hill which rises to 3203 feet and is separated from the Jilinga by the river Bokaro. Maran Burn hill lies south of the Damodar Valley between Hazaribagh and Ranchi districts attaining a height of 3445 feet.

Hazaribagh is a predominantly forest district and nearly half of the total area is covered by forests which are distributed almost uniformly throughout the district.

Sal is the most famous and predominant species of trees in the jungles of the district. Among other common species are bamboo, Khair, Salai, Simul, Mahua, Palas, Kusum, Kend, Asam, Piar and Bhelwa.

RIVERS. CANALS AND WATERWAYS

The district is divided into two main waterheads. One is served by the Damodar and its tributaries and the other by the Barakar. The Damodar rises in the Kharampat hill in Palamau and flows for 144 kms in the district. It is joined by the Garhi or Tandwa river near its entrance into the district where its bed is 1,326 feet above sea level. The Naikari, with drainage from the Ranchi plateau and further down the Bhera, joins the Damodar.The Rajrappa falls are situated near the confluence of the Damodar. The Barakar rises in cultivated fields near Ichak, about 11 kms north of Hazaribagh. It flows in the eastern direction till it joins the Damodar in the eastern part of Dhanbad district.

TOWNS, VILLAGES AND AMENITIES

The district is at present comprised of 3 sub-divisions, 15

Community Development Blocks. It has 23 towns.

The urban population of the district as percentage of total population in the census years 2001 is indicated below. It also shows the sex ratio (females per 1000 males) and density (population per sq. km.) in the urban population of the district in relation to the state:

State/ District	*Urban population as percentage of total population*	*Sex ratio, 2001 (Females per 1000 males)*			*Density (Population per sq. km.)*
	2001	*Total*	*Rural*	*Urban*	
Jharkhand	22.25	941	963	870	338
Hazaribagh	23.23	950	989	833	370

Amenities

Number (with percentage) of villages having one or more amenities in the undivided district of Hazaribagh as per 1991 census is given below:

Sl. No.	*Amenities*	*Number of inhabited villages*	*Percentage*
1.	Education	1840	55.04
2.	Medical	415	12.41
3.	Drinking Water	3343	100.00
4.	Post and Telegraph	293	8.76
5.	Market/Hat	230	6.88
6.	Communications	609	18.22
7.	Approach by Pucca Road	515	15.41
8.	Power Supply	789	23.60

COMMUNICATIONS

The district is well served by a network of good roads. It has National Highways, State Highways and roads managed by the Zila Parishad. Quite a few roads come under the Hazaribagh Mines Board, Forest Department and some small roads are managed by the Damodar Valley Corporation. The Grand Trunk Road (National Highway No. 2) covers some important places such as Hazaribagh and Barhi. The Barhi-Hazaribagh-Ranchi road is a part of N.H. 31 and the Barh-Rajauli road is a part of NH 31. The State Highways passing through the district are shown below alongwith their length in the district.

Road		*Length in kms*
Hazaribagh-Bagodar-Saraiya	—	64
Jamua-Kodarma	—	68
Hazaribagh-Simaria	—	57
The Important Zila Parishad roads are:		
Hazaribagh-Simaria		
Hazaribagh-Katkamsandi-Chatra	—	57
Hazarlbagh-Tandwa	—	—
Ramgarh-Dakagarha	—	49

Even unmetalled gravelled roads are open to vehicular traffic throughout the year except on unbridged sections during the rains.

The district headquarters at Hazaribagh is not directly connected by rail. The nearest railway station from this town is Hazaribagh Road situated at a distance of about 69 kms. Other important places in the district, viz., Patratu and Ramgarh are, however, on the rail head.

Riverways are not common in the district. Most of the rivers are shallow. Generally, they dry up in summer though they are in high floods during the monsoon. For these reasons. there is not much of river traffic in the district.

There is a fair weather landing air-strip for small planes at Hazaribagh, the district headquarters.

AGRICULTURE AND IRRIGATION

As the district is mostly covered by hills and jungles, the soil is rocky and sandy producing jungles and bushes. Some soils near the river beds are alluvial. The culturable lands are divided into two categories-lowlands and uplands. The former are fertile and very little manure is needed but the latter are not so.

Rice is the main crop of the district. Other important crops grown are bajra, maize, pulses (particularly arhar). No food crops mainly consist of oilseeds. The area under cash crops (sugarcane, etc.) is small.

Irrigation plays an important role in the agriculture economy of any district. However, in Hazaribagh district, due to the hilly topography of the area, there is not much scope for exploitation of surface water. The other means of irrigation left are exploitation of groundwater and taking recourse to lift irrigation. Tank irrigation is not very popular. Groundwater exploitation has also its limitation.

After independence, considerable attention has been paid to the provision of irrigational facilities in the district. Several major schemes have been taken up by the Damodar Valley Corporation. Among them mention may be made of Jurga Irrigation Scheme. Chharwa Dam and Gondo Dam. Besides, irrigational facilities have been extended in the district through a number of medium and minor irrigation schemes. *rahat* pumps. electric pumps, open boring tube-wells and hand-pumps. Recently the possibility of implementing dug-well scheme has increased due to the subsidy being given under I.R.D. scheme by the S.F.D.A. and financing by banks to the individual farmers. Likewise the subsidy for pumping sets is also given by the S.F.D.A and loans are being advanced on easy terms to the cultivators by the banks.

ANIMAL HUSBANDRY

The livestock found in the district are cattle (cows, bulls and bullocks) buffaloes, sheep, goats and pigs. The average yield of milk of the cows of the district is quite poor. Bullocks and buffaloes are also of small stature. They are not suitable for hard ploughing. The bulls are of inferior strain.

Dairying has not been taken up in the organised sector as an occupation and means of livelihood. Similar is the case of poultry. Only a few poultry farms have been opened in an organised manner. The district, however, offers an excellent potential for growth of dairy and poultry farms, being close to the industrial towns such as Bokaro, Ranchi, etc.

The rivers being hilly, there are no regular big fisheries even in the big rivers, namely, Damodar, Barakar and Kornar. The main fisheries consist of pisciculture in lakes, tanks, *bandhs* and ponds. Fish trade is in the hands of the *fishermen* who are located in Hazaribagh town, Ichak, Simaria and Chatra, under the pisciculture development programme, fish fry distribution centres have been opened in the above mentioned places.

INDUSTRIES

The district is richly-endowed with mineral resources so essential for industries. The rich mica mines located in parts of Hazaribagh Sadar form the backbone of the industrial activities in the district. Coal is yet another natural resource available in abundance in the district and coal mining activities employ a sizeable chunk of industrial workers of the district. The district of Hazaribagh is, in fact, famous for the best metallurgical coal in India.

Limestone, China clay and fire clay are also available in sizeable quantities in the district. Apart from the above, some minerals of less economic value found in the district are antimony, lead-ore, galena, molybdenite and tin.

Even though Hazaribagh district abounds in forest and mineral resources, not many large scale industrial units have come up. However, there has been considerable increase in medium and small-scale industrial establishments. Following are, the existing medium-scale industries in the district.

HANDICRAFTS

Cane and Bamboo work; metal-craft; papier-mache; Textiles

(embroidered); Textiles (printed); Textiles (woven) and Woodwork.

MINERALS AND ORES OCCURRENCES

Building Materials

The meta-gabbro occurring around Tirla and the amphibalites around Dumariatantoli.

Cassiterite

At Chappatand (24.7, 86.0). The cassitarite occurs in crystels of about equal dimensions with the other constituents of the rock but some times aggregates the exclusion of the other minerals. It also occurs at Nurunga (24.1, 86.1), Simratari (24.7, 85.8).

Coal

At Chope (24.1, 85.3), the smallest detached coal field in India, occupying about three-fourths of a square mile one seam of coal of poor quality 4 ft. in thickness and very limited in extent.

In the Gidi-A block, situated a furlong west of Gidi (23.7, 85.4), thirty two coal seams of which four are of considerable thickness, have been recorded. Twenty five seams have been recognised in the Saunda-B Block, about a mile North East of Saunda (23.7, 85.3).

In the Nalkari *nala* near Patratu Railway Station (23.7, 85.3), six coal seams are exposed, whose thickness varies from 3 to 25 ft.

At Ramgarh (23.6, 85.6). The total area of the field is about 65 sq. km.

Copper

Thinly disseminated grains of chalcopyrite are found in hornblende-diopside-granulite running for half a mile in length and forming a hillock south of Carisaraim (24.1, 85.5). Chalcopyrite associated with Pyrhotite is recorded in quartz veins near Toyar (23.5, 85.7).

Corundum

An occurrence of corundum around the Tutki Ghat, to the East of Hazaribagh.

Limestone

It occurs as beds interbranded with para-amphibolites and calc-silicate rocks on the border of Ranchi and Hazaribagh districts. The individual thickness of limestone band varies up to 10 ft. but the aggregate thickness of the bands in a particular zone is sometimes more than 150 ft.

Mica

The district is famous for Mica.

Minerals Water

There are four hot springs and one cold spring here. At Belkapi; (24.1, 85.7), at Duari (24.1, 85.2). At Katkamsandi (24.1, 85.2) at Kawa Gandhwani (23.7, 85.4).

Ochre

An occurrence of red ochre covering an area of 40 ft. by 30 ft. has been recorded on the western side of the *nala* west of Garea (24.1, 85.9).

Pyrites

Pyrites occurs as disseminations in quartzite near Khairo (24.1, 85.6), Lowabar (24.1, 85.9), Deoradih (24.1, 85.9), Jamumiya (24.1, 85.8).

Quartz

Occurrences of vein quartz have been reported from near Chonthia (24.5, 85.8) Basai (24.1, 85.8), Bandhakan (24.1, 85.8) Birmalli (24.2, 85.8). Ballia (24.1, 85.6), Swajatola (24.1, 85.7). White quartz occurs around Karma (24.4, 85.8). Bachaidih (24.2, 85.8), Dasarokhurd (24.3, 85.8).

Transparent to transluscent crystels or quartz with a maximum length of 2-1/2 inches have been located near Khaira (24.1, 85.6). White quartz with an occasional rosy thing occurs at Chandardih (24.4, 85.6), Nitanr (24.4, 85.7), Barkagaon (24.3,

85.6), Bijaia (24.3, 85.6 etc.

White quartz some times mixed with rosy quartz is also seen at Rangamati (24.5, 85.9), Naitani (24.4, 85.9), also occurs at Banasidih (24.4, 85.7).

Allanite

Allanite associated with epidote occurs at Bansodharwa (24.4, 85.6), Dhabudih (24.3, 85.7), Daldalia (24.3, 85.7), Bagro (24.4, 85.7), Parsabad (24.3, 85.7). Allenite also occurs in calc-silicate rocks near PETO (24.1, 85.5) and Barakar (24.0, 85.6).

Sillimanite

Occurrence of sillimanite in four quantities and in elongated crystels, varying from a fraclion of an inch to 3 inches, have been reported from between Ratithamai (24.4, 85.6) and Puto (24.4, 85.6) and also from south of Pipradih (24.3, 85.2) and North of Bansdih (24.4, 85.7). Small occurrences of sillimanite in mica-schists have been reported at Katio (24.5, 85.8) and Mahi Marwa (24.5, 85.9).

Felspar

Deposit of felspar are recorded within 6 to 9 kms. N.E. of Maheshmunda Railway station (24.23, 86.4) lying in the pegmatites near the village of Chamghara, Bariarpur, and Besodih.

Pegmatite zone runing from north of Marpa (24.13, 85.51) towards Karichatan (24.13, 85.58). The nalla running from Jhingibari (24.25, 85.58) to Lokea (24.2, 85.7). Pegmatites are being worked for felspar at Bandhakhara (24.1, 85.95). Workable desposits of felspar are recorded near Chichaki Railway station (24.11, 85.95) N.W of Barkradih (24.16, 85.96), and near Kubadih (24.18, 85.93).

Fire clay

Fire clay deposit in the Bokaro coalfield, Gunia (23.8, 85.83) Loiya (23.8, 85.63) and Mandu (23.8, 85.46), Devalgara (23.85, 84.96) Barkute (23.9, 84.96) Barditoli (23.81, 84.9) Manatu (23.9,

84.96) Tikatari (23.66, 85.03) Kurlongs (23.86, 84.95) Ara (23.83, 84.93) Bachra (23.7, 85.08) Belangi Hill (23.66, 85.03) Ray (23.7, 85.06).

Fire-clay deposits from the south Karanpura coalfield have been reported from a quarry near Hindigir Railway station (23.66, 85.16).

Garnet

Occurrence of medium sized garnets at Rati-Thamai (24.45, 85.6) and Puto (24.43, 85.56), Kusmaraja (24.1, 85.93) near Katio (24.5, 85.81).

Gemstone (Aquamarine)

Small crystals of aquamarine of a yellow colour are abundant near Tendwaha stream south of Mahabar hill.

Gemstone (Rock crystal):

Beautifully tinted rose quartz is often found in the pegmatites of the mica belt, particularly in the mines to the N.E. of Parsabad Railway station (24.3, 85.73).

Iron:

Near Hazaribagh (24.00, 85.41), Karanpura (23.83, 85.25), Kumaria (24.1, 85.93), Belgai (24.13, 85.78), Parasia (24.15, 85.8).

Kaolin:

Minor occurrences of Kaolin have been reported at Kutr Lowa (23.43, 85.7)

	Name of Industry	*Goods produced*
1.	M/s India Fire bricks & Insulation Co. Ltd., Marar, Ramgarh	Refractories
2.	Bihar Alloy Steel Ltd., Patratu	Alloy Steel
3.	Bharat Refractories, Marar, Ramgarh	Refractories
4.	Karanpura Development Co. Ltd. Sirka, Ramgarh.	Refractories
5.	Bihar Foundry & Castings Pvt. Ltd, Ramgarh.	Mini Steel Plant.
6.	Central workshop, Barkakana	Repairing Shop

Important Industries, 2000

Indo Asahi Glass Co. Ltd. Bhurkunda, P.O. Bhadaninagar, Distt. Hazaribagh, Bihar.

Manufacturer: Sheet glass including thinner grade ranging from 1.1 mm. Thickness, substantially required by the defence and civil health services, opthalmic lenses and desiliconised zircon products.

TRADE, COMMERCE AND EXPORT

The following table presents the most important commodities manufactured, exported from and imported in the 10 towns of Hazaribagh district.

Name of the town	*Most important commodities*		
	Manufactured	*Exported*	*Imported*
Barkakana	—	Coal	Rice
Barughutu	—	Coal	Cloth
Gidi	—	Washed coal	Raw coal
Hazaribagh	—	—	Food Stuffs
Patratu	—	Coal	Rice
Ramgarh Cantt.	Fire-bricks	Fire-bricks	Food-grains
Saunda	—	Coal	Rice
Sirka	—	Coal	Rice

Only in the town of Ramgarh Cantt. certain commodities are manufactured. Coal is the most important commodity exported from the towns in Hazaribagh district. Hazaribagh is the only town from where no commodity is exported but food-stuff is on its import list. Rice is the most important commodity to be imported in towns.

There are less number of organised markets in the district and sale and purchase in the rural areas usually takes place in the hats/markets spread over the whole district. The hats are the local markets where the local produce is generally bought and sold. Within the district the main markets are Hazaribagh.

TOURISM

Churchu. The village is situated about 19 kms south-east of Hazaribagh. There is an old temple in the village around which a large annual fair is held on the occasion of Ramnavmi.

Bokaro Falls. The Bokaro falls is situated in village Morangi, about 8 kms from Hazaribagh on the Hazaribagh-Ranchi Road. It is a beautiful picnic spot.

Banaso. The village is situated about 8 kms from Bishungarh and is famous for the Bhagwati Mahamaya Mandir located in it. It is said to have been constructed by Banasur, an important mythological figure, whose sovereignty extended to this area also. It is supposed to be a very ancient temple and a large number of sacrifices are made to propitiate Goddess Bhagwati.

Bishungarh. It is a beautiful waterfall lying 15 kms from Bishungarh and 6 kms from Konar Dam. Water in it remains available for the whole year. It is situated in the midst of forest and is a lovely picnic spot.

Ichak. The village is situated at a distance of 11 kms from Hazaribagh and is the headquarters of the block bearing the same name. Formerly it was the headquarters of the Ramgarh Raj, the remnants of which can still be seen. There are several old temples located in the village, important of which are the Sun temple, Shiva temple, Bansidhar temple, etc.

Konar Dam. Konar, the second of the four multi-purpose dams included in the first phase of the Damodar valley Project, is situated in Hazaribagh distict, across the Konar river, 9 kms. from Bishungarh.

Kanhari. A small hill, situated about 3 kms east of Hazaribagh town on the Hazaribagh-Jagishpur Road, is a favourite picnic spot.

National Park. It is situated about 22 kms north of Hazaribagh town in the midst of forest on Patna-Ranchi road.

The sanctuary attracts the attention of all visitors. It abounds in natural flora and fauna. There are a forest dak bungalow and a cottage for the stay of the visitors. There are four towers in the park each about 200 feet high.

Rajrappa. It has a waterfall near the confluence of Damodar and Bhera rivers, 38 kms north-east of Ramgarh and 14 kms north-west of Gola road railway station. There is a temple of Chhinnamastika Devi at the place where a large fair is held on the occasion of *Makarsankranti.*

Patratu. It is situated at a distance of about 35 kms from Ramgarh and is noted for its Thermal Power Station. It is also the headquarters of the block bearing the same name. It has got a rest house by the side of the dam and presents a very beautiful site. It is also a good picnic spot.

Suraj Kund. The place is situated about 38 kms. south-west of Hazaribagh on the Grand Trunk road and is famous for its hot springs. An annual fair is held on the occasion of *Makarsankranti.*

Tamasin. The place is located at a distance of about 25 kms to the north-east of Chatra on a *kutcha* road. It is famous for the image of goddess Bhagwati. It is also a beauty spot.

ZOO

(i) Chandrapura Deer Park, Soil conservation, Forestry East Division, Hazaribagh

(ii) Deer Park, For East Damodar Valley Corp.
Soil Conservation Department, Hazaribagh.

FAIRS AND FESTIVALS

Important fairs and melas organised in various parts of the district are mentioned below:

Makar Sankranti mela, Dussehra mela, Yatra mela, Kartik Purnima mela, Rath Yatra mela, Basant Panchmi mela.

EDUCATION

According to 2001 census, total literates (excluding the population in the age group of 0-6 years) in undivided district of Hazaribagh is 1,081,921 persons. Of these, 690,735 are males and 391,186 are females. In the rural areas of the district 722,108 persons (473,341 males and 248,767 females) are literates and in urban areas 359,813 persons (217,394 males and 142,419 females) are literates. The rate of literacy of this population to the total population, excluding 0-6 years age group according to 2001 census is shown below:

	Persons	*Males*	*Females*
Total	58.05	72.16	43.15
Rural	51.26	66.94	35.46
Urban	79.05	86.92	69:46

There are as many as 1840 villages in the district where educational facility of one type or other is available. Primary and middle school education facilities are generally available in all towns. The following table gives the details of the different categories of educational institutions per 10000 population in different towns of the district:

Name of the town	*Number per ten thousand population*			
	Higher Secondary/ Inter/PUC/ Junior College	*Secondary/ Matriculation*	*Junior Secondary/ Middle*	*Primary*
Barkakana	—	1.80	1.80	0.90
Barughutu	—	0.81	1.63	4.07
Gidi	—	—	1.54	0.77
Hazaribagh	0.12	1.12	3.37	5.74
Patratu	—	0.68	1.03	1.71
Ramgarh Cantt.	0.24	0.97	0.97	3.64
Saunda		0.71	1.41	0.85
Sirka	—	—	1.55	1.55
Total	0.09	0.84	1.96	2.80

COLLEGES (2000)

K.B. Womens College, Hazaribagh (Established 1963) Constituent College. Enrolment 2153, Teachers 31.

Markham College of Commerce, Hazaribagh (Established 1977) (Constituent College).

Ramgarh College, Ramgarh, (Established 1967), (Constituent College). Enrolment 2196, Teachers 24.

St. Collumbas College, Hazaribagh (1899) (Constituent College). Enrolment 4502, Teachers 77.

Annada College, Hazaribagh (Established 1979), Teachers 51. (Affiliated College)

Chotanagpur College, Ramgarh (Established 1977). Teachers 35. (Affiliated College)

Karmapura College, Barkagaon. (Affiliated College)

PTPS College, Patratu, (Affiliated 1972). Teachers 26. (Affiliated College)

Ram Narain Yadav Memorial Degree College, Barhi. (Affiliated College)

J.M. College, Bhurkunda, (Affiliated 1979). Teachers 54. (Affiliated College)

Jubilee College, Bhurkunda, (1980). Teachers 30. (Affiliated College)

(Above named colleges belong to Vinobha Bhave University, Hazaribagh, Established 1992).

MEDICAL

The availability of medical amenity of one type or other in the villages of this district is considerably low as only 415 villages have such amenity within the village.

The table below furnishes information regarding availability of beds in the medical institutions in different towns:

Name the towns	*Number of beds in medical institutions per 1000 population*
Barkakana	1.35
Barughutu	2.85

Gidi	1.16
Hazaribagh	7.36
Patratu	1.81
Ramgarh Cantt.	7.08
Saunda	2.47
Sirka	1.16
Total	3.65

The number of beds in medical institutions per 1000 population for urban areas of the district works out to be 3.65. This is the highest in case of Hazaribagh (M) having 7.36 beds per 1000 population and the lowest in Chatra (M) with only 0.92 beds per 1000 population. In Jhumri Tilaiya (M) no bed is available in medical institutions.

ADMINISTRATION

(i) Administrative Divisions:

Sub-divisions: Hazaribagh, Ramgarh. Barhi.

Community Development Blocks: Keredari, Barkagaon, Katkamsandi, Barhi, Ichak, Bishungarh, Hazaribagh, Churchu, Mandu, Patratu, Ramgarh and Golagh, Chauparan, Padma, Barkatha.

Towns and Urban Agglomerations with their Population, Sexratio, Decadal growth and Literacy rate (2001)

RAMGARH UA

Ramgarh Cantonment (CB)
Sirka (CT
Barkakana (CT)

HAZARIBAG UA

Hazaribag
Okni No.II

Town	Population	Percentage Decadal growth 1991-2001	Sex Ratio	Literacy Rate
Ara (CT)	14,181	22.25	853	68.38
Barughutu (CT)	21,091	26.15	863	82.49
Balkundra (CT)	5,369	-39.16	844	77.28
Barhi (CT)	9,933		887	72.23

Barkakana (CT)	16,872	22.88	866	78.77
Dari (CT)	7,382	14.61	907	74.13
Gidi (CT)	13,659	-5.70	820	79.09
Hazaribag (M)	127,243	30.07	874	86.84
Hesla (CT)	5,860	-	885	89.28
Kuju (CT)	18,049	21.85	837	71.11
Kedla (CT)	17,588	19.89	831	72.44
Lapanga (CT)	7,354	15.72	867	71.87
Meru (CT)	8,547	33.11	507	86.14
Okni No.11 (CT)	8,203	-	868	90.10
Orla (CT)	5,871	-	835	67.65
Patratu	32,132	-3.02	856	81.06
Palawa (CT)	9,757	55.51	903	73.49
Religara alias Pachhiari (CT)	7,470	-0.90	889	70.20
Ramgarh Cantonment (CT)	73,455	43.29	758	79.96
Saunda (CT)	85,037	10.88	806	73.71
Sewai (CT)	8,784	-	877	87.75
Sirka (CT)	20,170	16.37	876	66.20
Topa (CT)	5,008	-	862	73.49

(ii) Parliamentary constituencies and assembly segments:

No.* and *Name of Parliamentary Constituencies:

48-Hazaribagh.

No.* and *Name of Assembly Segments:

263. Barhi—Barhi police station in Hazaribagh Sadar sub-division; and Chauparan police station in Kodarma sub-division.

266. Barkagaon—Barkagaon police station and G.Ps. Terpa, Patratu, Koto, Palani, Haphua, Hariharpur Gegda, Deoria, Bargama, Pali, Salgo, Sanke, Jabo, Chaingara, Chikor, Lapanga, Ghutua, Barkakana, and Sidhwar-Kalan in Ramgarh police station in Hazaribagh Sadar sub-division.

267. Ramgarh—Ramgarh police station (excluding G.Ps. Terpa, Patratu, Koto, Palani, Haphua, Hariharpur, Gegda, Deoria, Bargarna, Pali, Salgo, Sanki, Jabo, Chaingara, Chikor, Lapanga,

Ghutua, Barkakana and Sidhwar-Kalan) and Gola police station in Hazaribagh Sadar sub-division.

268. Mandu—Mandu and Bishungarh police stations in Hazaribagh Sadar sub-division.

269. Hazaribagh—Hazaribagh police station in Hazaribagh Sadar sub-division.

Hazaribagh was in Hazaribagh West Lok Sabha constituency in 1952. The community wise breakup (OBE) in Hazaribagh is Muslims (13 per cent), Scheduled Castes (12 per cent), Scheduled Tribes (14 per cent), Kurmis (11 per cent), Ahirs (6 per cent) and Telis and Koeris around 5 per cent each. Among the Scheduled Castes, Bhuiyas (5 per cent) and Chamars (3 per cent) are dominant. Santals and Mundas are 4 per cent each while Oraons are 3 per cent.

OBSERVATIONAL ORGANIZATION

Surface observatories

The place lies under meteorological sub-Division; Bihar Plateau.

The place lies in

Latitude	:	23.9° North
Longitude	:	85.4° East
Altitude	:	611 m
Date of starting	:	1-8-1968

Hydrometeorological Stations for Climatological Purposes.

This instrument is located at various places in the district like, Barkatha, Barhi, Barkagaon, Bishnugarh, Ramgarh.

INSAT data collection platform

This instrument is at Patratu, located in

Latitude	:	23.6° North
Longitude	:	85.3° East
Altitude	:	365.5 m
Date of starting	:	May 1985

DISASTROUS WEATHER EVENTS

Coldwave:

January, 1981 moderate.

December, 1981 moderate.

1 January, 1982, moderate.

29-30 November, 1982 severe.

4-10 December, 1982, severe.

2-14 January, 1983, severe.

December 3rd and 4th week 1984, severe.

9-14 January 1985, severe.

2 January 1986, severe.

22-25 January 1987, severe.

January 1st week 1988, severe.

13-16 January 1989, severe.

27-31 December 1989, severe.

1-10 January 1990, severe.

January 1st and 2nd week 1992.

11 January 1995, severe.

Heatwave:

June 1st, 2nd, and 3rd week 1981.

1-7 July, 1982, moderate to severe.

28 May to 2nd June 1983, moderate to severe.

6 June 1983, severe.

7 June 1983, moderate.

2nd and 3rd June 1985, severe.

6 June 1985, severe.

Heavy Rains:

July 4th week to October 2nd week 1987, this area witnessed heavy rains, caused damaged to standing crops and cornstores.

Thurder storm:

16 July 1993, there was severe thunder storm, the wind speed was above 75 kms per hour, that caused damage to the houses and several trees, electric poles and telephone pole.

Lightning:

18 July, 1996, 24 persons, including 15 children died and 15 other injured at Kalaukula village under Barhi police station. On 30th August again there was disastrous lightining, many people reported died in this area.

ARCHAEOLOGICAL SITE

Banda	Dt Hazaribagh	Paleolithic Handaxes (4.2). IAR 1960-1.
Bargunda	Dt Hazaribagh	Hoard of copper objects found in 1850 (4.11) Foote, R.B., 1916 Indian
Karharbari	Dt Hazaribagh	A hoard of five pieces of smelted copper, three of which were unfinished shouldered celt, was found. Brown, C.J., 1917, Catalogue of Prehistoric Antiquities in the Indian Museum at Calcutta, Simla, pp.140-2.
Ramgarh	Dt. Hazaribagh	Early stone Age (Lower Palaeolithic (4.2) tools were found along the river Damodar IAR 1964-5.

DISTRIBUTION OF *SCHEDULED CASTE* POPULATION BY SEX DISTRICTWISE (1991)

	POPULATION		
	Total	Males	Females
HAZARIBAG			
	5,37,157	2,76,311	2,60,846
Bantar	176	93	83
Bauri	1,418	804	614
Bhogta	74,028	38,229	35,799
Bhuiya	1,90,033	97,572	92,461
Chamar, Mochi	1,20,452	60,888	59,564
Chaupal	1,165	518	647
Dabgar	314	171	143
Dhobi	26,906	13,708	13,198
Dom, Dhangad	5,497	2,970	2,527
Dusadh, Dhari, Dharhi	51,509	26,961	24,548
Ghasi	9,284	4,762	4,522
Halalkhor	281	134	147
Hari, Mehtar, Bhangi	1,654	916	738
Kanjar	143	81	62
Kurariar	141	92	49
Lalbegi	329	160	169
Musahar	8,804	4,539	4,265
Nat	90	48	42
Pan, Sawasi	981	594	387
Pasi	8,602	4,727	3,875
Rajwar	11,085	5,816	5,269
Turi	23,727	12,255	11,472
Unclassified	538	273	265

DISTRIBUTION OF *SCHEDULED TRIBE* POPULATION BY SEX DISTRICTWISE (1991)

	POPULATION		
	Total	Males	Females
HAZARIBAG			
	2,50,586	1,29,321	1,21,265
Asur	72	43	29
Baiga	511	257	254
Banjara	47	47	0
Bathudi	140	86	54
Bedia	36,938	19,014	17,924
Bhumij	433	184	249
Binjhia	498	307	191
Birhor	3,455	1,720	1,735
Birjia	318	188	130
Chero	95	54	41
Chick Baraik	421	233	188
Gond	800	449	351
Gorait	118	27	91
Ho	610	332	278
Karmali	28,925	14,731	14,194
Kharia	1,151	702	449
Kharwar	2,408	1,252	1,156
Khond	121	72	49
Kisan	567	334	233
Kora	183	119	64
Korwa	52	37	15
Lohara, Lohra	3,186	1,761	1,425
Mahli	7,310	3,780	3,530
Mal Paharia	2,092	1,103	989
Munda	52,254	27,398	24,856
Oraon	45,839	23,621	22,218
Parhaiya	878	499	379
Santal	60,633	30,669	29,964
Sauria Paharia	480	289	191
Savar	23	6	17
Unclassified	28	7	21

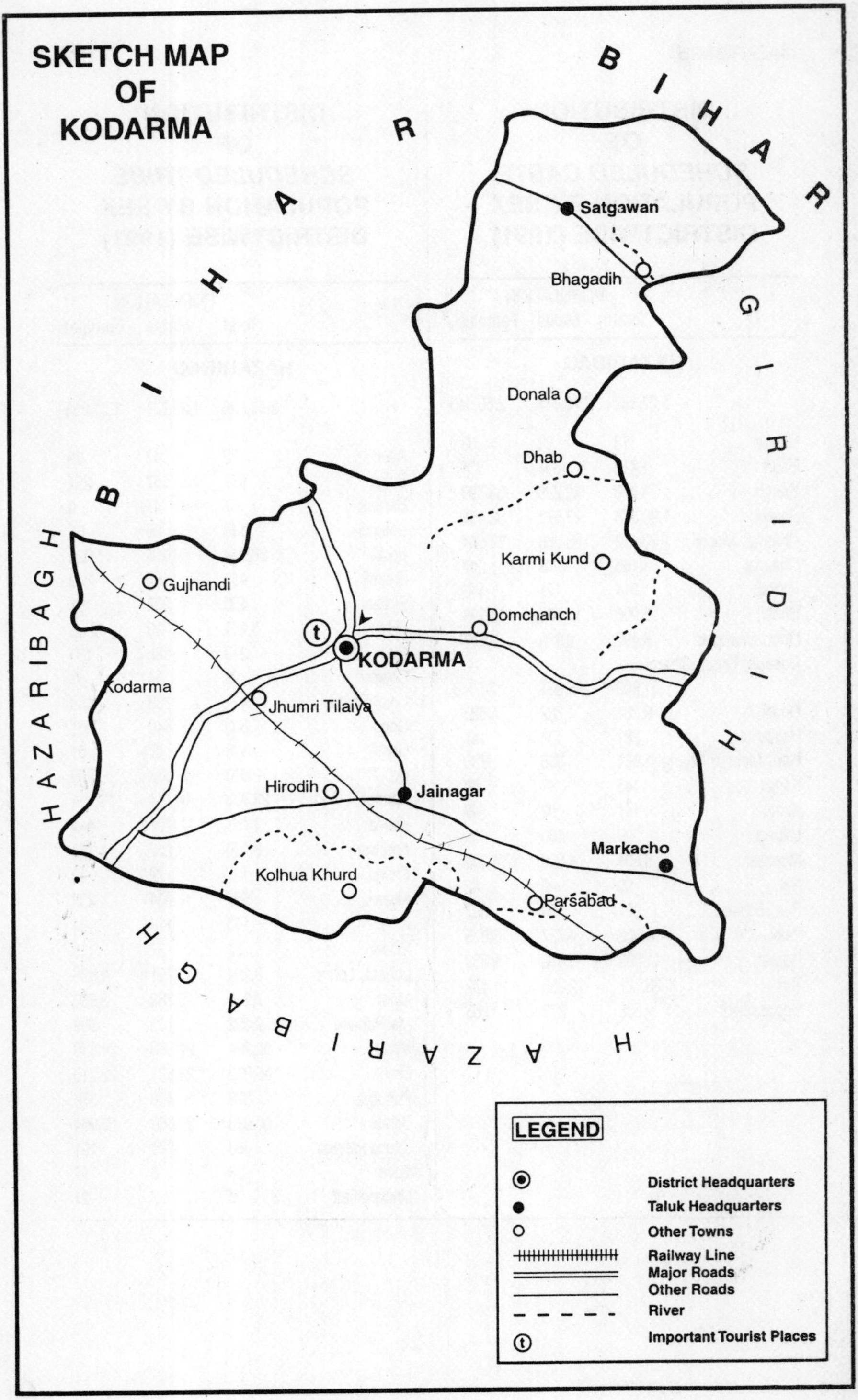

SKETCH MAP OF KODARMA
BIHAR
GIRIDIH
HAZARIBAGH
HAZARIBAGH
Satgawan
Bhagadih
Donala
Dhab
Karmi Kund
Domchanch
KODARMA
Gujhandi
Kodarma
Jhumri Tilaiya
Hirodih
Jainagar
Markacho
Kolhua Khurd
Parsabad
LEGEND
District Headquarters
Taluk Headquarters
Other Towns
Railway Line
Major Roads
Other Roads
River
Important Tourist Places

KODARMA

LOCATION AND AREA

Latitude : 24.2° North to 24.8° North.

Longitude : 85.2° East to 85.9° East.

Kodarma district forms the north-eastern portion of the North Chotanagpur division. It is bounded on the north-west by Nawada district of Bihar state, on the west by Gaya (Bihar) and Chatra districts, on the south by Hazaribagh district and on the east by Giridih district of Bihar. The district headquarters is located at Kodarma.

HISTORY

The district of Kodarma has been carved out as a result of the trifurcation of Hazaribagh district. It is comprised of one sub-division namely Kodarma and six Community Development Blocks namely Satgawan, Kodarma, Markacho, and Jainagar.

Since, as stated above, the district of Kodarma has been carved out from Hazaribagh district, its historical past is one and the same as of its parent district.

POPULATION (GENERAL, SC/ST)

Total population of the district as per 2001 Census is 498,683 persons of which 412,079 persons are returned from rural areas and the remaining 86,604 persons are returned from urban areas. The Scheduled Castes and Scheduled Tribes population of this district as per 1991 census are 104186 persons and 8978 persons respectively.

The Community Development Block-wise, population

distribution with sex ratio and literacy rate of this district is given below:

C.D. Block	Sex ratio Rural	Sex ratio Urban	Literacy rate Rural	Literacy rate Urban	Population Rural	Population Urban
KODARMA DISTRICT	**1026**	**888**	**47.90**	**79.52**	**412079**	**86604**
Satgawan	995	-	46.86	-	55,808	-
Kodarma	991	888	49.90	74.52	134,000	86,604
Jainagar	1,017	-	49.97	-	119,887	-
Markacho	1,101	-	43.38	-	102,384	-

LANGUAGES AND RELIGION

Main languages spoken in the district are Hindi and Urdu.

Religionwise breakup of population of this district is not available separately because it was the part of Hazaribagh district at the time of census-taking. The combined figures in this regard are provided in case of its parent district.

GEOGRAPHY AND PHYSICAL FEATURES

Annual Rainfall : 1240.6 mm
Temperature : Max. 42.40°C and Min. 4.50°C

Being the part of Chotanagpur plateau, it is thickly wooded and consists of a succession of hills. The average elevation varies from 300 to 1300 m high. Sal is the most famous and predominant species of trees in the jungles of the district. Among other common species are bamboo, khair, salai, simul, mabua, palas, kusum, kend, asam, piar and bhelwa.

RIVERS, CANALS AND WATERWAYS

Barsoti and Sakri are the main rivers of this district.

TOWNS, VILLAGES AND AMENITIES

The district is at present comprised of one sub-division and 4 Community Development Blocks. It has two towns.

COMMUNICATIONS

The district has a well net road communications. The Grand Trunk road or National Highway No. 2 passes through it. The Barhi- Rajauli road a part of National Highway No. 31 also passes through the district. The state highways run through the district is Jamui-Kodarma. The important Zila Parishad road is Chatra-Chauparan.

The district headquarters, i.e. Kodarma is connected by rail. The Grand cord line of Eastern railway runs through the district.

AGRICULTURE AND IRRIGATION

Paddy is the main crop of the district. The other crops grown are maize, bazra, pulses (particularly arhar). The cash-crops like sugar-cane grown in a very small area of this district.

The irrigational facilities have been provided in the district through a number of major medium and minor irrigation schemes. Several major schemes have been taken up by the Damodar Valley Corporation. Among them Tileiya Dam is the most important for irrigation in this district. Medium and minor irrigation schemes, rahat, pumps, electric pumps, open boring tube-wells and hand-pumps, are also prevalant in the district.

ANIMAL HUSBANDRY

The livestock population of this district comprised of cows, bulls, bullocks, buffaloes, sheep, goats and pigs. The quality of the livestock is, however, poor.

The district has veterinary hospitals and number of dispensaries which look after the welfare of animal wealth. Various schemes for cattle improvement have been undertaken by the district administration.

INDUSTRIES

The district is rich in Mica, a mineral of economic importance. One of the Mica mines of Jharkhand state is located in Kodarma sub- division. Despite the fact that the Mica, whose extensive deposits in this district are of importance within the country as also in some other countries, no large scale industrial unit has been set up here even today. However, there are a couple of medium and small scale industrial establishments.

HANDICRAFTS

Cane and Bamboo works; Dolls and toys work; Metal craft; papier-mache; textile's (embroidered) textiles (printed); Textiles (woven); wood work.

MINERALS AND ORES OCCURRENCES

Arsenic

At Dabur (24.6, 85.9) and Dhab (24.6, 85.8) Lumps of leucopyrite, and arsenide of iron, weighing several pounds, are occasionally found in the mica-bearing pegmatites near Dabur, on the Sukri River, and again about a mile S.S.W. of Dhab.

Beryl

Beryl occurs in a quartz-pegmatite ridge near Dumardiha. Beryl is fairly common in the mica-pegmatites of Kodarma forest.

Building Materials

The metamorphosed rocks like amphibolites, meta-dolerites and meta-gabbros from the northern part of the Kodarma is much suitable. The out-crops are easily accessible from Giridh—Domehants Kodarma road.

Mica

The mica deposits of the area are distributed along a belt of mica schists and associated genissorre granites extending from the Gaya district on the west for some 90 miles through Hazaribagh and Monghyr districts to Bhagalpur district on the east with a width reaching up to 16 miles. The more important part of this belt is along the disected northern edge of the Chotanagpur plateu, where numerous streams have exposed the mica bearing pegmatite veins by erosion. The main centres of activity have been the Kodarma Reserve Forest, Chatkari, Dhorakola, Domchanch, etc.

Monazite:

Small quantity of monazite and zircon are recorded in pink geneisses about a mile east of Bangaikalan (24.5, 85.7).

Lime

Apetite occurs abundantly in the mica-bearing pegmatites. Holland records that as an experiment 100 lbs. of the mineral were collected from the waste heaps at the Lakamandava mine near Kodarma (24.5, 85.6). Much larger quantities might easily be obtained, if the work were properly organised. The apetite contained 76 percent of phosphate lime.

Quartz

Quartz can be obtained as a bye-product of mica mining from pegmatites in the Kodarma (24.4, 85.5) area.

Columbite

At Kodarma (24.5, 85.6) specimens of columbite from the Government Forest near Kodarma were sent to the Geological Survey office. The specific gravity of the specimen was 6.19..

Silliminate

Occurrences of siliminate in fair quantities and in elongated crystals. Varying from a fraction of an inch to 3 inches have been reported from between Rathitamai (24.5, 85.6) and Puto (24.4, 85.6).

Gemstore (Apetite)

At Muhar Hill (24.71, 85.76).

Gemstore (Tourmaline)

Transparent green tourmaline with indicolite near Mani Mundar (24.61, 85.81).

TRADE, COMMERCE AND EXPORT

The following table provides information on most important commodities manufactured, exported from and imported into the town of this district alongwith the bank facility :

Name of the town	Most important commodities			Banks
	Manufactured	Exported	Imported	
Jhumri Tilatya	Micanite, iron rod and glass	Mica and micanite products	Rice, wheat and mustard oil	7

TOURISM

Ghorsima. The village is situated about 6 kms west of the block headquarters at Satgawan. It is noted for its Shiva temple around which an annual fair is held on the occasion of Shivaratri.

Tilaiya. Tilaiya is famous for the multipurpose dam of the D.V.C. and its rest house. It is situated at a distance of 22 kms south of Kodarma. The place has natural scenic beauty and is also known as picnic spot.

FAIRS AND FESTIVALS

Important fairs and melas organised in various parts of the district are mentioned below:

Shivratri fair, Basant Panchmi mela and Dussehra mela.

EDUCATION

According to 2001 census, total literates (excluding the population in the age groups 0-6 years) is 210,679 persons of these 142,440 are males and 68,239 are females. In the rural areas of the district 156,685 persons 109,614 males and 47,071 females are literates and in urban areas 53,994 persons (32,826 males and 21,168 females) are literates.

The following table gives details of different categories of educational institutions including stadia and public library available in the Jhumri Tilaiya of this district.

Name of the town	Educational institutions	Stadia	Public libraries, including reading rooms
Jhumri Tilaiya	Higher Secondary/ Intermediate School (1), Secondary /Matrlculation Schools (3), Junior Secondary and Middle Schools (5), Primary Schools (4)	—	PL : 2

COLLEGES (2000)

J.J. College, Jhumritelaiya (Established 1960). Enrolment 2605, Teachers 33. (Affiliated College)

(Above named college belong to Vinoba Bhave University, Hazaribagh, Established 1992).

MEDICAL

The table given below furnishes information regarding availability of medical facility in the town of this district including that of beds facility.

Name of the towns	*Medical institutions (with number of Beds)*	
Jhumri Tilaiya	Dispensaries (10, A-1, U-1, Hom-4)	—

ADMINISTRATION

(i) Administrative Divisions:

Sub-division: Kodarma.

Community Development Blocks: Satgawan, Kodarma, Markacho and Jainagar.

Towns and Urban Agglomerations with their Population, Sexratio, Decadal growth and Literacy rate (2001)

Town	Population	Percentage Decadal growth 1991-2001	Sex Ratio	Literacy Rate
Jhumri Tilaiya (M)	69,444	29.62	890	74.39
Kodarma (NA)	17,160	35.50	880	75.02

(ii) Parliamentary Constituencies and assembly segments:

No. **and** ***Name of Parliamentary Constituencies*** **:**

45-Kodarma.

No.* and *Name of Assembly Segments:

262. Kodarma—Kodarma and Satgawan police stations in Kodarma sub-division.

270. Barkatha—Barkatha and Jainagar police stations in Kodarma sub-division; and Ichak police station in Hazaribagh Sadar sub-division.

Kodarma was in Girdih Lok Sabha constituency in 1957, 1962, 1967 and 1971. The communitywise break up (OBE) in Kodarmais Muslims (15 per cent), Scheduled Castes (15 per cent), Scheduled Tribes (8 per cent), Ahirs (12 per cent) and Koeris and Telis around 5 per cent each. Kurmis, Brahmins, Rajputs are also present in some strength. Chamars (4 per cent) and Bhuiyas (3 per cent) are prominent among the Scheduled Castes while Santals (6 per cent) mainly constitute the Scheduled Tribes.

OBSERVATIONAL ORGANISATION

Hydrometeorological stations for climatological purposes.

Latitude : 24.4
Longitude : 85.5

DISASTROUS WEATHER EVENTS

Coldwave:

1st January 1982, moderate.
29-30 November 1982, severe.
4-10 December 1982, severe.
2-14 January 1983, severe.
December 3rd and 4th week 1984, severe.
9-14 January 1985, severe.
2 January 1986, severe.
22-25 January 1987, severe.
January 1st week 1988, severe.
13-16 January 1989, severe.
27-31 December 1989, severe.
1-10 January 1990, severe.

January 1st and 2nd week 1992.
11 January 1995, severe.

Heatwave:
1-7 July 1982, moderate to severe.
28 May to 2nd June 1983 moderate to severe.
6 June 1983, severe.
7 June 1983, moderate.

Heavy Rains:
July 4th week to October 2nd week 1987, this area witnessed heavy rains, caused damaged to standing crops and cornstores.

Thunder storm:
On 16th June 1993, this area witnessed severe thunder storm, caused damage to the houses, trees and electric poles.

Lightning:
18 July 1996, there was lightning in this area, caused damaged to the flowering crops.

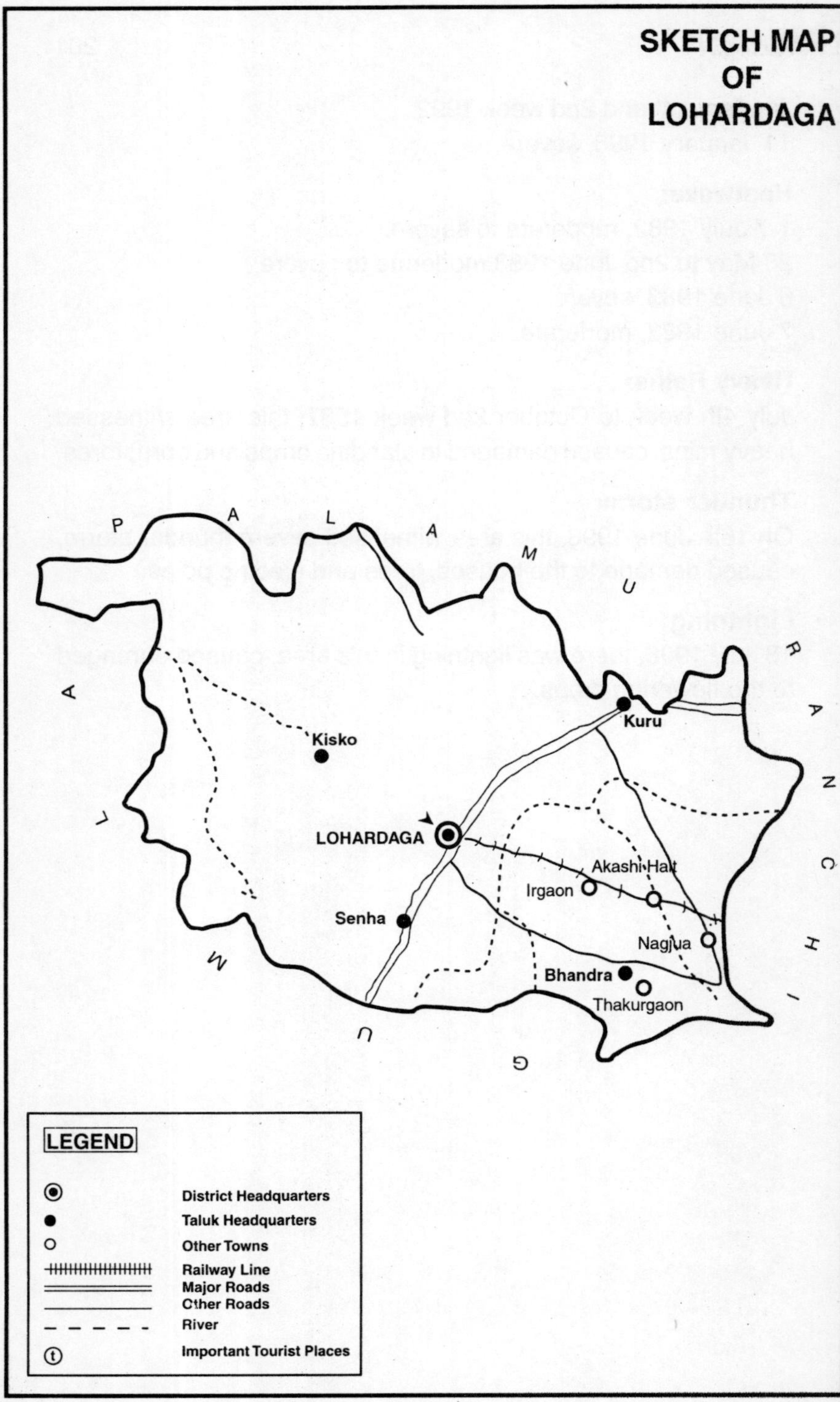
SKETCH MAP OF LOHARDAGA
P A L A M U
R A N C H I
G U M L A
Kuru
Kisko
LOHARDAGA
Akashi Halt
Irgaon
Senha
Nagjua
Bhandra
Thakurgaon
LEGEND
District Headquarters
Taluk Headquarters
Other Towns
Railway Line
Major Roads
Other Roads
River
Important Tourist Places

LOHARDAGA

LOCATION AND AREA

Latitude : 23.4° North to 24.8° North.
Longitude : 85.2° East to 85.9° East.

The district extends over an area of 1491 sq kms and is one of the smallest district of Jharkhand state. It is comprised within South Chotanagpur division and forms almost the central part of it. The district is bounded on the north by Palamu district, on the east by Ranchi district and on south as well as on west by Gumla district. Lohardaga is the district headquarters with the only town in this district.

HISTORY

Lohardaga is the original name of undivided Ranchi district which had come into existence after the creation of the non-regulation south-west frontier, as a result of the Kol insurrections in 1831-32. However, the name of the erstwhile district was changed in 1899 from Lohardaga to Ranchi. Immediately after the conduct of the 1981 census, the district of Ranchi split up into three districts, viz. Ranchi (consisting of old Ranchi Sadar and Khunti sub-divisions), Lohardaga (old Lohardaga sub-division). The historical past of Lohardaga is the same as of undivided Ranchi district.

POPULATION (GENERAL, SC/ST)

Total population of the district according to 2001 census is 364,405 persons, comprising of 184,405 males and 180,000 females. Rural population of the district is 318,201 persons (160,503 males and 157,698 females) and urban population is 46,204 persons (23,902 males and 22,302 females).

The Community Development Block-wise, population distribution with sex ratio and literacy rate of this district is given below:

C.D. Block	Sex ratio Rural	Sex ratio Urban	Literacy rate Rural	Literacy rate Urban	Population Rural	Population Urban
LOHARDAGA DISTRICT	**983**	**933**	**49.43**	**83.32**	**318201**	**46204**
Kisko	974	-	42.27	-	57,770	-
Kuru	991	-	53.48	-	83,889	-
Lohardaga	991	933	54.26	83.32	57,128	46,204
Senha	969	-	47.95	-	63,907	-
Bhandra	984	-	47.39	-	55,507	-

The Scheduled Castes and Scheduled Tribes population of the district as per 1991 census is 10919 persons and 162964 persons respectively. The rural-urban breakup of this population is indicated below:

Rural	(i)	Scheduled Castes	:	9441
	(ii)	Scheduled Tribes	:	157720
Urban	(i)	Scheduled Castes	:	1478
	(ii)	Scheduled Tribes	:	5244

The decennial growth rate of population of the district as a whole in relation to the state between the period 1991 and 2001 is presented below:

State/ District	*Decenntal growth rate of population (per cent) 1991-2001*		
	Total	*Rural*	*Urban*
Jharkhand	23.19	21.62	28.99
Lohardaga	26.14	23.75	45.47

LANGUAGES AND RELIGION

Main languages spoken in the district are Hindi, Bengali and Urdu.

Religionwise breakup of population is indicated below as per 1991 census:

Hindus: 213352, Muslims: 41442, Christians: 8743, Sikhs: 31, Buddhists: —, Jains : —, Other religions and persuasions : 25295, Religions not stated: 23.

GEOGRAPHY AND PHYSICAL FEATURES

Annual Rainfall : 972.0 mm
Temperature : Max. 36.00°C and Min. 6.00°C

Lohardaga is geographically a small area situated in south of Palamu district, surrounded by a number of lofty flat-topped hills, called *Pats.* The Pat area extends over the blocks of Bishunpur, Chainpur and Ghaghra and has an altitude of 2500 to 3000 feet above the sea level. Forests cover a considerable portion of the district. 'Dry Peninsular Sal' is the main type of forest found with patches of mixed forest towards the north-western part of the district. Bauxite is found in the region of Lohardaga.

RIVERS, CANALS AND WATERWAYS

The South Koel rises near Mandur (from the same ridge as the Subarnarekha) and flows in a north-westerly direction for some distance. It turns towards the south near Lohardaga and flows across the central part of the district to Singhbhum. Its main tributaries are the Kara and the Paras.

TOWNS, VILLAGES AND AMENITIES

The district, at present comprises of one sub-division, and 5 Community Development Blocks namely, Kisko, Kuru, Lohardaga, Senha and Bhandara. It has 1 town and 354 villages (353 inhabited villages and 1 uninhabited villages).

The urban population of the district as percentage of total population in 2001 census is indicated below. It also shows the sex ratio (females per 1000 males) and density (population per sq km) in the urban population of the district in relation to state:

State/ District	Urban population as percentage of total population	Sex ratio, 2001 (Females per 1000 males)			Density (Population per sq km)
	2001	Total	Rural	Urban	
Jharkhand	22.25	941	963	870	338
Lohardaga	12.68	976	983	933	244

Amenities

Number (with percentage) of villages having one or more amenities in the district as per 1991 census is given below:

Sl. No.	Amenities	Number of inhabited villages	Percentage
1.	Education	244	69.12
2.	Medical	50	14.16
3.	Drinking Water	353	100.00
4.	Post and Telegraph	49	13.88
5.	Market/Hat	47	13.31
6.	Communications	48	13.60
7.	Approach by Pucca Road	61	17.28
8.	Power Supply	144	40.79

COMMUNICATIONS

The district is well served by a network of good roads and all the block headquarters are connected by metalled roads. Municipal roads are maintained by the municipalities of Lohardaga. Considerable length of village roads has been constructed through Gram Panchayats. The district headquarter (i.e. Lohardaga) is connected with Ranchi by narrow gauge line of South-Eastern Railway.

AGRICULTURE AND IRRIGATION

With the gradual deforestation of the district more and more land is being brought under cultivation. The cultivable land of the district is divided into two classes viz. don and tanr. The don lands are the terraced lowlands on which mainly rice is grown and the tanr are the uplands which produce a coarse form of rice, millets, pulses and oil-seeds. The cultivators of this district depended mostly on a good rainfall for their crop of rice in pre-independence days. Artificial irrigation received some attention during Zamindari period, though this facility is not adequate even today. Wells, springs and ahars are the only traditional sources of irrigation.

ANIMAL HUSBANDRY

Cows, buffaloes, goats, pigs are the main livestock of the district. The cattle of this district are small and undersized which is largely due to lack of good pasturage and good fodder. Besides cattle, the cultivators keep large number of sheep and goats mainly for food purposes. The Munda in the past considered it almost a crime to drink the milk of a cow which they considered proper to leave entirely to the calf. The population of poultry birds has been steadily increasing in the district. Poultry is an indigenous cottage industry of the aboriginals of the district. For treatment, prevention and suppression of diseases of the livestock, there are a number of veterinary hospitals and dispensaries in the district.

INDUSTRIES

The district has a number of small scale industries at present. Metallic pots. *bidi* and soaps are manufactured here. In rural as well as urban areas rice mills are established which produce rice in good quantity.

HANDICRAFTS

Cane and bamboo works, Dolls and toys; wood work.

MINERALS AND ORES OCCURRENCES

Bauxite

According to A.K. Dey, who examined the bauxite deposits of Lahardaga area, the Bagrapat (23.5, 84.6) deposit is estimated to contain about 7000,000 tons and is most accessible. Other accessible deposits are at Khamar Pat (23.6, 84.7), Pokhra Pat (23.6, 84.6) and Bangla Pat (23.5, 84.6) and Dudhia Pahar (23.6, 84.6).

Clay

Deposit of white clay is reported at various point in the district.

Ochre

According to M.K. Roy Chowdhury, yellow and red lithomargic clays associated with laterite are occasionally seen in the Lohardaga (23.4, 84.7) area. Some thick bands of yellow clay and variegated material are exposed near Chuhimati (23.4, 84.4). The yellow clay can favourably be compared with Ochre and can be marketed after washing.

Kaolin

Kaolin Occurs at Bagru (23.46, 84.63), Lohardaga (23.45, 84.68).

TRADE, COMMERCE AND EXPORT

Lohardaga is the chief centre of trade in the undivided Ranchi district. The importance of this place has considerably increased with the opening and extension of railway facility. The chief articles of export of this district are: rice, vegetables and mahua. Metallic pots, *bidi* and soap are manufactured within the district. Wheat, sugar, kerosene oil, coal etc. are items of import. The table given below lists the most important commodities manufactured, exported from and imported in Lohardaga town:

Name of the town	*Most important commodities*			*Banks*
	Manufactured	*Exported*	*Imported*	
Lohardaga	Metalic pots, Bidi, Soap, Mahua	Rice, Vegetables K. Oil	Wheat, Sugar	4

TOURISM

The village Korambe is situated about 13 kms from block headquarters at Senha. It is famous for its temple having an idol said to be over 500 years old. Special prayers are offered on the occasion of Kartik Purnima (October-November). A Munda fair is also held on the occasion of Baisakhi Purnima (April-May). The Rath Yatra festival in the month of Asadh (June-July) is also celebrated with great enthusiasm.

FAIRS AND FESTIVALS

No major social or cultural event has taken place in the district during the last decade. Fairs and festivals are, however, held regularly in the district by different communities in complete harmony. The hats and melas are part and parcel of life of the common man in the district of Lohardaga. Important melas and fairs organised in various parts of the district are Karma Puja melas, Makar Sankranti mela, Rath Yatra mela, Shivaratri mela, Kartik Amawashya mela etc.

EDUCATION

According to 2001 census, total literates (excluding the population in the age group of 0-6 years) is 58,918 persons. Of these, 100,668 are males and 58,250 are females. In the rural areas of the district 126,060 persons (82,466 males and 43,594 females) are literates and in urban areas 32,858 persons (18,202 males and 14,656 females) are literates. The rate of literacy of this population to the total population, excluding 0-6 years age group according to 2001 census is shown below:

	Persons	*Males*	*Females*
Total	53.97	67.84	39.88
Rural	49.43	64.44	34.31
Urban	83.32	89.12	77.09

There are as many as 244 villages accounting for 69.12 per cent of the total number of inhabited villages in the district where educational facility is available. Primary and middle schools are available in the town. The following table gives the details of various types of educational institutions available in the only town of this district including the number of stadia and public libraries:

Name of the town	*Educational institutions*	*Stadia*	*Public libraries, including reading rooms*
1	*2*	*3*	*4*
Lohardaga	Shorthand Type writing Institutes (2), Secondary/Matriculation Schools (6), Junior Secondary and Middle Schools (8)	1	PL : 2

COLLEGES (2000)

B.S. College, Lohardaga (Established 1963) (Constituent College).

Madhusudan Lal Agrawal Mahila College, Lohardaga (Established 1984). (Affiliated College)

Ursuline Teachers Training College, Lohardaga. (Affiliated College)

(Above mentioned colleges belong to Ranchi University, Established 1960).

MEDICAL

The availablity of medical facility in the village is considerably low as only 14.16 per cent villages in the district have got it. The table given below furnishes information regarding various types of medical institutions available in the town of this district:

Name of the towns	*Number of beds in medical institutions per one thousand population*	
Godda	Hospital (4) :	30
	Dispensaries (6) :	—
	Family Planning Centre (1) :	—
	Others (8)	—

ADMINISTRATION

(i) Administrative Divisions :

Sub-divisions: Lohardaga.

Community Development Blocks: Kisko, Kuru, Lohardaga, Bhandra, Senha.

Towns and Urban Agglomerations with their Population, Sexratio, Decadal growth and Literacy rate (2001)

Town	Population	Percentage Decadal growth 1991-2001	Sex Ratio	Literacy Rate
Lohardaga (M)	46,204	45.47	933	83.32

(ii) Parliamentary Constituencies and assembly segments:

No. and Name of Parliamentary Constituencies:

53-Lohardaga (ST).

No. and Name of Assembly Segments:

314. Bishunpur (ST)—Bishunpur and Ghaghra police stations and Gumla police station (excluding Gumla municipality and G.Ps. Hurhuria, Ghatagaon, Asani, Chandali, Telgaon, Pugu, Bangaru, Karaundi, Dumardih and Murkunda) in Gumla sub-division; and Senha police station in Lohardaga sub- division.

315. Lohardaga (ST)—Lohardaga, Kuru and Kisko police stations in Lohardaga sub-division.

The communitywise breakup (OBE) in Lohardaga is Muslims (7 per cent), Christians (15 per cent), Scheduled Castes (6 per cent) and Scheduled Tribes (73 per cent). Of the Scheduled Tribes, Oraons (60 per cent) and Mundas (5 per cent) are the principal constituents. Other communities like Kurmi and Ahirs are present only in small numbers.

OBSERVATIONAL ORGANISATION

Hydrometeorological Stations for Climatological Purposes.

Latitude	:	23.4° North
Longitude	:	84.7° East
Date of starting	:	17-11-1985

This instruments work under Bhubaneshwar Flood Meterological Offices having facility of self rewarding raingauge.

DISASTROUS WEATHER EVENTS

Coalwave:

1st January 1982, moderate.
29-30 November 1982, severe.
4-10 December 1982, severe.
2-14 January 1983, severe.
December 3rd and 4th week 1984, severe.
27-31 December 1989, severe.
1-10 January 1990, severe.
January 1st and 2nd week, 1992.

Heatwave:

1-7 July 1982, moderate to severe.
28 May to 2 June 1983, moderate to severe.
6 June 1983, severe.
7 June 1983, moderate.

Heavy Rains:

July 4th week to October 2nd week 1987, this area witnessed moderate to heavy rains, caused damage to property and crops.

Lightning:

On 13th September 1996, the district observed disastrous lightning caused damage to standing flowering crops.

ARCHAEOLOGICAL SITE

Lohardaga	Dt Lohardaga	Megalithic [4.17.4] burials. Also a so-called 'Asura' site [14.4]. Roy, S.C., 1921, Jour Bihar & Orissa Res. Soc., 6.p.416. IAR 1963-4.

DISTRIBUTION OF SCHEDULED CASTE POPULATION BY SEX DISTRICTWISE (1991)

	POPULATION		
	Total	Males	Females
LOHARDAGA	10,919	5,573	5,346
Bantar	23	13	10
Bauri	144	72	72
Bhogta	509	247	262
Bhuiya	773	376	397
Chamar, Mochi	4,141	2,289	1,852
Chaupal	11	0	11
Dhobi	1,423	665	758
Dom, Dhangad	93	65	28
Dusadh, Dhari, Dharhi	919	435	484
Ghasi	512	235	277
Hari, Mehtar, Bhangi	183	91	92
Kurariar	8	0	8
Lalbegi	24	6	18
Musahar	144	96	48
Nat	15	6	9
Pan, Sawasi	3	3	0
Pasi	139	61	78
Rajwar	201	89	112
Turi	1,643	821	822
Unclassified	11	3	8

DISTRIBUTION OF *SCHEDULED TRIBE* POPULATION BY SEX DISTRICTWISE (1991)

	POPULATION		
	Total	Males	Females
LOHARDAGA	1,62,964	82,045	80,919
Asur	879	396	483
Baiga	30	9	21
Banjara	28	28	0
Bathudi	1	0	1
Bedia	21	21	0
Bhumij	66	46	20
Binjhia	33	32	1
Birhor	2	1	1
Birjia	426	226	200
Chick Baraik	159	73	86
Gond	47	19	28
Gorait	348	211	137
Ho	65	14	51
Karmali	52	32	20
Kharia	268	143	125
Kharwar	7,141	3,586	3,555
Kisan	3,827	1,892	1,935
Kora	30	20	10
Korwa	125	93	32
Lohara, Lohra	7,799	3,755	4,044
Mahli	5,376	2,779	2,597
Mal Paharia	1,502	881	621
Munda	5,905	3,080	2,825
Oraon	1,27,130	63,857	63,273
Parhaiya	661	359	302
Santal	893	399	494
Sauria Paharia	127	83	44
Savar	10	10	0
Unclassified	13	0	13

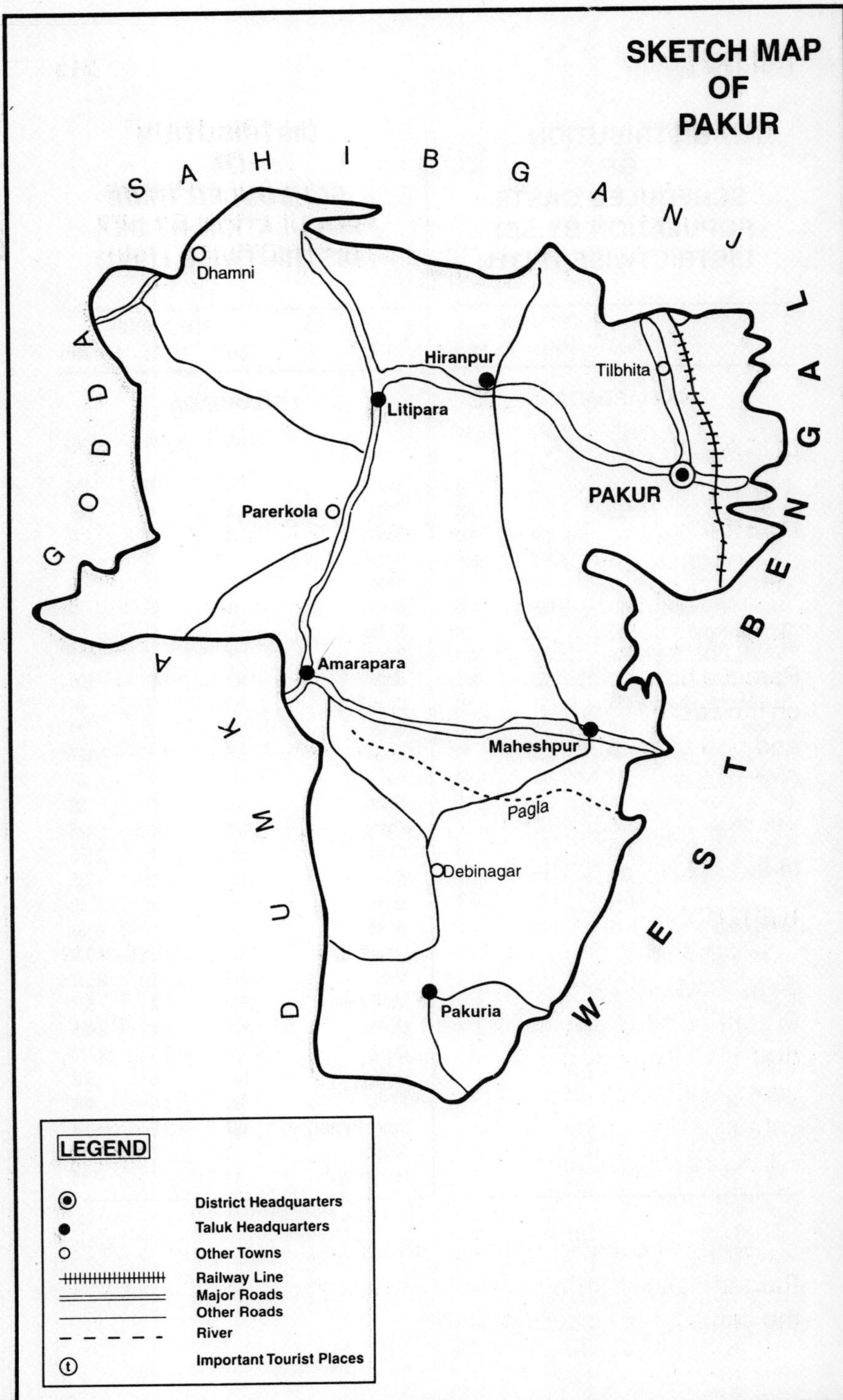
SKETCH MAP OF PAKUR
SAHIBGANJ
GODDA
DUMKA
WEST BENGAL
Dhamni
Hiranpur
Litipara
Tilbhita
PAKUR
Parerkola
Amarapara
Maheshpur
Pagla
Debinagar
Pakuria
LEGEND
District Headquarters
Taluk Headquarters
Other Towns
Railway Line
Major Roads
Other Roads
River
Important Tourist Places

PAKUR

LOCATION AND AREA

Altitude	:	350 m (Hiranpur)
Latitude	:	24.2° North to 24.7° North
Longitude	:	87.4° East to 87.9° East

The district of Pakur is situated in the eastern portion of Jharkhand state, comprised within the newly created Santhal Pargana division. It is bounded on the north by Sahibganj district, on the east by West Bengal state, on the south by Dumka district and part of West Bengal state, and on the west by Dumka and Godda districts.

The district take its name from Pakur town which is the seat of the district administration.

HISTORY

The district of Pakur has been carved out as a separate district due to the bifurcation of Sahibganj district. According to the said bifurcation, Pakur sub-division of erstwhile Sahibganj district separated from it and attained the status of a separate district. At present, this district is comprised of one sub-division namely Pakur and six Community Development Blocks namely Litipara, Amrapara, Hiranpur, Pakur, Maheshpur and Pakuria..

Since, the district of Pakur formed part of erstwhile Santhal Pargana district till a couple of years ago, its historical past is the same as of its parent district.

POPULATION (GENERAL, SC/ST)

Total population of the district as per 2001 Census is 701,616 persons of which 665,602 persons are retained from rural areas and the remaining 36,014 persons are retained from urban areas. The Scheduled Castes and Scheduled Tribes population of this district as per 1991 census are 21484 persons and 278331 persons respectively.

The Community Development Block-wise, population distribution with sex ratio and literacy rate of this district is given below:

	Sex ratio		Literacy rate		Population	
C.D. Block	Rural	Urban	Rural	Urban	Rural	Urban
PAKUR DISTRICT	**961**	**899**	**28.14**	**72.59**	**665602**	**36014**
Litipara	955	-	24.28	-	87,536	-
Amrapara	938	-	29.28	-	53,283	-
Hiranpur	959	-	35.58	-	68,092	-
Pakaur	970	899	21.13	72.59	197,008	36,014
Maheshpur	958	-	30.65	-	170,482	-
Pakuria	966	-	35.50	-	89,201	-

LANGUAGES AND RELIGION

Hindi is the main language spoken in the district.

Separate religionwise breakup of population is not available, because it was the part of Sahibganj district at the time of census taking.

GEOGRAPHY AND PHYSICAL FEATURES

Annual Rainfall : 1383.0 mm

Temperature : Max. 40.00°C and Min. 4.00°C

The district is consists of uplands, undulations, long ridges and depressions. This area has plenty of fertile lands and is intensively cultivated.

RIVERS, CANALS AND WATERWAYS

At a distance from the eastern boundary of the district, Ganga passes through it. The other rivers in the district are Gumani, Bansloi, Palsi and Brahmani.

TOWNS, C.D. Block and Subdivision

The district is comprised of one sub-division and six Community Development Blocks. It has one town.

COMMUNICATIONS

The district of Pakur is well served by road transport. All the Community Development Blocks headquarters are connected with the district headquarters by black-topped roads.

The district headquarter is connected by Eastern Railway.

AGRICULTURE AND IRRIGATION

Main crops of the district are paddy and maize. Groundnuts, sweet potatoes and khesari are also widely grown in this district. Irrigational facilities are not adequate in this district. Well is the most common source of irrigation, but this is not a *very* dependable source. The major part of the district being rocky, it is difficult to dig wells. The undulatory nature of land makes it possible to store rain water by bunding. Seepage ponds are also found. Apart from being dependent upon rains, these are by no means adequate. The result is that failure of rains invariably involves failure of crops except in small pockets.

ANIMAL HUSBANDRY

The livestock population of the district includes cows, buffaloes, sheep, goats and pigs.

There are a number of veterinary hospitals and dispensaries spread over the entire district. Treatment, prevention and suppression of diseases of the livestock are the main functions of the veterinary institutions.

INDUSTRIES

The district is deprived of any major industry .However, there are a few small scale industries which are engaged in manufacture of stone chips, lac and *bidi*.

MINERALS AND ORES OCCURRENCES

Building Materials

Trap is being quarried for road metal and railway ballast near Malpahari situated about 3 miles S.W. of Pakur Railway station.

Coal

Occurrence of inferior coal in Damini-Koh, a Government Estate comprised within the subdivisions of Dumka, Pakaur, Godda and Rajmahal. The coal seams are less than 4 ft. in thickness.

Fire-clay

Dhumabhita (24.7, 87.53), Simlong (24.75, 87.5), Telbhita (24.8, 87.46).

Gemstone (Agate)

Dumarchir (24.58, 87.51) and Garasungla (24.65, 87.4).

Glass-making Materials

Bedded sandstones of the Damuda series exposed in the Rajmahal coal fields near Mangal Hat (25.08, 87.85) and Pir Pahar (25.1, 87.83).

Iron

At Garasingla (24.65, 87.4), Chirudhi (24.51, 87.48), Amarapara (24.53, 87.56).

Kaolin

At Bagmara (24.63, 87.45), Rajabhita (24.68, 87.48), Ghagri (24.74, 87.46), Mangal Hat (25.08, 87.78), Sidpur (25.1, 87.76)

TRADE, COMMERCE AND EXPORT

The table given below presents information on most important commodities, manufacturing, exported from and imported in Pakur town of this district.

Name of the town	*Most important commodities*			*Banks*
	Manufactured	*Exported*	*Imported*	
Pakur	Stone chips, Lac and *Bidi*	Stone chips, Lac and *Bidi*	Sugar, Cement and , Coal	3

TOURISM

Aliganj. The village is situated south of Pakur town. It contains a fortress about 150 years old which is said to have been the stronghold of the Santhals during the Santhal rebellion of 1854-55.

Birkiti. The village which is also known as 'Birkhatta' lies about 10 kms south of Maheshpur. It was the site of a bitter battle between the local Rajput chief, Raja Udit Narain Singh and Nawab Murshid Kuli Jafar Khan of Murshidabad in the early 18th century. The ruins of the fort of the aforesaid chief can still be seen.

Debinagar. The village is situated 16 kms south-west of Maheshpur. It contains the remnants of temples and houses said to have been built by a local Raja Udai Narayan Singh. The ruins of the tunnel which once connected this place with village Birkiti can still be seen.

Pakur. Pakur town is the administrative headquarters of the district. The Pakur Raj family is an old well known family. Several institutions in the district owe their origin to the generosity of this family. During the Santhal rebellion of 1855 the town was destroyed by the Santhals who came in thousands and plundered the Bungalow's and the Rani's Palace. They resorted to loot and carried away many valuables.

The town has a tower named Matello Tower, 30 ft high and 20 ft diameter. It was built in 1856 to provide protection to the railway officials. Guns can be fired from the top of it.

FAIRS AND FESTIVALS

Fairs and festivals are held regularly in the district. The most important seasonal fairs organised in the district are on the occasions of Shivratri and Shravana Sombari, apart from those held at the time of Durga puja and Diwali.

EDUCATION

According to 2001 census, total literates (excluding the population in the age group of 0-6 years) is 171,056 persons. Of these 115,149 are males and 55,907 are females. In the rural areas of the district 149,115 persons (102,537 males and 46,578 females) are literates and in urban areas 21941 persons (12,612 males and 9,329 females) are literates. The rate of literacy of this population excluding 0-6 years age of group according to 2001 census is shown below.

	Persons	*Males*	*Females*
Total	30.54	40.19	20.44
Rural	28.14	37.91	17.96
Urban	72.59	78.63	65.77

The following table gives details of different categories of educational institutions including public library available in the Pakur town of this district.

Name of the town	*Educational institutions*	*Stadia*	*Public libraries, including reading rooms*
Pakur	Secondary/Matriculation Schools (4), Junior Secondary and Middle Schools (8)	—	PL : 1

COLLEGES (2000)

K K M College, Pakur (Established 1966) Constituent College. Enrolment 1068, Teachers 26.

Evening College, Pakur (1993). Enrolment 326, Teachers 24. (Affiliated College)

S K M College, Maheshpur Raj, (1982), Teachers 66. (Affiliated College)

(Above named colleges belong to Siddhu Kanhu University, Dumka, Established 1992).

MEDICAL

The table given below furnishes information regarding availability of medical facility in Pakur town of this district including that of beds facility.

Name of the towns	*Medical institutions (with number of Beds)*	
Godda	Hospital (1)	20
	T.B. Clinic (1)	10
	Family Planning Centre (1)	6

ADMINISTRATION

(i) Administrative Divisions :

Sub-division: Pakur.

Community Development Blocks: Litipara, Amrapara, Hiranpur, Pakur, Maheshpur and Pakuria.

Towns and Urban Agglomerations with their Population, Sexratio, Decadal growth and Literacy rate (2001)

Town	Population	Percentage Decadal growth 1991-2001	Sex Ratio	Literacy Rate
Pakaur (M)	36,014	37.24	899	72.59

(ii) Parliamentary Constituency and Assembly segments

No. **and** ***Name of Parliamentary Constituencies*** **:**

26-Rajmahal (ST).

No. **and** ***Name of Assembly Segments:***

150. Litipara (ST)—Litipara, Amrapara and Hiranpur police stations in Pakur sub-division; and Gopikandar police station in Dumka Sadar sub-division.

151. Pakur—Pakur police station in Pakur sub-division; and Barharwa police station in Rajmahal sub-division.

152. Maheshpur (ST)—Maheshpur and Pakuria police stations in Pakaur sub-division.

OBSERVATIONAL ORGANISATION

Hydrometeorological Stations for Climatological Purposes.

This instrument is in Hiranpur, worked under Flood meteorological offices. Asansol. Hiranpur lies in

Latitude	:	24.7° North
Longitude	:	87.7° East
Altitude	:	350m
Date of starting	:	3-8-1961

DISASTROUS WEATHER EVENTS

Coldwave:

1st January 1982, Moderate.
29-30 November 1982, severe.
4-10 December 1982, severe.
2-14 January 1983, severe.
December 3rd and 4th week 1984, severe.
27-31 December 1989, severe.
1-10 January 1990, severe.
January 1st and 2nd week 1992.

Heatwave:

1-7 July 1982, moderate to severe.
28 May to 2nd June 1983, moderate to severe.
6 June 1983, severe.
7 June 1983, severe.

Drought:

August, and September 1st week 1982.

The drought was of moderate category, transplantation of paddy crop badly affected.

Flood and Heavy Rains:

In August 3rd and 4th week this area witnessed heavy rains and flood.

July 4th week to October 2nd week 1987 this area witnessed heavy rains caused damaged to the property and corn stone.

Thunderstorm:

22 May 1988 there was a thunderstorm in this area caused heavy damage to the thatched houses, telephone poles and the trees.

SKETCH MAP OF PALAMU

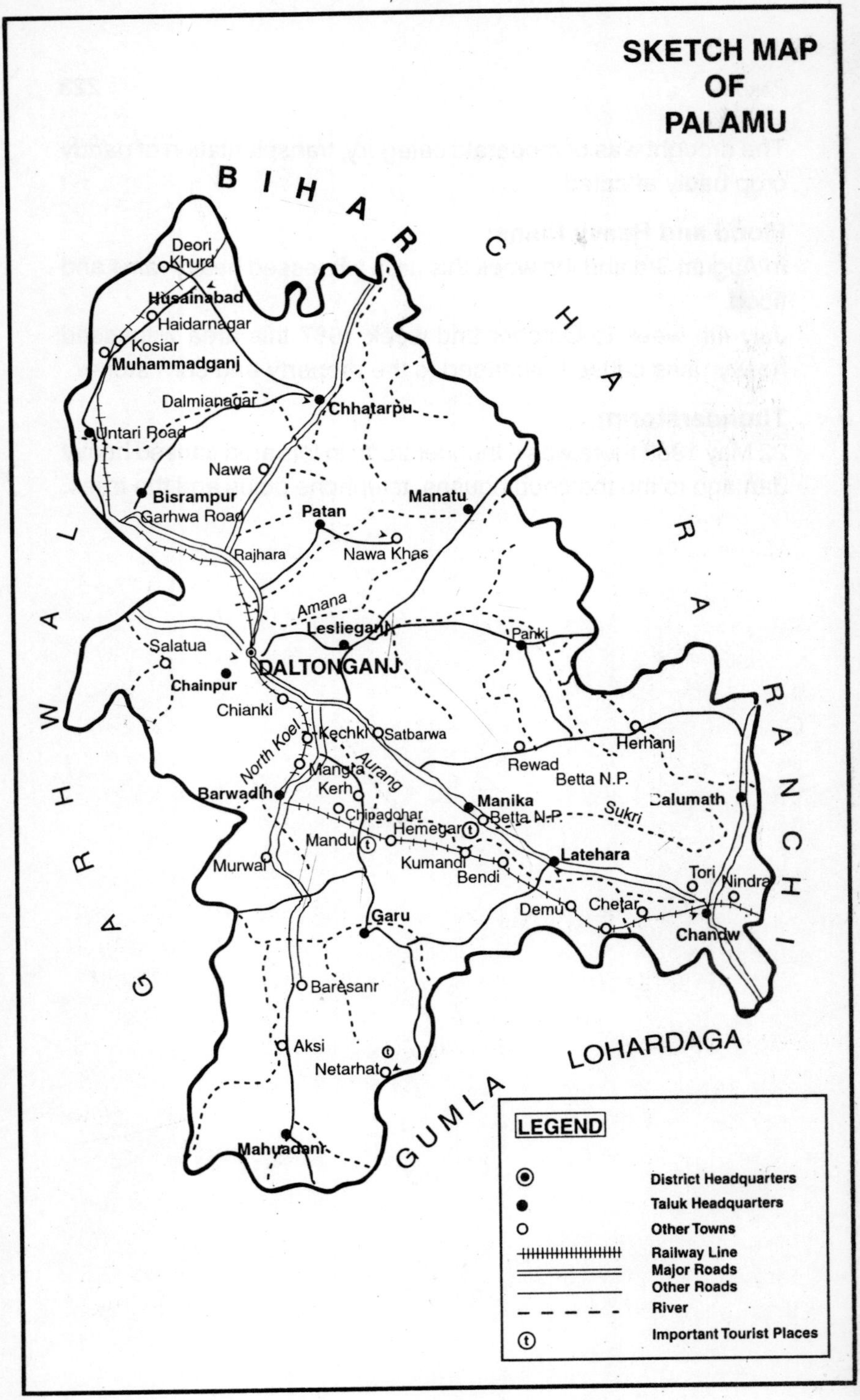

PALAMAU

LOCATION AND AREA

Altitude : 221 m

Latitude : 23.4° North to 24.6° North

Longitude : 84° East to 84.9° East

The district is bounded on the north by Rohtas and Aurangabad districts of Bihar state, on the east by Gaya (Bihar), Chatra and part of Ranchi districts, on the south by Lohardaga and Gumla districts and on the west by Surguja district of Chhattishgarh state and Garhwa district. The district of Palamau lies in the south-western part of the State. It is comprised within the Palamau division. Total area of the district is 7976 sq kms The district headquarters is located at Daltonganj.

HISTORY

The district was constituted on the 1st January, 1928. Just after the movement of 1857, Palamau had been formed Into a separate subdivision with the headquarters at Daltonganj. In 1871 *Parganas* Japla and Belaunja were transferred from Gaya to Palamau. Tori *Pargana* was also added to it in 1891. Daltonganj town Is the headquarters and the principal town of the district situated on the Koel river. The town has taken Its name after Colonel Dalton, Commissioner of Chotanagpur in 1861.

The early history of Palamau is shrouded in legends and traditions. Since the district consisted mostly of forest tracts, the territory seldom engaged the attention of invading armies, and the area remained outside the pale of influence of empires which were established in other parts of modern Bihar. The area was probably inhabited by autochthonous tribes in the past. The Kharwars, Oraons and Cheros, three aboriginal races practically ruled over this tract. Inscriptions and other relics which have been found Indicate a fairly developed civilization 'inspite of the jungles and comparative inaccessibility of the area. The Oraons had their headquarters at Rohtas Garh in the then Shahabad district (which included the present district of Bhojpur and Rohtas) and there is every indication that for some time a portion of Palamau was ruled from the headquarters of Rohtas Garh. The Cheros reigned in Palamau for nearly 200 years and the most famous of Chero rulers was Medni Rai who according to tradition made himself Lord Paramount of the southern portion of Gaya and of large portions of Hazaribagh and Surguja (in Madhya Pradesh). His son, Pratap Rai built a fort at Palamau separate from the fort that had been built by his father.

Prior to the domination of Palamau by the Cheros, Rakshel Rajputs held sway over the district. They in turn had supplanted early Marhatta settlers of whom, however, no trace is to be found now. They have probably been assimilated in the indigenous population.

A factual history of Palamau, therefore, commences with the 16th century. In 1538 Sher Shah had sent one of his officers to control the turbulent chiefs and free the Grand Trunk Road from their exploits against travellers. The influence of the Mughals extended to Palamau during the reign of Emperor Akbar when it was invaded by Raja Man Singh in 1574. The troops left by him were, however, driven out in 1605 when Akbar died.

In 1629, Emperor Shahjehan appointed Ahmad Khan as the Subedar of Patna, and Palamau was given to him as his Jagir .Ahmad Khan imposed an arrival tribute of Rs. 1,36,000. The non-payment of this tribute by the Chero rulers of Palamau led to three successive invasions by the Muhammadans. The first invasion took place in the reign of Pratap Rai. The

Muhammadan army was headed by Shaista Khan, the governor of Bihar. The army reached the fort of Palamau, defeated Pratap Rai and extracted a tribute of Rs 80,000 after which Shaista Khan left in 1642.

The second invasion was caused by internal bickerings. As a result of this Pratap Rai, after negotiations, agreed to pay an annual tribute of one lakh of rupees. On the recommendation of Itaikad Khan, successor of Shaista Khan, Emperor Shahjehan gave Palamau to him as a military fief on a jama of 2.5 lakhs of rupees.

Inspite of the success of these invasions, the payment of tribute by the Chero chiefs was never regular. As a last resort, Daud Khan, governor of Bihar, left Patna with a strong force in 1660 and inspite of heavy drawbacks and difficult terrain, reached within three kilometres of Palamau. There was an engagement and fighting which lasted three days, after which the fort was captured. Palamau was then placed in charge of Muhammadan Faujdar. But this system was done away with soon and Palamau was placed under the direct control of the Viceroy of Bihar in 1660. In 1720 Palamau was again invaded by Subedar Sarballand Khan. But actual fighting was warded off by the payment of one lakh of rupees in cash and in the shape of diamonds.

As in some other districts, here also the British intervened at others' invitations. The circumstances leading to the establishment of Bihar rule in Palamau sowed the seed of disaffection and enmity between the dispossessed Cheros and their new masters. The first intervention of the British in the affairs of the Chero Raj of Palamau occurred in 1772 owing to the protracted internecine quarrels between two rival Chero factions (1722-70). Two candidates claiming to be the rightful Raja, one Gopal Rai, grandson of Jaikishun Rai, the other Chitrajit Rai, grandson of the murdered ruling chief, Ranjit Rai, brought their suits to the British. The British, more interested in revenue collection than in family quarrels, decided to occupy the fort of Palamau. As Chitrajit's Dewan, Jatnath Singh, refused to agree to this even in return for recognition of Chitrajit's claim, the controlling council at Patna decided to support the cause of Gopal Rai. The fort was occupied by the British in February, 1771 and Gopal Rai was installed as the ruler on his agreeing to pay an annual tribute of Rs 12,000. Gopal Rai was, however, removed after trial in 1776. There followed a scramble for power. Bishwanath Rai, his minor brother, succeeded him while Gajraj Rai became the manager. But their position was assailed by Sugandh Rai and Sheo Prasad Singh. However, Gajraj Rai could continue due to the support of the collector of Ramgarh. Meanwhile in 1780 Daljit Rai, brother of Chatrapti Rai, attempted to revive the fortune of the house of Medni Rai. The Governor ordered that Bishwanath Rai, the third brother of Gopal Rai and not Gajaraj or Sugandh, was the successor to the gaddi. Since this order was resisted Major Crawford was sent to Palamau with military force to restore peace. Major Crawford managed to capture Gajaraj and Sugandh. Raja Bishwanath Rai died in 1783. He was followed by Churaman Rai who came of age in 1793.

Churaman Rai succeded in resuming the estate of his weaker tenants. His action provoked the tenantry, and led to the Chero insurrection in 1800. The leader was Bhukhan Singh, a Chero. The British came with a force and suppressed the insurrection but by that time the Raja and the administration had been reduced to bankruptcy. An Assistant Collector of Bihar was appointed to look after the revenue collection in the western part of the province. Parry, the Assistant Collector who took over in 1811 made the first settlement of revenue in 1812.

He annulled the Sanad granted by Churaman Rai and took over direct collection. The Palamau estate was attacked. In 1812, the sale of Palamau estate was authorised and it was accordingly sold for Rs. 51,000 against arrears amounting to Rs. 65,000. The assessment of the estate was reduced to Rs. 9,000 in 1814 when it was granted to Ghanshyam Singh of Deo as a reward for his help to the British in suppressing Cheros and the Kharwars.

In 1813 there was an uprising organised by great Jagirdars. This led to the attachment of the estates of Chainpur, Ranka, Lokaya, Bisrampur and Obra. The Kok rebellion of 1832 had its impact in Palamau also. The Cheros and the Kharwars rose against the administration, and non-tribal Hindus and Muslims. The insurgents were, however, defeated in an engagement with the British forces near Latehar.

During the 1857 Movement, Palamau was the most severely-affected district of the Chotanagpur plateau.

The brothers Nilambar and Pitambar were chiefs of the Bhogta clan of the Kharwar tribe, who held ancestral jagirs. Immediately after they heard movement against the British rule, they made up their minds to declare independence. They were joined by many Chero jagirdars. On 21st October, 1857 a force of 500 persons was organised which was led by Nilambar and Pitambar. They attacked Raghubar Dayal at Chainpur since he had sided with the British. From there they proceeded to Leslieganj and caused heavy destruction. Lt. Graham, with only 50 persons at his disposal, could not do much to thwart the insurgents. The entire country-side appeared to be up in arms. Lt. Graham was besieged in the house of Raghubar Dayal. In December two companies arrived under Major Cotter. He was able to capture Devi Bakshi Rai, one of the principal leaders of the movement. In January Col. Dalton, the Commissioner of Ranchi himself came to Palamau and captured the Palamau Fort. Ultimately the insurgents were captured and peace was restored soon afterwards. It is noteworthy that the movement in Palamau was no mere sepoy mutiny but an uprising of the indigenous population of the district.

Palamau played an important part in the freedom movement of the country. The Bihar Students' Conference was held at Daltonganj in 1920 under the presidentship of Rev. C.F. Andrews.

The participants included Mazharul Haque. Mahatma Gandhi and Dr Rajendra Prasad visited Daltonaganj in 1927. The August disturbances in 1942 had their echoes in Palamau. The people of Palamau took active part in all the subsequent movements which led to the country's independence.

The jurisdiction of the district has remained intact in the last few decades and it has remained unaffected as a result of the reorganisation of districts which took place after the 1971 Census. The district was divided into two parts vlz. Palamau and Garhwa after the conduct of 1991 census. According to the said bifurcation, the Garhwa sub-division was upgraded and attained the status of a separate district.

POPULATION (GENERAL, SC/ST)

Total population of the district according to 2001 census is 2,092,004 persons. Rural population of the district is 1,967,070 persons and urban population is 124,934 persons.

The Community Development Block-wise, population distribution with sex ratio and literacy rate of this district is given below:

	Sex ratio		Literacy rate		Population	
C.D. Block	Rural	Urban	Rural	Urban	Rural	Urban
PALAMU DISTRICT	**941**	**906**	**43.36**	**79.62**	**1967070**	**124934**
Hussainabad	931	906	50.59	65.74	203278	27,362
Hariharganj	927	-	48.87	-	87,499	-
Chhatarpur	933	-	35.45	-	166,843	-
Pandu	934	-	45.86	-	74,464	-
Bishrampur	924	-	45.95	-	133,862	-
Patan	926	-	45.28	-	146,139	-
Manatu	933	-	37.09	-	97,622	-
Panki	937	-	39.82	-	123,820	-
Manika	970	-	33.45	-	64,633	-
Satbarwa	961	-	42.63	-	52,541	-
Lesliegahj	965	-	50.90	-	79,345	-
Daltonganj	915	880	62.25	86.66	92,078	71,307
Chainpur	925	-	39.48	-	177,013	-
Barwadih	939	864	36.79	78.12	70,839	7198
Mahuadanr	963	-	57.30	-	66,159	-
Garu	956	-	36.52	-	25,447	-
Latehar	979	881	38.24	72.27	87,999	19,067
Balumath	975	-	34.51	-	136,010	-
Chandwa	961	-	41.06	-	81,419	-

The Scheduled Castes and Scheduled Tribes population of the district as per 1991 census is 221303 persons and 150667 persons respectively. The rural-urban breakup of this population is indicated below:

Rural	(i)	Scheduled Castes	:	217808
	(ii)	Scheduled Tribes	:	149811
Urban	(i)	Scheduled Castes	:	3495
	(ii)	Scheduled Tribes	:	856

The decennial growth rate of population of the district as a whole in relation to the state between the period 1991 and 2001 is presented below:

State/ District	*Decennial growth rate of population (per cent) 1991-2001*		
	Total	*Rural*	*Urban*
Jharkhand	23.19	21.62	28.99
Palamau	26.80	27.20	20.81

LANGUAGES AND RELIGION

Main languages spoken in the district are Hindi and Urdu.

Religionwise breakup of population of the undivided district of Palamau is indicated below as per 1991 census :

Hindus: 2118329, Muslims: 281578, Christians: 43046, Sikhs: 898, Buddhists: 37, Jains: 249, Other religions and persuasions: 7050, Religion not stated: 4.

GEOGRAPHY AND PHYSICAL FEATURES

Annual Rainfall	:	1023.5 mm
Temperature	:	Max. 44.90°C and Min. 2.90°C

The average elevation of Palamau is about 1200 feet above the mean sea level, the highest point being Netarhat. The district comprises two natural divisions. The first constitutes the erstwhile *Parganas* of Palamau and Tori which has the characteristics of

Chotanagpur Plateau proper. The second natural division comprises the erstwhile *Pargana* of Japla which was transferred from Gaya district of Palamau in 1871. This division is almost devoid of hills lying along the bank of the Sone and north-east corner of the district and similar in characteristics to the adjoining parts of Gaya.

The hills in the district are widely scattered. Many of the ranges consist of crystalline and metamorphic rocks and rise up to 3000 feet. Another class consists of hills formed of sandstones or conglomerates and constitutes the long ranges east of the Koel some 200 to 300 feet high but some rising higher such as the Latehar peak which is 910 feet high from the surrounding area and 2051 feet above mean sea level. The third category of hills comprise the *pats* or plateaus on the south which are formed of crystalline rock with their summits capped with sandstone trap or laterite. Some of the important hills are Kotam south of Garu police station and Kumandih between Garu and Latehar.

RIVERS, CANALS AND WATERWAYS

The general line of drainage is from south to north towards the Sone, which forms north-western boundary of the district. The principal rivers are Koel and its tributaries, the Auranga and the Amanat. There are also a host of smaller streams, most of which are mere mountain torrents with rock strewn beds. The Koel, Auranga and Amanat have their upper ridges characterised by high banks. The bed of the Koel is rocky for a small length from the north of its confluence with Auranga after which it is sandy. It is generally dry in the summer when boat traffic is not possible up to Daltonganj. The Auranga rises near Sohinda and flows in the north-westerly direction for about 80 kms till it joins the Koel. The Amanat rises in Hazaribagh and flows in the westerly direction to join the Koel.

The Sone enters the district on its north-west corner and then flows towards north. The Sadabah, which literally means ever flowing flows some 27 kilometres north of Daltonganj and is noted chiefly because of an irrigation scheme completed there.

TOWNS, VILLAGES AND AMENITIES

The district is at present comprised of 2 sub-divisions, 19 community development blocks. It has 5 towns.

The urban population of the district as percentage of total population in the census years 2001 is indicated below. It also shows the sex ratio (females per 1000 males) and density (population per sq km) in the urban population of the district in relation to the state:

State/ District	*Urban population as percentage of total population*	*Sex ratio, 2001 (Females per 1000 males)*			*Density (Population per sq km)*
	2001	*Total*	*Rural*	*Urban*	
Jharkhand	22.25	966	973	931	338
Palamau	5.97	974	976	953	240

Amenities

Number (with percentage) of villages having one or more amenities in the undivided district of Palamau district as per 1991 census is given as follows:

Sl. No.	*Amenities*	*Number of Inhabited Villages*	*Percentage*
1.	Education	2145	65.46
2.	Medical	498	15.20
3.	Drinking Water	3277	100.00
4.	Post and Telegraph	341	10.41
5.	Market/Hat	285	8.70
6.	Communications	824	25.14
7.	Approach by Pucca Road	720	21.97
8.	Power Supply	886	26.91

COMMUNICATIONS

Roads. Although no National Highway runs through the district it has a good number of state roads. Among the main roads are the following :

(i) Daltonganj—Ranchi road which runs from Daltonganj through Latehar and Chandwa for 155 kms.

(ii) Daltonganj—Aurangabad road runs through Chhatarpur and Hariharganj for 70 kms within the district from where Aurangabad on the Grand Trunk Road is only 26 kms away.

(iii) Chandwa—Balumath-Chatra road runs through Balumath for 37 kilometres in the district and joins Dobhi on the G.T. Road.

Besides, there are a number of district board roads, the most important of which is Daltonganj-Garhwa Road. Various roads maintained by the Forest Department help in easy transport of forest produce.

Railways. A branch of the Eastern Railway runs from Dehri-on-Sone to Gomoh. It runs through the district from Japla to Mahua Milan via Garhwa Road, Daltonganj, Latehar .

Rivers. There is hardly any traffic by boat.

Airways. There is a small landing ground at Chianki, 5 kilometres from Daltonganj .

AGRICULTURE AND IRRIGATION

Rice is the main crop of the district accounting for a little less than one-third of the gross area sown. Maize and wheat form other important crops. Among the non-food crops grown, the major portion is covered by oil, seeds. Sugar-cane is the cash crop of the district. It is mostly grown in the valley in the north and in the central part of Pa!amau.

The uncertainty of a well distributed monsoon underscores the importance of artificial methods of irrigation for successful crop raising. There are a large number of rivers and streams in the district, but in most of them the supply of water diminishes rapidly or fails entirely soon after the end of the rains.

The system of artficial irrigation prevalent in the district consists of three main types, viz. major irrigation schemes, medium irrigation schemes and minor irrigation schemes. The major irrigation schemes provide a perennial supply of water both during the kharif and rabi seasons while medium irrigation schemes are intended to supply assured irrigation to paddy crop during the intervening drought periods in the kharif season. The minor irrigation schemes include minor bandh, ahar, pyne, wells. etc. These are low cost schemes and their maintenance cost is also low. The are more suited to the local requirement as these can provide water in areas where major schemes cannot work.

The district is not noted for fish. The rivers are mostly hilly and their currents are very sharp and so there is very little possibility for breeding. In the summer season almost all the rivers except Sone become dry. During rainy season certain varieties of fish are found in the river Koel. During other seasons fish becomes rare in Palamau. In order to develop fisheries, nurseries have been started at a few important centres in the district. Carp breeding scheme is also in operation in Daltonganj. The feasibility of using reservoirs for fish-breeding is being examined. There is a fish sanctuary in the Sone near Japla. The fishes are mostly found in tanks. However, the district has a few very big tanks where fish could be bred.

ANIMAL HUSBANDRY

The livestock population of the district includes cattle (cows, bulls and bullocks), buffaloes, sheep, goats and pigs.

The district has a veterinary hospital and a number of dispensaries. They are manned by veterinary surgeons. Various schemes for cattle improvement are functioning in the district. Bullocks play a great part in agriculture. Bullocks of Shahabadi breed are gradually replacing the local breeds of poor and small-sized bullocks.

There is a good scope for the development of poultry in the district. It is an important subsidiary occupation of the local tribal population. However, there is no system of proper housing and feeding. Both in the urban as well as rural areas, poultry is kept in free range. With the rapid industrialisation of the neighbouring districts the scope of export of poultry from this district has increased considerably.

INDUSTRIES

A century ago, Palamau was noted for cotton weaving. There was a big cultivation of cotton, which led to a flourishing cloth weaving industry.

The district contains deposits of various minerals. The important minerals which are available for commercial exploitation are coal, limestone, fireclay, bauxite and laterite. Coal has the most important place among mining and heavy industries. Another important large scale industry is the Sone Valley Portland Cement Co. Ltd. Works at Japla. It is one of the units of the Sahu Jain group of industries.

There are a number of small units spread over the district for crushing stone and preparation of stone chips. The cultivation of lac is widely spread in the district and lac industry is a valued subsidiary occupation of the cultivators. *Biri* making industry is also widespread throughout the district.

The major forest produce consists of timber, bamboo, firewood and charcoal. The district has vast natural resources but they are still to be fully exploited. There is a great potentiality for the bamboo pulp industry in the neighbourhood of Chipadohar. There is also great potentiality for the development of plywood factory in Palamau. It has also tremendous resources for fire bricks factory and the catechu industry.

MINERALS AND ORES OCCURRENCES

Beryl

Large crystel of beryl occur at Dhangaon (24.1, 84.2) and near Banai (24.1, 84.3) in mica-pegmatiteo.

Building Materials

Epidiorites at Sagardinva (24.0, 83.9) and basic intrusions Lesleiganj (24.1, 84.2), Ara (24.1, 84.6) and Harkuwa (24.1, 84.5) are suitable for use as road metal. The massive epidiorite forming the eastern flank of the narrow ridge between Netarhat (23.5, 84.5) and the larger plateau to the south, and the trap rock exposed below the scrap between Gamharpat (23.4, 84.2) and Tewarpanitoli (23.4, 84.3) may be used as road metal.

The granite and granite gnesis and the dolerites lying in the Muhammadganj (24.4, 83.9) area may be used as road metal.

Laterite occurrences near the road between Gamharia and Senha (23.4, 84.7) constitute a potential source of Road metal.

Clay

Deposits of clay are found near Tupu Kalan and Mungar in the neighbour-hood of Latehar (23.7, 84.5). The clay is plastic and does not fuse when fired up to 1300°C. The Tupu Kalan clay is white firing and that of Munjar is reddish-brown.

The beds of clay up to 5 ft. thick associated with Barakar rocks are also recorded at Semariatanr (23.7, 84.4), Parsahi (23.7, 84.4), Bendi (23.7, 84.4), Tubed (23.8, 84.6)

Coal

At Aurunga (23.8, 84.3). The total area is 145 sq. km., but workable coal is confined to the rocks of the Barakar group, which cover an area of about 90 sq. km. several coal seams occur, some of them up to 40 ft. in thickness. The coal is rich in ash and moisture.

At Daltonganj (24.1, 84.1), Coal of poor quality was discovered on the Amanat River near Singra (24.1, 84.1). The total area is about 300 sq. km. of which only 50 sq. km. are occupied by the Barakar. Several thin seams occur, and with the exception of a 29 ft. seam at Rajhara (24.2, 84.1) and Pandua (24.2, 84.1) the seams rarely exceed more than 5 ft. in thickness. The coal is non-caking in character.

At Hutar (23.8, 84.1). The total area is about 110 sq. km. of which 90 sq. km. are occupied by the Barakar group. Five seams are known, thin over much of the area, but in places they thicken. One seam of 13 ft. 8 inches thickness is known. A four foot thick coal seam occurs at Binda (23.8, 83.8).

Copper

Some traces of copper ore was found when sinking a well at Daltonganj (24.1, 84.1). Disseminated in beds of schistore gnesiss.

Lead and Silver

Ball records the finding of weathered fragments of galena on the surface near Barikhap (23.9, 84.8)

Limestone

Isolated patches of limestone occur over a belt extending east and west parallel to the coal fields between Ramgarh and Palamau. At Olhepat (23.8, 84.7) on the eastern edge of the Ausanga coal field.

Mica

Considerable amount of muscovite occurs in pegmatites near Daltonganj (24.1, 84.1) Lesliganj (24.1, 84.2) etc. The mica flakes range in size from 1-1/2 inches to 2 inches by 1 inch in size. However the flakes are not suitable for commercial purposes.

Mineral Water

At Jarom (23.8, 84.55) Ball record a spring here in the bed of the Tataka River. Temperature of water is 55.5°C, discharge not copious but steady. Water emits H_2s sand CO_2.

Ball records another spring at Kokraha Or Thata (23.8, 84.1). Temperature of water is 66°C, discharge copious. Water is strongly impregnated with H_2s.

Fire clay

The fire clay in the vicinity of Mahuamilan (23.7, 84.81) Lohsinghnatoli (23.7, 84.8) Ambatanertoli (23.71, 84.8) Amiatanartoli (23.73, 84.81) and Chitarpur (23.76, 84.78).

Fire-clay also occurs as seams in the Barakar stage in the Pandwa (24.16, 84.6) Rajhora (24.16, 84.01) Hutar colliery (23.81, 84.1) Anwankar (23.78, 84.1).

Garnet

Occurrence of crystals of garnet at Pandwa and Kachwatanr (24.05, 84.11).

Gemstone (Diamond)

Diamond of considerable value are reported to have come from the workings near south river (23.26, 84.28).

Graphite

At Khamdih (23.96, 84.21), Haluman (23.93, 84.21), Bari Khas (23.85, 84.21), Sorka (23.96, 84.5), Ajlatua (23.96, 84.06), Sirka (23.96, 83.76), Tulbula (24.25, 84.03), Arapur (24.1, 84.55), Kusri (24.5, 84.33), Murma (23.9, 84.28), Kathautia (23.9, 84.28), Kui (22.85, 84.3).

At Kita (23.76, 84.56), Arapur (24.23, 84.03) and Hatai Khas (24.23, 84.01) near Daltonganj.

Iron

At Rajbar (23.78, 84.68) Balungar (23.83, 84.71), Morwai (23.76, 84.15), Nawadih (23.83, 84.08), Gore (23.63, 83.96)

TRADE, COMMERCE AND EXPORT

The table given below presents the most important commodities manufactured. exported from and imported into different towns of Palamau district :

Name of the town	*Most important commodities*		
	Manufactured	*Exported*	*Imported*
Daltonganj	Bambooware	Timber	Rice
Deori kalan	Cement	Cement	Rice
Hussainabad	Blanket	Groundnut	Rice
Latehar	—	Wood	Rice
Netarhat	—	—	Rice

TOURISM

Amjharia. The village is situated about 11 kms off Chandwa, on the road from Bar-sidar to Ranchi. It is a place of great scenic beauty which attracts tourists. It has a Forest Rest House situated on the summit of a hill, commanding a picturesque view of the area.

Dundu. The village lies about 25 kms from the block headquarters at Manatu. It is noted for its *mahua* tree under which the villagers dance on the occasion of *Karma* festival and *Jitia* (Jiwitputrikavrat). The tree is believed to have special powers.

Garu. The village is the headquarters of the development block bearing the same name and is situated on the southern bank of the river Koel. The area is renowned for wild game hunting. Elephants are found in large number in the forests.

Gulgulpat. The place is situated at an altitude of 3900 feet above mean sea level and lately it was named as Jawaharpat in the memory of Shri Jawahar Lal Nehru. It contains dense forests. There are many peacocks in the area. The scenery in this area is very picturesque particularly between July and September.

Kantifalls. The village is situated on the Chandwa-Kuri road about 6 kms from village Senha. It is a lovely spot for picnic as it lies amidst forests.

Kechki. It is a village close to Auranga bridge and is an important centre for export of forest produce, particularly bamboos. It is an attractive place for picnic and well worth a visit by the tourists.

Kulku. It is situated at the confluence of the rivers Koel and Haraya and is noted as a place of scenic beauty. It has a forest bungalow which commands a fine view up and down the river.

Loda falls. It is situated in the interior of the district about 14 kms from Mahuadam and is also known as 'Burha Ghagh'. The water falls from a height of 450 feet. It is said to be the highest fall in the state. It lies on the Burha river which forms the border between Jharkhand and Madhya Pradesh for some distance.

Palamau fort. The fort is situated on a hill in a dense forest by the side of river Auranga about 5 kms, from the National Park, Betla and 19 kms from Barwadih. The fort is ascribed to the Chero, Raja, Medni Rai. An annual *Adivasi* fair is held here in the month of November.

Tatha. It is located at a distance of about 51 kms from Daltonganj. It is noted for a hot spring, which draws a large number of visitors in the winter.

Daltonganj. It is a municipal town and the headquarters of the district. The town was founded in 1862 by Colonel Dalton, the then Commissioner of Chotanagpur, after whom it has been named.

Netarhat. It is a hill station in Mahuadanr community development block and is at an altitude of about 3,800 feet above the mean sea level. Apart from its natural beauty, it is noted for its beautiful sunrise and sunset. Netarhat township has an agriculture farm and the Netarhat Residential Public School established in 1954 which has enhanced its importance. It attracts a large number of tourists every year for whom the tourist department of state government has provided a beautiful tourist bungalow.

FAIRS AND FESTIVALS

Imporant fairs and melas organised in various parts of the district are mentioned below:

Shivratri mela, Makar Sankaranti mela, Kartik Purnima mela, Paush Purnima mela, Maghi Purnima mela, Ram Navami mela, Paush Amawashya mela.

EDUCATION

According to 2001 census, total literates (excluding the population in the age group of 0-6 years) is 766,490 persons. Of these, 520,077 are males and 246,413 are females. In the rural areas of the district 681,228 persons (470,534 males and 210,694 females) are literates and in urban areas 85,262 persons (49,543 males and 35,719 females) are literates. The rate of literacy of this population to the total population, excluding 0-6 years age group according to 2001 census is shown below:

	Persons	*Males*	*Females*
Total	45.67	59.76	30.50
Rural	43.36	57.86	27.80
Urban	79.62	86.84	71.39

Primary and middle school facilities are generally available in all towns. The following table gives details of different categories of educational institutions per ten thousand population in different towns of the district:

Name of the town	*Number per ten thousand population*			
	Higher Secondary/ Inter/PUC/ Junior College	*Secondary/ Matriculation*	*Junior Secondary/ Middle*	*Primary*
Daltonganj	0.19	1.35	2.69	5.58
Deori Kalan	—	2.10	2.10	2.10
Hussainabad	—	0.69	2.08	1.38
Latehar	—	1.60	8.78	2.39
Netarhat	—	6.88	—	3.44

COLLEGES

G L A College, Daltonganj, (Constituent College).

J S N Mahila College, Daltonganj (Established 1969) (Constituent College).

Janata Sheoratri College, Daltonganj (Established 1970) (Constituent College).

SSJS Namodhari College Garhwa (Established Constituent College).

A.K. Singh College, Japla, (Established 1984). (Affiliated College)

B N Singh College, Daltonganj (Established 1984). (Affiliated College)

S G J Singh Namdhari College, Garhwa (1980). (Affiliated College)

St. Tulsidas College, Rahela (Established 1985). (Affiliated College)

(Above named colleges belong to Ranchi university, Ranchi. Established, 1960).

MEDICAL

The table below furnishes information regarding availability of beds in the medical institutions in different towns of the district :

Name of the towns	*Number of beds in medical institutions per 1000 population*
Daltonganj	2.31
Deori Kalan	1.26
Hussainabad	0.48
Latehar	1.99
Netarhat	2.06

ADMINISTRATION

(i) Administrative Divisions

Sub-divisions : Daltonganj, Hussainabad, Latehar, Chatarpura.

Community Development Blocks: Bishrampur, Hussainabad, Hariharganj, Chhatarpur, Patan, Manatu, Panki, Leslie ganj, Daltonganj, Barwadih, Manika,Balumath, Chandwa, Latehar, Garu, Mahuadanr, Pandu, Satbarwa, Chainpur.

Towns and Urban Agglomerations with their Population, Sexratio, Decadal growth and Literacy rate (2001)

Town	Population	Percentage Decadal growth 1991-2001	Sex Ratio	Literacy Rate
Barwadih (CT)	7,198	8.37	864	78.12
Daltonganj (M)	71,307	26.60	880	86.66
Deorikalan (CT)	3,929	-	913	64.83
Hussainabad (NA)	23,433	35.40	905	65.90
Latehar (NA)	19.067	26.46	881	72.27

(ii) Parliamentary Constituencies and assembly segments

No.* and *Name of Parliamentary Constituencies:

44-Chatra, 53-Lohardaga (ST), 54-Palamau (SC).

No.* and *Name of Assembly Segments:

Chatra

318. Panki—Panki, Lesliganj and Manatu police stations in Palamau Sadar sub- division.

316. Latehar (SC)—Latehar (N.A.C.), (G.Ps. Pochra, Lutl, Kaima, Kura, Bishunpur, Mungar, Nindir, Laharpur and Zalim in (Latehar police station, Chandwa and Balumath police stations in Latehar sub- division.

Lohardaga (ST)

317. Manika (ST)—Latehar police station (excluding Latehar (N.A.C.) and G.Ps. Pochra, Luti, Kaima, Kura, Bishunpur, Mungar, Nindir, Laharpur and Zalim), Barwadih, Garoo and Mahuadanr police stations in Latehar sub-division.

Palamau (SC)

319. Daltonganj—Daltonganj and Chainpur police stations in Palamau Sadar sub-division; and Bhandaria police station in Garhwa sub-division.

322. Bishrampur—Bishrampur police station in Palamau Sadar sub-division; and Majhiaon police station in Garhwa sub-division.

323. Chhatarpur (SC)—Chhatarpur and Patan police stations in Palamau Sadar sub-division.

324. Hussainabad—Hussainabad and Hariharganj police stations in Palamau Sadar sub-division.

Palamau was in Palamau cum Hazaribagh cum Ranchi Lok Sabha constituency in 1952. The communitywise breakup [OBE] in Palamau is Muslims (12 per cent), Scheduled Castes (27 percent), Scheduled Tribes (14 per cent), Ahirs (7 per cent) and Brahmins, Kahars and Rajputs around 5 per cent each. Others present in some numbers are Koeris and Tells. Bhuiyas (10 per cent), Chamars (7 per cent) and Dosadhs (5 per cent) are dominant among the Scheduled Castes. Oraons and Kharwars, around 5 per cent each, are most numerous among the Scheduled Tribes.

OBSERVATIONAL ORGANISATION

Surface Observatories

This facility is available at Daltonganj. The instrument work under, meteorological sub-division, Bihar Plateau, M.C. Patna. The instrument lies in

Latitude	:	24.1° North
Longitude	:	84.1° East
Altitude	:	221m
Date of starting	:	19-4-1888.

Agricultural Meteorological Station

It is an Ordinary Meteorological station lies in

Latitude	:	24.4° North
Longitude	:	84.1° East
Altitude	:	229 m
Date of starting	:	1-1-1976

Hydrometeorological Station for Climatological Purposes: This instrument facility is available at Chandwa and Khalari. These instrument lies in

Chandwa

Latitude : 23.7° North
Longitude : 84.7° East
Altitude : 524 m
Date of starting : 1-2-1951

Khalari

Latitude : 23.7° North
Longitude : 85.1° East
Altitude : 457 m
Date of starting : 12-5-1948

Flood Meteorological Offices

This instrument facility is available at Balumath Hariharganj, Japla, Latehar, Panki

Balumath

Latitude : 28.8° North
Longitude : 84.8° East
Altitude
Date of starting : 28-11-1978

Hariharganj

Latitude : 24.5° North
Longitude : 84.8° East
Date of starting : 18-12-1978

Japla

Latitude : 24.6 North
Longitude : 83.9° East
Altitude
Date of starting : 11-05-1975

Latehar

Latitude : 23.7° North
Longitude : 84.5° East
Date of starting : 25-11-1978

Panki

Latitude : 24.1° North
Longitude : 84.5° East
Altitude
Date of starting : 6-12-1978

DISASTROUS WEATHER EVENTS

Coldwave:

1st January 1982, moderate.
29-30 November 1982, severe.
4-10 December 1982, severe.
2-14 January 1983, severe.
December 3rd and 4th week 1984 severe.
27-31 December 1989, severe.
1-10 January 1990, severe.
January 1st and 2nd week 1992.

Heatwave:

1-7 July 1982, moderate to severe.
28 May to 2nd June 1983, moderate to severe.
6 June 1983, severe.
7 June 1983, moderate.

Drought:

August-September and October 1982 Kharif crop very badly hit as rain fall was 50 per cent of the normal in these areas.
March 2nd week 1993. Acute shortage of drinking water and fodder reported. Hundred of cattle heads perished due to fodder shortage.

Floods and Heavy Rains:

August 3rd and 4th week 1984, this area witnessed flood and heavy rains, several people died and cattle perished.
July 4th week and August 1985, this area witnessed heavy rains, several people died, and crops was damaged.
July 4th week to October 2nd week 1987 this area witnessed heavy rains, caused damaged to the property and corn store.

Lightning:

3 July 1994, there was lightning in this area, three persons died and Four other injured at village Allandia under Chandwa Latehar police station.

Hail Storm:

On 19th March 1996. It was heavy hailstorm. Several houses damaged and extensive damage to crop reported.

ARCHAEOLOGICAL SITE

Andhari Pahar Chalwa	Dt. Palamau	Middle Palaeolithic (4.3) sit, IAR 1970-1
Bhagadeh Ramana	Dt Palamau	Middle Stone Age (Middle Palaeolithic (4.3) site. IAR 1971-2.
Bhavanalpur	Dt Palamu	Middle Stone Age (Middle Palaeolithic (4.3) site. IAR 1971-2.
Chopali Pahar	Dt. Palamau	Middle Stone Age (Middle Palaeolithic (4.3) site. IAR 1970-1.
Dhajawa Pahar	Dt Palamau	Middle Stone Age (Middle Palaeolithic (4.3) site. IAR 1970-1.
Dhekulia	Dt Palamau	Scrapers, pionts, blades, knives, burins and awls were found. The industry shows a tendency towards the Late Stone Age (Mesolithic (4.5) tradition. IAR 1965-6.
Dhonka Pahar	Dt Palamau	Middle Stone Age (Middle Palaeolithic (4.3) site. IAR 1970-1.
Ghotama	Dt Palamau	Middle stone age (Middle Palaeolithic [4.3] site. IAR 1971-2.
Ghutara	Dt Palamau	Middle stone age (Middle Palaeolithic [4.3] site. IAR 1970-1.
Hami	Dt Palamau	Nineteen bar-celts and six flat celts of copper were found on the bank of a small river (4.11). Jour. Bihar & Orissa Res. Soc., 2, 1916, p.481-4.
Hardi	Dt Palamau	Middle Stone Age (Middle Palaeolithic (4.3) site. IAR 1971-2.
Isunpera	Dt Palamau	Middle Stone Age (Middel Palaeolithic (4.3) site. IAR 1971-2.
Jhari Pahar	Dt Palamau	Middle Stone Age (Middle Palaeolithic [4.3] site. IAR 1970-1.

Korwa	Dt. Palamau	Middle Stone Age (Middle Paleolithic [4.3] site. IAR 1971-2.
Kuharbena	Dt. Palamau	Middle Stone Age (Middle Palaeolithic [4.3] site. IAR 1971-2.
Lal Mijaura	Dt. Palamau	Middle Stone Age (Middle Palaeolithic [4.3] site. IAR 1971-2.
Mahudih	Dt. Palamau	Middle Stone Age (Middle Palaeolithic [4.3] site. IAR 1971-2.
Marvania	Dt Palamau	Rich microlithic site yielding a large number of geometric and non-geomet ric tools such as lunates, burins, points and blades. A few Upper Palaeolithic [4.4] blades were also picked up.
Pathardiha Raji	Dt. Palamau	Middle Stone Age (Middle Palaeolithic [4.3] site.
Pratappur	Dt. Palamu	Rich microlithic site IAR, 1959-60.
Saguna	Dt. Palamau	A flat cell of copper.
Namadiharamana	Dt. Palamau	Middle stone age site (4.3) IAR 1971-2.
Thelidagaramana	Dt. Palamau	Middle stone Age Middle Palaeolithic (4.2) site.
Urjungigarhwa	Dt. Palamau	Middle stone Age, Middle Palaeolithic (4.3) site IAR 1971-2.
Vahipara	Dt. Palamau	Middle stone Age. Middle Palaeolithic (4.3) site. IAR 1971-2.

DISTRIBUTION OF *SCHEDULED CASTE* POPULATION BY SEX DISTRICTWISE (1991)

	POPULATION		
	Total	Males	Females
PALAMU			
	6,14,560	3,17,616	2,96,944
Bantar	138	63	75
Bauri	475	278	197
Bhogta	35,305	17,937	17,368
Bhuiya	2,11,920	1,08,816	1,03,104
Chamar, Mochi	1,72,091	89,603	82,488
Chaupal	252	143	109
Dabgar	1,448	829	619
Dhobi	31,051	15,538	15,513
Dom, Dhangad	3,177	1,660	1,517
Dusadh, Dhari, Dharhi	1,06,713	55,320	51,393
Ghasi	7,422	3,977	3,445
Halalkhor	309	136	173
Hari, Mehtar, Bhangi	363	228	135
Kanjar	18	18	0
Kurariar	19	16	3
Lalbegi	20	10	10
Musahar	1,560	876	684
Nat	427	205	222
Pan, Sawasi	14	2	12
Pasi	6,998	3,379	3,619
Rajwar	28,010	14,895	13,115
Turi	6,494	3,494	3,000
Unclassified	336	193	143

DISTRIBUTION OF *SCHEDULED TRIBE* POPULATION BY SEX DISTRICTWISE (1991)

	POPULATION		
	Total	Males	Females
PALAMU			
	4,43,266	2,26,486	2,16,780
Asur	246	100	146
Baiga	1,518	652	866
Banjara	104	68	36
Bathudi	73	41	32
Bedia	50	22	28
Bhumij	189	54	135
Binjhia	62	40	22
Birjia	2,527	1,295	1,232
Chero	58,923	30,371	28,552
Chick Baraik	958	397	561
Gond	3,536	1,951	1,585
Gorait	44	41	3
Ho	299	172	127
Karmali	78	16	62
Kharia	2,398	1,326	1,072
Kharwar	1,31,035	66,886	64,149
Khond	74	63	11
Kisan	14,921	8,025	6,896
Kora	480	163	317
Korwa	17,844	9,420	8,424
Lohara, Lohra	14,426	7,767	6,659
Mahli	1,159	657	502
Mal Paharia	1,707	943	764
Munda	19,225	9,026	10,199
Oraon	1,57,271	79,972	77,299
Parhaiya	12,739	6,210	6,529
Santal	1,105	655	450
Sauria Paharia	199	113	86
Savar	68	40	28
Unclassified	8	0	8

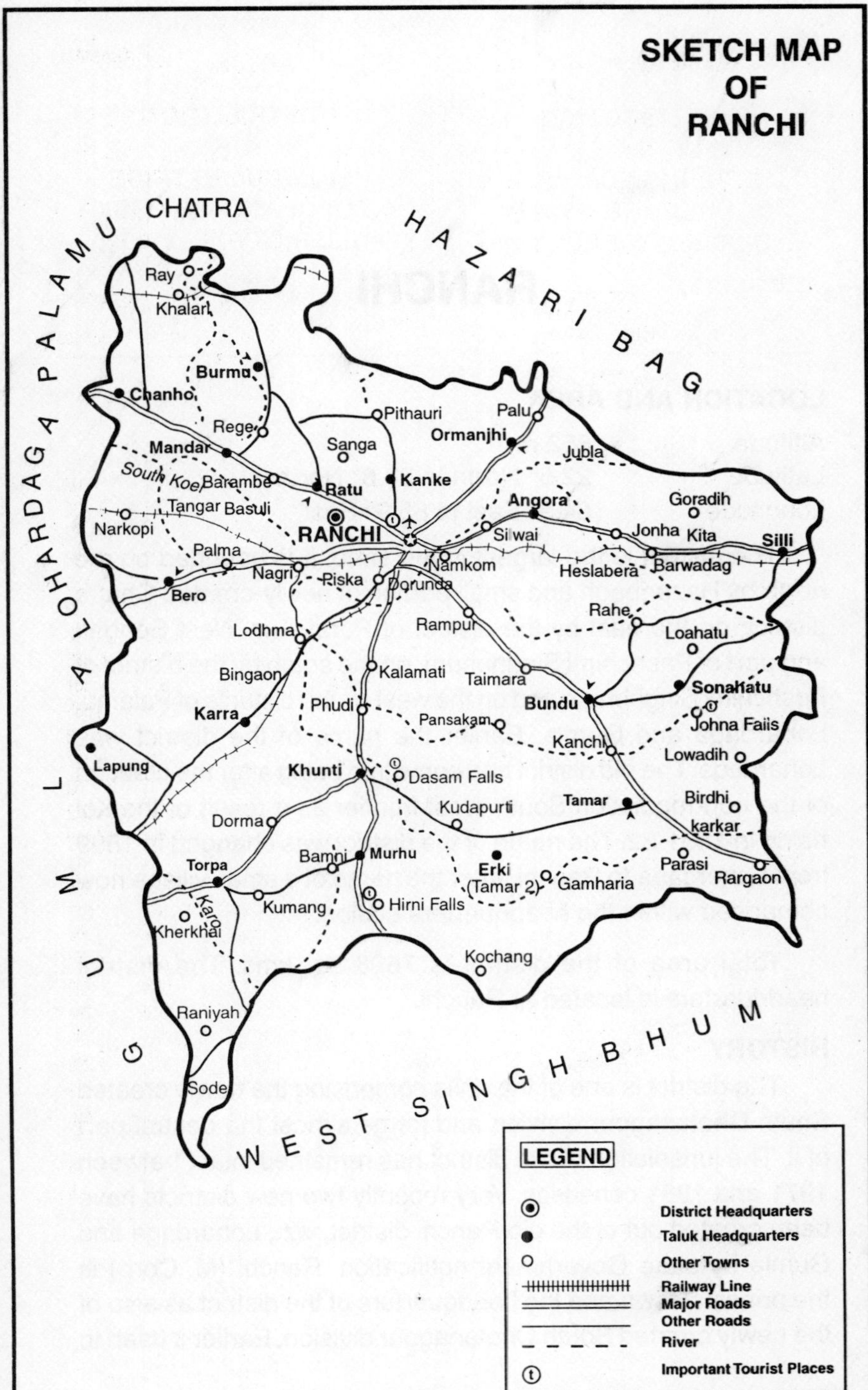
SKETCH MAP OF RANCHI
CHATRA
HAZARIBAG
PALAMU
LOHARDAGA
GUMLA
WEST SINGHBHUM
Ray
Khalari
Burmu
Chanho
Rege
Mandar
South Koel
Barambe
Ratu
Pithauri
Sanga
Kanke
Palu
Ormanjhi
Jubla
Angora
Goradih
Tangar Basuli
Narkopi
RANCHI
Silwai
Jonha
Kita
Silli
Palma
Nagri
Piska
Dorunda
Namkom
Heslabera
Barwadag
Bero
Rahe
Lodhma
Rampur
Loahatu
Bingaon
Kalamati
Taimara
Sonahatu
Phudi
Pansakam
Bundu
Johna Falls
Karra
Kanchi
Lowadih
Lapung
Khunti
Dasam Falls
Tamar
Birdhi
Kudapurti
karkar
Dorma
Torpa
Bamni
Murhu
Erki
(Tamar 2)
Gamharia
Parasi
Rargaon
Karo
Kumang
Hirni Falls
Kherkhai
Kochang
Raniyah
Sode
LEGEND
District Headquarters
Taluk Headquarters
Other Towns
Railway Line
Major Roads
Other Roads
River
Important Tourist Places

RANCHI

LOCATION AND AREA

Altitude	:	652 m
Latitude	:	22.5° North to 23.6° North
Longitude	:	84.9° East to 85.9° East

The district is the largest in the state. It is bounded on the north by Hazaribagh and small portion of newly-created Chatra district, on the east by the district of Purulia (in West Bengal) and part of Pashchimi Singhbhum, on the south by the district of Pashchimi Singhbhum and on the west by the districts of Palamu, Lohardaga and Gumla. Earlier the name of the district was Lohardaga. The old district had come into being after the creation of the non-regulation South West frontier as a result of the Kol rising in 1831-32. The name of the district was changed in 1899 from Lohardaga to Ranchi, after the name of a small village now comprised within the headquarters station.

Total area of the district is 7698 sq. kms. The district headquarters is located at Ranchi.

HISTORY

The district is one of the units comprising the newly created South Chotanagpur division and forms almost the central part of it. The jurisdiction of the district has remained intact between 1971 and 1981 censuses. Very recently two new districts have been created out of the old Ranchi district, viz., Lohardaga and Gumla by state Government notification. Ranchi (M. Corp) is the principal town and the headquarters of the district as also of the newly created South Chotanagpur division. Earlier it used to be the summer capital of the then Bihar state and the headquarters of Chotanagpur division.

In ancient times the tract which corresponds to the district of Ranchi and the neighbouring parganas was in the undisturbed possession of the Munda and Oraon tribes and was known to the Aryans as *Jharkhand* or the 'forest territory'. The entire tract was presumably beyond the pale of direct Hindu influence in ancient India. However, Jarasandh, the mighty emperor of Rajgriha in the Mahabharat period might have excercised some kind of loose supervision over the area. Similarly, Mahapadmanand Ugrasen of Magadh, who subdued the entire country up to Orissa, might have gained some control over *Jharkhand* as well. Possibly, the area was included in the Magadh Empire during the reign of Ashoka (273-232 B.C.).

With the decline of Mauryan power, king Kharavela of Kalinga led an army through *Jharkhand* and ransacked Rajgriha and Pataliputra. Later, Samudra Gupta (335-380 A.D.) must have passed through the area on his expedition to the Deccan. The Chinese traveller Itsing is believed to have journeyed through the Chotanagpur plateau in course of his travels to Nalanda and Bodh Gaya.

The Chotanagpur Raj is believed to have been set up in 5th century A.D. after the fall of the imperial Guptas. Phanimuket was elected the first king. It is said that he was found by the side of a tank under the protection of a Nag (Snake). Hence the dynasty founded by him was named the Nag Dynasty.

The entire Chotanagpur plateau was referred to as *Jharkhand* by the Muhammedan historians. Throughout the Turko-Afghan period (1526), the area remained virtually free from external influence. It is only with the accession of Akbar to the throne of Delhi in 1556 that Muslim influence penetrated *Jharkhand*, then known to the Mughals as Kokrah. In 1585, Akbar sent a force under the command of Shahabaz Khan to reduce the Raja of Chotanagpur to the position of a tributary *Kokrah* was included in the Subah of Bihar, as mentioned in the *Ain-i-Akbari.*

After the death of Akbar in 1605, the area presumably regained its independence. This necessitated an expedition in 1616 by Ibrahim Khan, Fateh-Jang. governor of Bihar and brother of Queen Noorjehan. Ibrahim Khan defeated and captured Durjan Sal, the 46th Raja of Chotanagpur. The king was imprisoned in Gwalior Jail. He was later released by the Emperor and allowed to resume his previous position as an independent chief. After that the relations between the Moghul emperors and the Khokra Jharkhand chiefs continued to be somewhat friendly and peaceful. A stipulated revenue of Rs 6000 was regularly paid.

In 1632, Chotanagpur was given as Jagir to the Governor at Patna for annual payment of Rs 1,36,000. During the reign of Muhammad Shah (1719-1748). Sar Baland Khan, the Governor of Bihar, marched against the Raja of Chotanagpur and forced his submission. Another expedition was led by Fakhruddoula, Governor of Bihar. in 1731. He came to terms with the Raja of Ramgarh who owed allegiance to the Raja of Chotanagpur. The district seems to have enjoyed almost an unbroken peace from 1624, when Durjan Sal was released till the appearance of the British in 1772.

The *Divani* of Bengal, Bihar and Orissa was granted by Emperor Shah Alam II to the East India Company in 1765. This *Diwani* included Chotanagpur as a part of Bihar. The internecine quarrels and depredations of the Raja of Gidhaur, the Raja of Ramgarh and the rival claim between Gopal Rai and Chitrajit Rai for the Kingdom of Palamu. This situation led the British to take an active interest in this area. In December 1771 Captain Camac attacked Palamu and put Chitrajit Rai as the Raja. The history of Ranchi for some time thereafter is interlinked with the history of Palamu, Hazaribagh and Singhbhum.

During the operations of Captain Camac against the Raja of Palamu, Dhupnath Shahi, Raja of Chotanagpur rendered useful service to the British. He acknowledged the authority of the Company and offered to pay an annual tribute of Rs 12,000 instead of Rs 6,000 fixed under the Muslim rule. However, arrears in payment resulted in an expedition against him in 1773, as a result of which an agreement was reached stipulating enhanced payment of Rs 15,000 per year. The Raja was allowed to retain his hold on the internal administration.

Captain Camac was succeeded in 1780 by Chapman, the first civilian administrator of Chotanagpur. The so-called 'conquered provinces' were formed into a district under the name of the Ramgarh Hill Tract in 1780 which lasted till 1833. The district of Ranchi was not directly included in this unit but was added under the designation ofTributory *Mahal* of Chotanagpur. Chapman was at the same time the Judge and the Magistrate and Collector of the district. There was an Adivasi insurrection at Tamar in 1789 which could be quelled only by the use of force. Sporadic disturbances continued for six years more.

Disputes between the Raja and his brothers led to further disturbances in 1807-08. A force was sent under Major Roughsedge. The Diwan of the Raja who was primarily responsible for the trouble, was apprehended and jailed. The Raja paid up arrears of revenue and settled his disputes with her brothers. Six police thanas were also set up in 1809, marking the beginning of end of the feudal authority of the Raja. This also marked the induction of non-tribal revenue collecting agents who later oppressed the aboriginal tenants.

The discontent among the tribal population evidenced in the earlier insurrections, found an outlet in the Kol insurrections of 1831-32. The immediate cause for it was the humiliation caused to Mundas by the Sikh and Muslim *thikadars* (intermediaries in revenue collection). The Mundas got together in Laukha village near Tamar and plundered and destroyed many villages held in farm by Sikh and Muslim *thikadars*. They were overpowered by the forces led by captain Wilkinson in 1832.

Ranchi has attracted many Christian missions which have contributed much to the growth of education in the district. The earliest Christian missionaries reached the district in 1845 and the first conversions of tribal population to Christianity took place in 1850.

The 7th and 8th native companies of the Ramgarh Battalion stationed at Hazaribagh rose in revolt on the 30th July. When news of this reached Col. Dalton (who was then the Commissioner of Ranchi), he sent Lt. Graham with two companies of the Ramgarh Light infantry, thirty horsemen and two guns to disarm the regiment at Hazaribagh. This force left Ranchi on 1st August. Meanwhile, the insurgents at Hazaribagh started marching to Ranchi by the road via Badam. Getting news of this the infantry with Lt. Graham also rose against British authority and commenced their return journey to Ranchi. Lt. Graham proceeded to Hazaribagh with the cavalry which remained loyal to him and reached there on the 2nd August. The deserters from Lt. Graham's contingent returned to the army station at Doranda and successfully exhorted the sepoys there to rise against the British authority. In view this, Col. Dalton left Ranchi for Hazaribagh.

This insurgent troops at Doranda burnt the offices and courts of the district office and some bungalows and set free the prisoners in jail. They expected the insurgents from Hazaribagh to join them but when the latter did not reach Doranda, they set out in the third week of September to join Babu Kuer Singh in Shahabad. They were attacked and defeated on the 2nd October 1857 at Chatra under a British force commanded by Major English. Meanwhile, Col. Dalton returned to Ranchi on 22nd September with a contingent of force. The courts were reopened and peace and order restored.

The infiltration of the British in the political horizon of Chotanagpur also synchronised with a great socio-economic revolution. Agrarian discontent against the imposition of *begari* (forced labour) and illegal enhancement of rent by the intermediaries resulted in Sardari agitation, so called due to the instigation and leadership provided by the Sardars. By 1887, the movement had grown and many Munda and Oraon cultivators refused to pay rent to landlords. The Sardari agitation (or Laaj as it was called), was at its height in 1895 when a socio-religious leader named Birsas Munda appeared on the scene. The importance of his role in the social history of Ranchi is borne out by the appelation of Birsa Bhagwan given to him.

The movement led by Birsa Munda was half agrarian and half religious. It had a direct connection with agrarian unrest and also appeared to have been influenced by Christian ideas. Birsa Munda was an apostate from Christianity. His teaching was partly spiritual and partly revolutionary. He proclaimed that the land belonged to the people who had reclaimed it from forests, and therefore, no rent should be paid for it. He asserted that he was the Messiah and claimed divine powers of healing.

Birsa's crusade brought about an armed uprising, of the deluded peasantry which was, quickly supressed. Birsa died in jail in 1900.

A religious movement among the Oraons was initiated by Jatra Oraon of Bishunpur police station in 1914. The Tana Bhagat movment, as it was called, also had its genesis in agrarian issues and particularly the economic dispartiy between Christian converts and the traditional or *sansari* Oraons. The non-cooperation movement launched by Jatra Oraon and his associates soon spread even to Palamu and Hazaribagh.

The district played an Important role in the national freedom movement. Under the guidance of Ganesh Chandra Ghosh, Ranchi became an important centre of work for the followers of Revolutionary Party. Ranchi was the venue of a meeting between Mahatma Gandhi and Sir Edward Albert Gait, Lieutenant Governor of Bihar and Orissa on 4th June and again on 2nd September 1917 in the context of the Champaran Indigo Planters repressive measures against the *raiyats* of that district. The

Champaran agrarian law was subsequently passed under the name of Bihar and Orissa Act I of 1918.

The non-cooperation movement in Ranchi district followed the pattern as elsewhere in India. The movement caught the imagination of the people particularly the Tana Bhagats and a large number of them attended the Gaya session of the Congress in December 1922 which was presided over by Deshbandhu Chittranjan Das. These Tana Bhagats returned home deeply impressed with the message of freedom movement. Barefooted they used to trek over long distances with Congress flag in their hands and they carried the message to the masses in the interior. They attended the meetings organised by the non-cooperation workers.

On 5th October 1926, a Khadi exhibition was opened at Ranchi in the presence of Shri Rajendra Prasad in the local Arya Samaj Hall. The Tana Bhagats also attended it. This was part of the constructive programme launched by Mahatma Gandhi after he had suspended the Non-Cooperation Movement in 1922. The Simon Commission was boycotted in 1927. On 4th April 1930, Tarun Singh (Youth League} of Ranchi organised a meeting in the local municipal park which was attended by a large number of students from different educational institutions. The leaders appealed to them to join the Civil Disobedience Movement.

The Salt Satyagraha which was launched at the behest of Mahatma Gandhi, received great response in Ranchi district. In the wake of the Quit India Revolution of 1942, the arrest of national leaders led to strikes, processions, demonstrations and also disruption of the lines of communications. The district took an active part in the subsequent events which led to the country's independence in 1947.

POPULATION (GENERAL, SC/ST)

Total population of the district according to 2001 census is 2,783,577 persons, comprising of 1,436,423 males and 1,347,154 females. Rural population of the district is 1,806,682 persons (916,230 males and 890,452 females) and urban population is 976,895 persons (520,193 males and 456,702 females).

The Community Development Block-wise, population distribution with sex ratio and literacy rate of this district is given below:

C.D. Block	Sex ratio Rural	Sex ratio Urban	Literacy rate Rural	Literacy rate Urban	Population Rural	Population Urban
RANCHI DISTRICT	**972**	**878**	**55.06**	**84.31**	**1806682**	**976895**
Burmu	936	838	51.35	73.82	100.102	43,774
Kanke	939	879	60.17	85.26	162,197	862,850
Ormanjhi	951	-	57.40	-	76,096	-
Angara	981	-	52.12	-	102,990	-
Silli	963	897	60.06	83.11	97,936	11999
Sonahatu	988	-	56.52	-	94,991	-
Namkum	949	838	59.78	83.72	103,572	10,496
Ratu	966	-	61.34	-	128,712	-
Mandar	975	-	57.61	-	98.,899	-
Chanho	962	-	55.21	-	83,806	-
Bero	977	-	57.39	-	131,515	-
Lapung	1,003	-	47.94	-	53,289	-
Karra	1,005	-	51.49	-	90,824	-
Torpa	1,014	-	60.16	-	77,142	-
Rania	1,017	-	52.91	-	33,793	-
Murhu	983	-	51.13	-	72,664	-
Khunti	1,000	906	46.74	80.40	63,512	29271
Baudu	977	901	53.35	71.29	53,517	18,505
Erki (Tamar II)	972	-	40.26	-	67,455	-
Tamar I	972	-	50.20	-	114,270	-

The Scheduled Castes and Scheduled Tribes population of the district as per 1991 census is 123239 persons and 964422 persons respectively. The rural-urban breakup of this population is indicated below:

Rural	(i)	Scheduled Castes	: 84516
	(ii)	Scheduled Tribes	: 810602
Urban	(i)	Scheduled Castes	: 38723
	(ii)	Scheduled Tribes	: 153820

The decennial growth rate of population of the district as a whole in relation to the state between the period 1991 and 2001 is presented below :

State/ District	Decennial growth rate of population (per cent) 1991-2001		
	Total	Rural	Urban
Jharkhand	23.19	21.62	28.99
Ranchi	25.72	21.79	33.70

LANGUAGES AND RELIGION

Main languages spoken in the district are Hindi, Bengali and Urdu.

Religion-wise breakup of population is indicated below as per 1991 census:

Hindus: 1189510, Muslims: 229181, Christians: 190109, Sikhs: 5169, Buddhists: 224, Jains: 1371, Other religions and persuasions: 227572, Religion not stated: 137.

GEOGRAPHY AND PHYSICAL FEATURES

Annual Rain fall : 1462.7 mm

Temperature : Max. 41.80°C and Min. 5.30°C

The district of Ranchi comprises two broad natural divisions, viz.

(i) The lower Chotanagpur plateau, and

(ii) The Ranchi Plateau proper,

The lower Chotanagpur plateau, with an average elevation of 500 to 1000 feet above the sea level, comprises a small area in the north-eastern part of the district extending over Silli Sonahatu and Tamar blocks. The rest of the district, which may broadly be termed as the Ranchi plateau, has an average elevation of 2000 feet above the sea level, though the land is undulating. The highest portion of the plateau is comprised of a ridge lying about 16 kms south-west of Ranchi city. The main rivers of the district, the Subarnarekha and the South Koel, emanate from this ridge. The highest summits are found in the range of hills in the extreme west, stretching from Birpokhar (3621 feet above sea level, on the northern border of the district. The hills are Oria (3493 feet), Bardag (3216 feet) and Hutar (3209 feet), all within Palamu district. Bulbul (3351 feet) lies on the Palamu border. In the range which stretches to south from Bulbul is the Saru Pahar (3615 feet), the highest point in the district.

Isolated hills are found in the central plateau. The most noteworthy of them is the Marang Buru (2434 feet), situated 16 kms south of Ranchi. It is the sacred hill of the Mundas. The Ranchi hill (2423 feet) is also worthy of mention.

RIVERS, CANALS AND WATERWAYS

The Subarnarekha,the South Koel and the Sankh are the principal rivers of the district.

The Subarnarekha originates near Ratu. It flows in an easterly direction in the district until it descends from the plateau at Hundru (about 38 kms east of Ranchi). Here the plateau ends abruptly and the Subarnarekha comes suddenly upon a sheer drop of about 300 feet, giving rise to a splendid fall which is a great attraction for tourists.The river flows through the district of Singhbhum for almost 112 kms. leaving it at its south eastern extremity. It then flows on through Midnapur district of West Bengal and enters the Bay of Bengal after traversing a course of 474 kms.

The South Koel rises near Mandar (from the same ridge as the Subarnarekha) and flows in a north-westerly direction for some distance. It turns towards the south near Lohardaga and flows across the central part of the district to Singhbhum. Its main tributaries are the Kara and the Paras.

The Sankh rises in the north-western part of the district near the Rajadera plateau. It flows in a southerly direction along the western part of the district.

The North Koel originates at Tendar and flows north entering Palamu near Rud.

TOWNS, VILLAGES AND AMENITIES

The district is at present comprised of one sub-division and 20 community development blocks. It has 8 towns and 2057 villages (2038 inhabited villages and 19 uninhabited villages).

The urban population of the district as percentage of total population in the census 2001 is indicated below. It also shows the sex ratio (females per 1000 males) and density (population per sq km) in the urban population of the district in relation to the state:

State/ District	*Urban population as percentage of total population*	*Sex ratio, 2001 (Females per 1000 males)*			*Density (Population per sq. km.)*
	2001	*Total*	*Rural*	*Urban*	
Jharkhand	22.25	941	963	870	338
Ranchi	35.09	938	972	878	362

Amenities

Number (with percentage) of villages having one or more amenities in undivided district of Ranchi as per 1991 census is given below:

Sl. No.	*Amenities*	*Number of inhabited villages*	*Percentage*
1.	Education	1451	71.20
2.	Medical	364	17.86
3.	Drinking Water	2038	100.00
4.	Post and Telegraph	239	11.73
5.	Market/Hat	355	17.42
6.	Communications	275	13.49
7.	Approach by Pucca Road	223	10.94
8.	Power Supply	459	22.52

COMMUNICATIONS

Roads. The district is well-served by a network of good roads and has been called the motorist's paradise.

The chief roads emanating from Ranchi city are :

	Roads	*Length (in kms)*
1.	Ranchi-Bundu-Tamar-Chandil Jamshedpur (NH 33)	115
2.	Ranchi Ramgarh Hazaribagh (NH 33)	91
3.	Ranchi-Chaibasa-Jamshedpur	202
4.	Ranchi-Netarhat	154
5.	Ranchi-Daltonganj	163
6.	Ranchi-Gumla -Simdega-Rourkela	270

Of these, the first two are National Highways. Ranchi district has a good number of metalled roads and almost all the block headquarters are connected by such roads.

Railways. The opening of the Purulia-Ranchi branch of the Bengal-Nagpur (now south-eastern) Railway brought the railway to the district. The Gomoh-Barkakana-Daltonganj section of the Eastern Railway (opened in 1927) runs for about 26 kms through Ranchi district. It has a rail head at Ranchi Road (which lies in Hazaribagh district), situated about 51 kms from Ranchi town, with the opening of the Chandrapura Main section in the South-Eastern Railway. Ranchi is directly connected by trains from the then State capital Patna.

Besides the broad gauge line referred to above, there is a narrow gauge line running from Ranchi to Lohardaga over a distance of 67 kms. Ranchi is also connected with Rourkela by rail.

Airways. There is an aerodrome at Hinoo, near Ranchi city. Ranchi is on the air-map of India and there are daily flights to Kolkata, Patna and Delhi.

AGRICULTURE AND IRRIGATION

Rice is the main crop of the district. It covers the major portion of the gross area sown. Wheat, on the other hand, covers a very small proportion of the total gross area sown. Among the non-food crops grown, oil seeds are the most important.

The cultivators of Ranchi district depend on a good rainfall for their crop of rice. In the pre-indpendence days, the irrigation received some attention at the hands of the erstwhile zamindars. The British govemment as such paid little attention to the irrigation needs of the district.

The hill streams remain almost dry except in the rainy season and do not offer as much scope for irrigation as the perennial rivers. Artificial irrigation facility in the district is not adequate. The wells, springs and nahars are the only traditional sources of irrigation.

In the post-independence days several schemes have been executed by the government, the important among them being Aradih, Resa, Kita Nandani, Bucha-Opa, Ranchi etc. The district, however, still requires more facilities. of irrigation through major, medium and minor irrigation schemes in order to ensure a regular source of water supply and assured irrigation to the paddy crops as also other crops.

ANIMAL HUSBANDRY

The cattle of Ranchi district are small and undersized which is largely due to lack of good pasturage and good fodder. In the remote parts there is still ample pasturage in the jungles, but owing to the tension of cultivation the area is rapidly decreasing. Besides cattle, the cultivators keep large number of sheep and goats, mainly for food purposes. The Mundas in the past considered it almost a crime to drink the milk of a cow which they considered proper to leave entirely to the calf.

There has been a concerted effort on behalf of the state government to improve the breed of the cattle by way of distribution of stud bulls of Mariana and Tharparkar varieties. In order to upgrade the cattle quickly and also at low cost, artificial insemination centres with sub-centres have been opened in the district. Distribution of frozen semen has also been introduced in the district.

There are a number of veterinary hospitals and dispensaries spread over the entire district. Treatment, prevention and suppression of diseases of the livestock are the main functions of the veterinary institutions.

The population of poultry has been steadily increasing in the district. Poultry farms have been opened at a number of places. Concerted efforts are being made to improve the breed of the poultry in the district. Poultry is an indigenous cottage industry of the aboriginals of the district who invariably keep poultry.

INDUSTRIES

In the post-independence period there has been extensive industrial and mining activities in the district of Ranchi, the notable among them being the establishment of Heavy Engineering Corporation (HEC) Hatia. The rapid development of Ranchi city bears ample testimony to the powerful industrial revolution coming in the wake of the exploitation of the district's vast mineral resources.

In the earlier part of 20th century, the only industries of any importance in the district were the collection and manufacture of lac which was carried on principally in Bundu in Khunti sub-division and the manufacture of tea apart from the cottage industries carried on by the village artisans.

At present, among the large industrial establishments of the district, mention may be made of the

(i) Heavy Engineering Corporation, Hatia

(ii) Associated Cement Co. Ltd,. Khelari Cement Works, Khelari

(iii) Indian Aluminium Company Ltd. Muri-Alumina Works, Muri

(iv) Government Vaccine Institute, Ranchi

(v) High Tension Insulation Factory, Namkum

(vi) Electric Equipment Factory, Tatisilvai
(vii) Indian Oxygen Ltd.
(viii) Mahalakshmi Fibre Ltd.
(ix) Nalanda Ceramics Ltd.
(x) Cement Factory, Khelari
(xi) Usha Martin Black Co.
(xii) Catholic Press, Purulia Road, Ranchi
(xiii) A.M. Arathoon Private Ltd, Murhu
(xiv) Ranchi Distillery, Ranchi
(xv) Hindpiri Lac Factory, Hindpiri, Ranchi
(xvi) Chotanagpur Engineering Works

Important Industries, 2000

Jenson and Nicholson (India) Ltd. Tupudana, Ranchi.

Manufacturer: Paints, pigments, varnishes and allied products such as weighfeeders, railway wagon weighing devices, belt weighers, solid flow proportioning and measuring devices on stream and automatic calibration devices. The company also carries on hotel business.

Mahalakshmi Fibers and Industries Ltd. P.O. Ormanjhi, Ranchi, Jharkhand.

Manufacturer: Cotton yarn.

Usha Martin Industries Ltd. Tatisilwai, Ranchi.

Manufacturer: Wire drawing and allied machines, wire rods, wire ropes, wires, billets, rolled products, hydraulic machines including presses, proof loading machines and accessories, equipment and materials for prestressed concrete system etc. M/s R.B. Agencies Ltd., M/s P. K. Estates Ltd. and M/s Umil Lease Finance Co. Ltd. are the subsidiary companies.

Usha Beltron Ltd. Tatisilwai, Ranchi.

Production of jelly filled telecommunication cable.

HANDICRAFTS

Cane and Bamboo works; Dolls and toys works; Metal-craft, papier-mache, Textiles (embroidered); Textiles (printed); and Wood work.

MINERALS AND ORES OCCURRENCES

Asbestos

Samples of poor quality asbestos were reported to have been found near Itakeel (Itki, 23.3, 85.1).

Barytes

Some veins of barytes associated with galena extended E.W. through Silwai (23.4, 85.4) and Bangaibera (23.3, 85.5) about 20 km east of Ranchi.

Berytes occurs with vermiculite at Ulatutoli (23.4, 85.5), Bahea (23.4, 85.5) Tiliajaratoli (23.4, 85.5) and Baniajaratoli (Hamlet 23.66, 85.53) minor occurrences of barytes are recorded near Supatoti (23.36, 85.9) and Karamtoli (23.3, 85.1).

Old working for barytes of poor quality are noticed in the area south of Angara (23.4, 85.5).

Building Materials

Beautifully tinted yellow-green epidosite which may be used as a decorative stone occurs in south Ranchi, N.W. of Dasauri (22.9, 85.6) and south of Ragudih (22.9, 85.6) south of Jate (22.9, 85.2) the rock is finely banded.

Calc-silicate rocks, amphibolites and hybrid granulites occurring close to the Ramgarh-Ranchi road have been quarried for road metal.

Sericite-quartz-schist occurring near Tamer (23.1, 85.65), Piskahatu (23.1, 85.6) Amlesa (23.1, 85.7) and Jegodakai (23.1, 85.7) and granite gneiss near Bagdisenengtoli (23.1, 85.6) could be used for building purposes.

Cassiterite

Occurrences of Cassiterite have been reported from the hills north of Paharsingh (23.4, 85.7) near the contact of pegmatite and calc-silicate rocks.

Chromite

Chromite occurs in Hotag hill (23.35, 85.83).

Clay

Two deposits of clay have been reported to occur near Haridih (23.45, 85.8) and Sursu (23.45, 85.7). The reserve near Haridih are estimated at about 200,000 tons of crude clay for a thickness of 15 ft. The deposit is close to the Subarnarekha River and 2 miles from Sondimra Railway station.

Lead and Silver

At Sili (23.35, 85.9), Galena is also recorded to occur near Silivai (23.4, 85.45). Galena associated with sphalerite and pyrite in small lenses and pockets of garnetiferous granulite have been reported from near Matatu (23.46, 85.5).

Limestone

Several small bands of crystalline limestone have been located near Jabla (23.5, 85.6), Urba (23.6, 85.5) Haritoli (23.55, 85.5) and Halbadih (23.4, 85.5)

Ochre

Black carbonaceous phyllite, which may be easily powdered and used as a black pegments occurs at Papirda (22.9, 85.6) and in Kudda (22.9, 85.8). Large quantity of fine purplish red clay occur on the ridges S.W. of Kubasa (22.9, 85.7) Brown earths are associated with manganese ore at Leda Buru (22.46, 85.36).

Steatite

Steatite and talc-schist ranging from talc-chlorite-schist to deposit of almost pure fine-grained massive talc occur within the main Dalma lava suite to the north of Kuddadih (22.9, 85.8) and south of Banudih (22.9, 85.8).

Vermiculite

Good quality vermiculite occurs in small veins or lenses in granite-gneisses at Benijaratoli (23.4, 85.5).

Graphite

At Mandu (23.53, 85.48) and Hindebeli (23.5, 85.56)

Kawlin

At Ulatu (23.61, 85.13), Dhawtatoli (23.61, 85.21), Bagda (23.58, 85.25), Chirhufoli (23.56, 85.21), Guwatotoli (23.65, 85.8), Ichhapini (23.48, 85.15)

Gold

At Sonapet (22.88, 85.73), Birgaon (23.5, 85.71).

Graphite

At Manatu (23.53, 85.48) and Hindebeli (23.5, 85.56).

Kaolin

At Ulatu (23.61, 85.13), Dhawtatoli (23.61, 85.21), Bagda (23.58, 85.25), Chirhutoli (23.56, 85.21), Guwatotoli (23.65, 85.8), Ichhapini (23.48, 85.15).

TRADE, COMMERCE AND EXPORT

The table given below lists the most important commodities manufactured, exported and imported in the towns of district :

Name of the town	*Most important commodities*			*Banks*
	Manufactured	*Exported*	*Imported*	
Bundu	Lac, Button, Steal Materials	Shellac, Rice Vegetable	Wheat, Coal, Edible oil	3
Khelari	Cement	Cement, Coal, Limestone	Rice, Wheat, Maize	1
Khunti	Furniture, Earthen pot, Shellac	Lac, Timber, Vegetable	Salt, K. Oil Foodgrains	3
Muri	Alumina Powder	—	Rice, Wheat, Coal	2
Kamke	Handloom Cloth	Handloom, Vegetable,	Rice, Thread, Cloth, Milk	1
Ranchi	Oxygen, Cement Hume Pipes Iron goods and Machinery	Vegetable, Cement, Hume pipes, Agricultural tools and implements	Food-grains, Iron rods and sheets paper	36

The chief centres of trade in the district are Ranchi, Palkot, Gobindpur and Bundu. Apart from the railways a considerable amount of trade still goes by road. In the wilder parts of the district, pack bullocks are also used for transporting grains from one place to another. The chief articles of export after a good harvest are oil seeds and rice. Timber stick lac is also exported to different manufacturing centres. Other items of export are hide and skins, tea. bones. etc. Sugar, salt. kerosene oil, coal and manufacturing articles are the principal items of import.

TOURISM

Barenda. The village is situated at the foot of a hillock about 14 kms east of the block headquarters at Sonahatu. It was formerly the seat of the Nagbansi Rajas.

Basangarh. It is a tola of village Hatia in Khijri block situated about 10 kms south of Ranchi city. Thakur Bishwanath Sahi of this village was hanged for taking an active part in the movement of 1857.

Chakahatu. The village is situated about 11 kms east of the block headquarters at Sonahatu and about 26 kms north-east of Bundu town. The place is noted for the large burial ground of the Mundas stretching over several hectares of land containing many thousands of sepal charal stones (Sasandiries).

Derang. It is a small village situated about 16 kms south of the block headquarters at Torpa. It is noted for the famous pigeon waterfall.

Itaki (Itaki Thakurgaon). It is situated about 26 kms west of Ranchi city. The place is noted for its tuberculosis sanatorium, one of the largest in the country.

Jagannathpur. The village falls in Khizri block and is situated about 10 kms south-west of Ranchi city. It stands on a high rocky hill commanding an extensive view of the surrounding plateau. It has the largest temple in the district resembling the temple of

Lord Jagannath at Puri in Orissa state. The Rath-Yatra festival held here every year attracts a large number of people.

Jaria (Jariagarh). The village lies in Karra block, situated about 35 kms west of Khunti. The village is famous for its Dussehra Mela. Mahabir Jhandas (flags with images of Lord Hanuman) are taken out on the occasion of Ramanavami and the festival is also celebrated with great show.

Kaimbo. The village is situated about 16 kms south of the block headquarters at Mandar. It has two large Shiva temples around which a large annual fair is held on the occasion of Shivaratri.

Ratu. The village which is headquarter of a development block bearing the same name, is situated about 13 kms west of Ranchi city. It is the seat of the erstwhile Maharaja of Chotanagpur. Large fairs are held in the village on the eve of the Durga Puja and Rath-Yatra.

Bhorra. It is a small village situated about 6 kms south of the block headquarters at Ratu and about 11 kms south-west of Ranchi city. It is famous as the place of origin of the river Koel. According to local saying the river originated from tears of extreme devotion to Koeli, a household deity.

Chalkad. The village is situated about 26 kms south of the block headquarters at Erki and about 56 kms south of Khunti. It is noted as the birth place of Birsa Munda also known as Birsa Bhagwan. A fair is held here on 3rd June every year to commemorate his birth anniversary.

Gautamdhara fall (Johna fall). It is an important waterfall, situated about 43 kms south-east of Ranchi city. A large annual fair is held on the occasion of *Makar Sankranti.*

Hundru fall. The village Hundru, which lies in Angara block, is situated about 45 kms north-east of Ranchi city. It contains the famous Hundru fall of ten called a Tourists Paradise'. A fair is held here on the occasion of *Makar Sankranti* every year.

Kairo. The village is situated about 16 kms south of the block headquarters at Karra. It has a dilapidated palace and two big tanks known to have been built by king Hiralal Nath Sahdeo. The throne constructed by him still exists in the village. There is a well in his palace compound which never dries up and is unfathomable. The village also has a 200 year old temple which is built in lime and mortar .

Ulihatu. The village is situated in Erki block about 29 kms. east of Khunti. It is noted as the native place of Birsa Munda.

Ranchi. Ranchi is one of the important cities and capital town of Jharkhand state. It has a municipal corporation. It is located in the central plateau at a height of 2128 feet above mean sea level. It is also the headquarters of Ranchi district as also of newly-created South Chotanagpur Division. It used to be the summer capital of the then Bihar state and the headquarters of the old Chotanagpur division. Some of the important landmarks in the city are: the Jain Mandir,Tagore Hill and the Ranchi Dam. The location of headquarters of the Central Coalfields Ltd. (CCL), the Heavy-Engineering Corporation and the Hindustan Steel Limited has considerably changed the face of the city and made Ranchi an important industrial centre.

As already stated, Ranchi is known for its salubrious climate and beautiful scenic spots close by. It has a moderate summer and bracing winter. It was due to the climatic factors that Ranchi had been selected to be the summer capital of the then Bihar state. It attracts visitors from different parts of the state during summer.

ZOO

Bhagwan Birsa Biological park; Birsa Mrig Vihar.

MUSEUM

Bihar Tribal Welfare Research Institute; Museum, Department of Anthropology.

HOTELS

Hotel Yuvraj Palace, (Govenrment approved) 4 star.
Access: 2 kms. from air port, 1 km from Railway station and 5 kms. from Down Town Area.
Rooms: 25- All double.

Hotel Arya, (Government Approved) 3 star.
Access: 17 kms. from Airport, 2 kms. from Railway station.
Rooms: 29.

Hotel Chinar, (Goverment Approved), 3 star. Access: 7km fram Airport, 3km from Railway Station 2.5km from Bus Stand. Rooms 43 Double 39, Suites: 4

Hotel Ranchi Ashok : (Government Approved) 3 Star. Access: 35 kms from Airport, 2 kms from Railway station, 2.5 kms from Bus stand.

Kwality Inns, (Government approved) 3 star.
Access: 3 kms from Airport, 30 kms from Railway staiton, 0.5 km from Bus stand. Rooms: 36.

Hotel Yuvraj, (Government approved) 2 star. Access: 2 kms from Airport, 1 km from Railway station, 1/2 km. from central Bus stand. Rooms: 35.

Hotel Highland Inn, (Government approved).
Access: 2 kms from Airport, near to Railway staiton and Bus stand.

FAIRS AND FESTIVALS

Important fairs and melas organised in various parts of the district are mentioned below:

Dussehra mela, Rath Yatra mela, Jyeshtha Yatra mela, Muharram mela, Ram Navami mela, Kuchu mela, Bishu mela, Mage mela, Makar Sankranti mela, Buru mela, Chhath Parab mela.

EDUCATION

According to the 2001 census, total literates (excluding the population in the age group of 0-6 years) is 1,537,826 persons.

Of these, 941,317 are males and 596,509 are females. In the rural areas of the district 820,581 persons (528,044 males and 292,537 females) are literates and in urban areas 717,245 persons (413,273 males and 303,972 females) are literates. The rate of literacy of this population to the total population, excluding 0-6 years age group according to 2001 census is shown below:

	Persons	Males	Females
Total	65.69	77.76	52.77
Rural	55.06	69.90	39.80
Urban	84.31	90.79	76.86

There are as many as 1451 villages, accounting for 71.20 per cent of the total number of inhabited villages in the district where educational facility of one type or other is in all the towns. The following table gives the details of various types of educational institutions available in different towns of the district inculding the number of stadia and public libraries :

Name of the town	*Educational institutions*	*Stadia*	*Public libraries, including reading rooms*
Bundu	Higher Secondary/ Intermediate/ PUC School (1), Secondary/Matriculation (1), Junior Secondary and, Middle Schools (4)		
Ranchi	Shorthand, Typewriting Training Institutes (10), Higher Secondary to Junior Secondary and Middle Schools (72)	1	PL : 10
Kanke	Secondary/Matriculation Schools (2) Junior Secondary and Middle Schools (2)	—	—

Khunti	Secondary/Matriculation Schools (3), Junior Secondary and Middle Schools (6)	—	PL : 1
Muri	Secondary/Matriculation Schools (1), Junior Secondary and Middle Schools (3)	—	PL : 2
Khelari	Higher Secondary School (1), Secondary/Matriculation Schools (2), Junior Secondary/Middle Schools (2)	—	—

COLLEGES, 2000

Birsa College, Khunti, (Established 1962). (Constituent College)

College of Nursing, (Established 1978). (Constituent College)

Doranda College, Doranda, Ranchi (Established 1951). (Constituent College)

J N College, Dhurwa, (Established 1972). (Constituent College)

Mandar College, Mandar, (1972 (Constituent College)

Marwi College, Ranchi, (Constituent College).

P P K College, Bundu, (Constituent College).

B. L. Singh Yadav College, (Established 1972). (Constituent College).

Ranchi College, Ranchi (Established 1926). (Constituent College)

Ranchi Womens College, (Established 1950). (Constituent College)

S S Memorial College, (Constituent College).

Central Institute of Psychiatry, Kanke (Affiliated College)

Chotanagpur Law College, (Established 1954) (Affiliated College)

Gossner College, (Established 1972). (Affiliated College)

Government Teachers Training College, Ranchi (Affiliated College)

Government Womens Teachers Training College, Ranchi (Affiliated College)

KO College, Ratu, (Established 1984) (Affiliated College)

Maulana Azad College Ranchi (Established 1971) (Affiliated College)

Millat Teachers Training College, Ranchi (Affiliated College)

Millat Womens College, Ranchi (Established 1983) (Affiliated College)

National Institute of Foundry and Forge Technology, Ranchi (Affiliated College)

Nirmala College, Ranchi (Established 1969), (Affiliated College)

Rajendra Medical College, Ranchi (Established 1960) (Affiliated College)

Ram Manohar Lohia College, Ranchi (Established 1980) (Affiliated College)

St. Joseph College, Torpa, Ranchi (Established 1980) (Affiliated College)

St. Xaviers College, Ranchi (Established 1954) (Affiliated College)

Yogoda College, Dhurwa, Ranchi (Established 1967) (Affiliated College)

(These colleges belong to Ranchi university, Ranchi. Established 1960)

College of Forestry Kanke (Established 1979). Enrolment 25, Teachers 18. (Constituent College)

Ranchi Agricultural College, Kanke, (Established 1955). Enrolment 860, Teachers 150.

Ranchi College of Veterinary Science and Animal Husbandry, Kanke, (Established 1961). Enrolment 66, Teachers 62. (Affiliated College)

(These Colleges belong to Birsa Agriculteral University. Established 1980).

Birla Institute of Technology, Mesra.

MEDICAL

The availability of medical institutions in the villages is not much satisfactory as only 17.86 per cent villages in the district have got it,

The table below furnishes information regarding availability of medical institutions in the urban areas of the district.

Name of the towns	*Medical institutions (with number of beds)*	
Bundu	Hospital (1) :	12
	Dispensary (1) :	—
	Family Planning Centre (1) :	—
Itaki	Dispensaries (2) :	—
	T.B. Centre (1) :	415
	Health Centre (1) :	
	Family Planning Centre (1) :	
Kanke	Hospitals (2) :	2220
	Dispensary (1) :	—
	Family Planning Centre (1) :	—
Khelari	Hospitals (2) :	30
	Dispensaries (1) :	—
Khunti	Hospital (1) :	14
	Family Planning Centre (1) :	—
	Others (2) :	—
Muri	Hospital (1) :	—
	Dispensary (1) :	—
Ranchi	Hospitals (6) :	2575
	Dispensaries (8) :	—
	T.B, Centres (2):	55
	Nursing Homes (15) :	319

NEWSPAPERS

Prabhat Khabar, it is a Hindi daily newspaper having circulation above 81,000.

Ranchi Express, it is a big Hindi daily newspaper and the circulation is 77078.

Aj: It is categorised a medium daliy and the circulation is above 37 thousand.

Apni Ranchi: It is a Hindi weekly, having circulation 29000.

Maqjid Dawat: A Hindi monthly.

Jharkhand Ki Pukar: A Hindi monthly.

Judiciary Today: Bilingual, Monthly.

ADMINISTRATION

(i) Administrative Divisions :

Sub-divisions : Ranchi Sadar, Khunti.

Community Development Blocks : Burmu, Mandar, Chanho, Bero, Lapung, Ratu, Namkum, Kanke, Ormanjhi, Angara, Silli, Sonahatu, Tamar I, Bundu, Erki (Tamar II), Khunti, Murhu, Karra, Torpa, Rania.

Towns and Urban Agglomerations with their Population, Sexratio, Decadal growth and Literacy rate (2001)

RANCHI UA

Ranchi (MC); Kanke (CT)

Town	Population	Percentage Decadal growth 1991-2001	Sex Ratio	Literacy Rate
Bundu (NA)	18,505	15.20	901	71.29
Churi (CT)	25,075	27.72	804	77.38
Kanke (CT)	16,396	5.86	877	84.90
Khelari (CT)	18,699	31.87	886	69.07
Khunti (NA)	29,271	21.04	906	80.40
Muri (CT)	11,999	16.02	897	83.11
Ranchi (M.Corp)	846,454	41.24	879	85.27
Tati (CT)	10,496	-	838	83.72

(ii) Parliamentary constituencies and assembly segments:

No.* and *Name of Parliamentary Constituencies:

49-Ranchi, 52- Khunti (ST).

No.* and *Name of Assembly Segments:

Khunti

301. Tamar (ST)—Tamar, Erki and Bundu police stations in Khunti sub-division.

302. Torpa (ST)—Torpa and Rania police stations and G.Ps. Gumru, Gobindpur, Tilmi, Lapa, Jariagarh, Urikel and Hutub in Karra police station in Khunti sub-division; and Bano police station in Simdega sub-division.

303. Khunti (ST)—Khunti and Murhu police stations and Karra police station (excluding G.Ps. Gumru, Gobindpur,Tilmi, Lapa, Jariagarh, Urikel and Hutub) in Khunti sub-division.

Ranchi

304. Silli—Silli police station, G .Ps. Barwadag, Tati, Jonha, Kashidih, Merha, Ambajharia and Kontatoli in Angara police station in Ranchi Sadar sub-division; and Sonahatu police station in Khunti sub-division.

305. Khijri (ST)—Ormanjhi, Namkum and Hatia police stations and Angara police station (excluding G .Ps. Barwadag. Tati, Jonha, Kashidih, Merha. Ambajharia and Kontatoli) in Ranchi Sadar sub-division.

306. Ranchi—Ranchi municipality in Ranchi Kotwali police station in Ranchi Sadar sub-division.

307. Hatia—Jaganathpur, Ratu and Doranda police stations and Ranchi Kotwali police station (excluding Ranchi municipality) in Ranchi Sadar sub-division.

308. Kanke (SC)—Kanke, Ranchi Sadar, Burmu and Khelari police stations in Ranchi Sadar sub-division.

Lohardaga (ST)

309. Mandar (ST)—Bero, Mandar and Lapung police stations in Ranchi Sadar sub-division.

Ranchi was in Ranchi West parliamentary constituency in 1952 and in Ranchi East parliamentary constituency in 1957 and 1962. The communitywise breakup (OBE) in Ranchi is Muslims (13 per cent), Christians (7 per cent) , Scheduled Castes (6 per cent) and Scheduled Tribes (39 per cent). Among the Scheduled tribes, Oraons (19 per cent) and Mundas (14 per cent) are most numerous. Kurmis (6 per cent), ahirs (4 per cent) and Rajputs and Telis around 3 per cent each are also present.

Khunti was in Ranchi West Lok Sabha constituency in 1952, 1957 and 1962. The communitywise break up (OBE) in Khunti is Christians (27 per cent), Scheduled Castes (7 per cent) and Scheduled Tribes (73 per cent). This is a Munda dominated constituency. Mundas comprise 60 per cent of the population. Oraons, the other important Scheduled Tribe have 5 per cent presence. Other communities like Kurmis and Ahirs are present only in small numbers.

OBSERVATIONAL ORGANISATION

Surface Observatories

Ranchi has the facility of surface observatories. The instrument work under meteorological sub-division, Bihar Plateaus. The instrument lies in

Latitude	:	23.3° North
Longitude	:	85.3° East
Altitude	:	652 m
Date of starting	:	20-9-1955.

Agricultural Meteorological stations:

This facility is available at Kanke, the instruments lies in

Latitude	:	23.4° North
Longitude	:	85.3° East
Altitude	:	675
Date of starting	:	20-9-1976

Hydrometeorological Stations for Climatological Purposes

This instrument is working at two places in the district i.e. at

Burmu and Mandar. These places lies in

Burmu

Latitude	:	23.5° North
Longitude	:	85.2° East
Altitude	:	622 metre
Date of starting	:	31-1-1951

Mandar

Latitude	:	23.4° North
Longitude	:	85.1° East
Altitude	:	671 metre
Date of starting	:	1-5-1948

Upper Air Observatories

Radiosonde Ascent: Date of starting 10-4-1978

Radio/Radar wind Ascent: Date of starting 25-1-1972.

Radiation station

This instrument was started in February 1986

Aeronautical Meteorological Observatories

There are at present 76 aviation meteorological observatories in India. This facility is available in Ranchi. These maintain current weather watch at aerodromes or important locations along and near air routes, provide service for the use of air-craft and air traffic control units.

Storm Detection Radar Station:

This instrument is located at airports, weather Radars capable of detecting thunder storms and precipitation areas within a radius of 150 to 400 kms. around the station. This instrument facility is available in Ranchi.

DISASTROUS WEATHER EVENTS

Coldwave:

1st January 1982, moderate.

29-30 November 1982, severe.

4-10 December 1982, severe.

2-14 January 1983, severe.

December 3rd and 4th week 1984, severe.
27-31 December 1989, severe.
1-10 January 1990, severe.
January 1st and 2nd week 1992.

Heatwave:
1-7 July 1982, moderate to severe.
28 May to 2 June 1983, moderate to severe.
6 June 1983, severe.
7 June 1983, moderate.

Floods and Heavy Rains:
July 4th week and in August 1985 this area witnessed heavy rains. Paddy crop damaged.
July 4th week to October 2nd week 1987 this area witnessed moderate to heavy rains. Crops damaged.

Lightning:
On 13th September 1996, this district witnessed lightning. Many people reported killed and injured.

ARCHAEOLOGICAL SITE

Anigara	Dt. Ranchi	Burial site.
Baheya	Dt Ranchi	So called Asura site (14.4) yielding copper vessels, ornaments and a polished bronze dish. Jour, Bihar & Orissa Res. Soc. 6, 1921, pp.412-13
Bamla	Dt Ranchi	Dolmens and microliths (4.5). IAR 1960-1.
Bandua	Dt Ranchi	A flat copper celt (4.11) Patna Museum Collection
Bansjore	Dt. Ranchi	Microlithic Blades, flakes and caras (4.5). IAR 1960-1.
Bartola	Dt Ranchi	21 flat copper celts (4.11), Jour, Bihar & Orissa Res. Soc., 1915 p.127
Barwe	Dt Ranchi	Late stone age (Mesolithic [4.5] site. IAR 1965-6.
Belwadag	Dt Ranchi	Asure site (14.4). A Kushan coin (3.1) of Huviska, stone implements and beads were also found. Roy, S.C. 1915, in Jour. Bihar & Orissa Res. Soc., 1, pp. 230-4.

Bhakuadih	Dt Ranchi	Microliths (4.5). IAR 1960-1.
Bichana	Dt Ranchi	A flat copper celt (4.11). Orissa Museum collection.
Bichna	Dt Ranchi	Site yieldig potsherds, stone celts, beads, iron arrowheads, copper axe-head, etc, Roy, S.C. 1915, Jour. Bihar & Orissa Res. Soc., 1, pp. 240-2
Bighatoli	Dt Ranchi	Microliths (4.5). IAR 1963-4
Binda	Dt Ranchi	Prehistoric site yielding chisel of schistose stone, polished but broken celt of gneiss, broad flat-bladed exe-head, large elongated celt of schist, a small triangular polished celt of quarlzite and a small hatchet of quartz (4.6.4.). Roy. S.C., 1916, in Jour. Bihar & Orissa Res. Soc. 2, p.68
Birta	Dt Ranchi	Microliths (4.5).IAR 1965-6
Budhudih	Dt Ranchi	Microliths and an Asura habitation (14.4) site. IAR 1964-5.
Burhadi	Dt Ranchi	Prehistoric site yielding a stone celt (4.6.4). Proc., Asiatic Soc. Bengal, 1870, p. 268
Burju	Dt Ranchi	Prehistoric site yielding polished chisel (4.6.4), Roy, S.C., 1916 in Jour. Bhiar & Orissa Res. Soc., 2, p.67
Buruhatu	Dt Ranchi	Prehistoric site yielding a broken chisel of state and broken and polished chisel of quartzite (4.6.4). Roy, S.C., 1916, in Jour. Bihar & Orissa Res. Soc., 2, p.75.
Buruma	Dt Ranchi	So-called Asura site (14.4) yielding cop per bracelets and earthen jars, pots and cups. Roy, S.C., 1921, in Jour. Bihar & Orissa Res. Soc., 6, pp. 413-20
Chacho Nawatoli	Dt Ranchi	Prehistoric site yielding a traingular polished celt (4.6.4) Jour, Bihar & Orissa Res. Soc. 2, 1916, p.66
Chainpur	Dt Ranchi	Middle and Late Stone Age Middle Palaeolithic (4.3) and Mesolithic (4.5) site. IAR 1965-6
Chendagutu	Dt Ranchi	Chisel of schist (4.6-1). Jour. Bihar & Orissa Res. Soc., 3, 1916, p. 68
Chenegutu	Dt Ranchi	Chisel of schist, a broken broadbladed axe of schist, a rectangular polished chisel of basait and other chisels (4.6.4). Jour. Bihar & Orissa Res. Soc., 2, 1916, p.67

Chiraundi	Dt Ranchi	Asura habitation (14.4) site. IAR 1964-5
Chakahatri	Dt. Ranchi	So called Asurs burial ground (14.4) comprising tombs mostly of the dolmen form. Asialtic Soc Bengal, 1873, p.116
Damari	Dt Ranchi	Microliths (4.5). IAR 1965-6.
Dargama	Dt Ranchi	Five copper celts were found near a water channel (4.11). Jour. Bihar & Orissa Res. Soc. 1, 1915, p.239;6, 1921, p. 417
Daruharu	Dt Ranchi	Microliths (4.5). IAR 1960-1
Diankel	Dt Ranchi	Microliths (4.5). IAR 1964-5
Digri	Dt Ranchi	Asura burial site (14.4) consisting of grave-stones under which large earthen jars were discovered contain ing bones and in some cases copper or naments or stone beads. Roy, S.C., in Jour, Bihar & Orissa Res. Soc., 1, 1915, p.243
Dubalabera	Dt Ranchi	Lower Palaeolithic (4.2) site. IAR 1965-6.
Dulna	Dt Ranchi	Site situated on then. bank of the river Katri. Bricks can be seen on the sur face. Patil, D.R., 1963, Antiquarian Remains in Bihar, Patna, p. 122.
Erkia	Dt Ranchi	Site yieldig grey pottery and a small iron chisel. Patil, D.R., 1963. Antiquarian remains in Bihar, patna, p.123.
Gora	Dt Ranchi	Site yielding a stone ceremonial stool and an elongated broadbladed axe of siliceous rock Rov. S.C. 1916, in Jour. Bihar & Orissa Res. Soc., 2, p.71; 1918, 4, p.412.
Guram	Dt Ranchi	Microliths (4.5). IAR 1960-1.
Hansa	Dt Ranchi	Burial ground market by about a hun-dred horizontal slabs and vertical pill ars. Patil, D.R., 1962, Antiquarian Re mains in Bihar, Patna, pp.159-60.
Harin	Dt Ranchi	Microliths 94.5. IAR 1960-1.
Ite	Dt Ranchi	Site yielding a thin elongated but mostly chipped and slightly polished celt of schist. Roy, S.C., 1916, in Jour. Bihar & Orissa Res. Soc., 2, p.69

Jamatoli	Dt Ranchi	Late stone age (Mesolithic [4.5] site. IAR 1965-6.
Janumpiri	Dt Ranchi	A small polished stone celt (4.6.5) was found. Roy, S.C., 1916., in Jour. Bihar & Orissa Res., Soc., 2, p68.
Jurdag	Dt Ranchi	A Palaeolithic implement (of unspeci fied nature), of quartzite was found). Roy, S.C., 1918, In Jour, Bihar & Orissa Res. Soc., 3, p.157.
Jamatoli	Dt Ranchi	Late Stone Age (Mesolithic [4.5] site. IAR 1965-6.
Janumpiri	Dt Ranchi	A small polished stone celt [4.6.5] was found. Roy, S.C. 1916, in Jour Bihar & Orissa Res. Soc. 2, p.68
Jurdag	Dt Ranchi	A Palaeolithic implement (of unspeci fied nature) of quartzite was found. Roy, S.C., 1918, In Jour Bihar & Orissa Res. Soc., 3, p.157
Kakra	Dt Ranchi	Chisel of basalt and a small polished celt of quartzite. Roy, S.C., 1918, In Jour Bihar & Orissa Res. Soc.,23, p.67
Kamdera	Dt Ranchi	Two flat copper celts [4.11]. Patna Mu seum collection.
Kandra	Dt Ranchi	Late Stone Age (Mesolithic [4.5]) site. IAR 1965-6.
Kanthar-toli	Dt Ranchi	So-called Asura site [14.4]
Kochedega	Dt Ranchi	Microliths (of unspecified nature). IAR 1963-4.
Kuchajharia	Dt Ranchi	Microlithic tools, both geometric and non-geometric, were collected. Though coarse grey and red wares were also found, their contemporaneity with the microliths is not certain. IAR 1959-60.
Kunjla	Dt Ranchi	Asura site [14.4] 4 km s.s.w of Khunti. The mound is covered with brick and pottery. Excavation exposed ruins of a brick house, almost complete on plain, measuring 19X6 m. The antiquities dis covered in the excavation included a good number of iron objects. The pot tery is coarse in fabric, thick in sec tion and made of badly levigated clay with small bits of quartz. Roy S.C., 1915, in Jour. Bihar & Orissa Res. Soc., 1. p.237. Excavated by A. Ghosh (not published).

Kurumgarh	Dt Ranchi	Tools of the Early, Middle (Lower, Mid dle Palaeolithic [4.2.,3] and Late Stone (Mesolithic [4.5] Ages. IAR 1965-6.
Lupungdi	Dt Ranchi	Burial site indicated by gravestones under which large earthen jars contain ing bones and sometimes copper or naments and stone beads were found. Roy, S.C., 1915, in Jour Bihar & Orissa Res. Soc., 1, p.243.
Maranghada	Dt Ranchi	Megaliths [4.17.4]. IAR 1965-6.
Maranghatu	Dt Ranchi	Megaliths [4.17.4]. IAR 1965-6.
Pangura	Dt. Ranchi	A Neolithic [4.6.5] polished chisel of dark-green gneiss was found.
Pokla	Dt. Ranchi	So called Asura (14.4) burial site consisting of the remains of a graveyard marked by slabs of stone and a scpulchral stone pillar.
Sabia	Dt. Ranchi	Early stone Age (Lower Palaeolithic (4.2) tooks like choppers hand axes and scrapers in the valley of subarnerekha IAR 1964-5.
Khuntitoli	Dt. Ranchi	A hamlet close to the subdivisional town of Khunti, with a large number of megalithic burials (4.17.4). IAR 1965-6, P.10
Murud	Dt. Ranchi	So called Asura site (14.4) yielding a copper chain, bronze ear rings and an elongated crude of phyllitic rock.
Namkum	Dt. Ranchi	Early stone age Lower Palaeolithic (4.2) implements such as chhoppers, hand axes and scrapers were found. Flaksblades on quartz and quartzite were also collected from this valley of the subarnarekha and sapahi near Namkum. IAR 1964-5.
Nawadih	Dt. Ranchi	Late stone age Mesolithic (4.5) site.
Nawagaon	Dt. Ranchi	Palaeolithic (4.2) hand axes. IAR 1965-6.
Nichitpur	Dt. Ranchi	Microlith of unspecified nature. IAR 1965-6.
Omto	Dt. Ranchi	Prehistoric site yielding a heavy broad bladed axe made of highly polished ornamental quartzite.
Oskea	Dt. Ranchi	So called Asura (14.4) burial site with smelting Kiln.
Salgi	Dt. Ranchi	A small chisel of geneiss.

Saradkel	Dt. Ranchi	On the east bank of the Tajna at a distance of about 9 km to the east of the subdivisional town of Khunti.
Saurigaon	Dt. Ranchi	Burial ground and so called Asura site 14.4. Burial yielded bones, copper, ornaments and beads.
Sembua	Dt. Ranchi	A polished but crude chisel of schist was found.
Senegutu	Dt. Ranchi	A broad polished axe of geneiss was found.
Sodaj	Dt. Ranchi	A highly polished wedge shaped chisel of dark-green quartizite was found.
Sonahatu	Dt. Ranchi	Microliths (of unspecified nature) and small dolmens. IAR 1961-2.
Soparan	Dt. Ranchi	Polished celt and chisels (4.6.5).
Tamar	Dt. Ranchi	Stone age site yilding blades, lunates and finely worked pots IAR 1968-9.
Tanti Silwali	Dt. Ranchi	Early stone age (Lower Palaeolithic (4.2) tools like chopper, hand-axes and scrapers were found in the valley of the Subarnarekha IAR 1964-5.
Toner	Dt. Ranchi	So-called Asura (14.4) site.
Torankhel	Dt. Ranchi	Fragmentary axe of gneiss.
Torpa	Dt. Ranchi	Microlethics (of unspecified nature) IAR 1964-5.
Udhuru	Dt. Ranchi	Microliths. IAR 1964-5.

DISTRIBUTION OF *SCHEDULED CASTE* POPULATION BY SEX DISTRICTWISE (1991)

	POPULATION		
	Total	Males	Females
RANCHI			
	1,23,239	64,292	58,947
Bantar	477	201	276
Bauri	1,059	590	469
Bhogta	13,683	6,969	6,714
Bhuiya	4,218	2,156	2,062
Chamar, Mochi	13,487	7,363	6,124
Chaupal	248	140	108
Dabgar	94	46	48
Dhobi	15,467	8,264	7,203
Dom, Dhangad	6,065	3,207	2,858
Dusadh, Dhari, Dharhi	5,605	3,185	2,420
Ghasi	27,467	13,955	13,512
Halalkhor	247	104	143
Hari, Mehtar, Bhangi	2,029	983	1,046
Kanjar	166	137	29
Kurariar	253	113	140
Lalbegi	62	41	21
Musahar	1,814	999	815
Nat	416	200	216
Pan, Sawasi	15,274	7,734	7,540
Pasi	1,874	1,132	742
Rajwar	3,000	1,543	1,457
Turi	9,769	4,991	4,778
Unclassified	465	239	226

DISTRIBUTION OF *SCHEDULED TRIBE* POPULATION BY SEX DISTRICTWISE (1991)

	POPULATION		
	Total	Males	Females
RANCHI			
	9,64,422	4,90,510	4,73,912
Asur	73	49	24
Baiga	209	113	96
Banjara	20	6	14
Bathudi	27	1	26
Bedia	25,821	13,254	12,567
Bhumij	335	173	162
Binjhia	1,760	919	841
Birhor	374	188	186
Birjia	83	58	25
Chero	178	134	44
Chick Baraik	14,132	7,225	6,907
Gond	1,208	591	617
Gorait	1,977	1,064	913
Ho	555	321	234
Karmali	8,109	3,913	4,196
Kharia	5,848	3,179	2,669
Kharwar	579	324	255
Khond	47	41	6
Kisan	1,515	811	704
Kora	579	313	266
Korwa	291	156	135
Lohara, Lohra	57,267	29,766	27,501
Mahli	21,494	11,122	10,372
Mal Paharia	3,985	2,177	1,808
Munda	4,61,002	2,30,951	2,30,051
Oraon	3,51,694	1,81,249	1,70,445
Parhaiya	387	233	154
Santal	3,639	1,703	1,936
Sauria Paharia	704	270	434
Savar	15	6	9
Unclassified	515	200	315

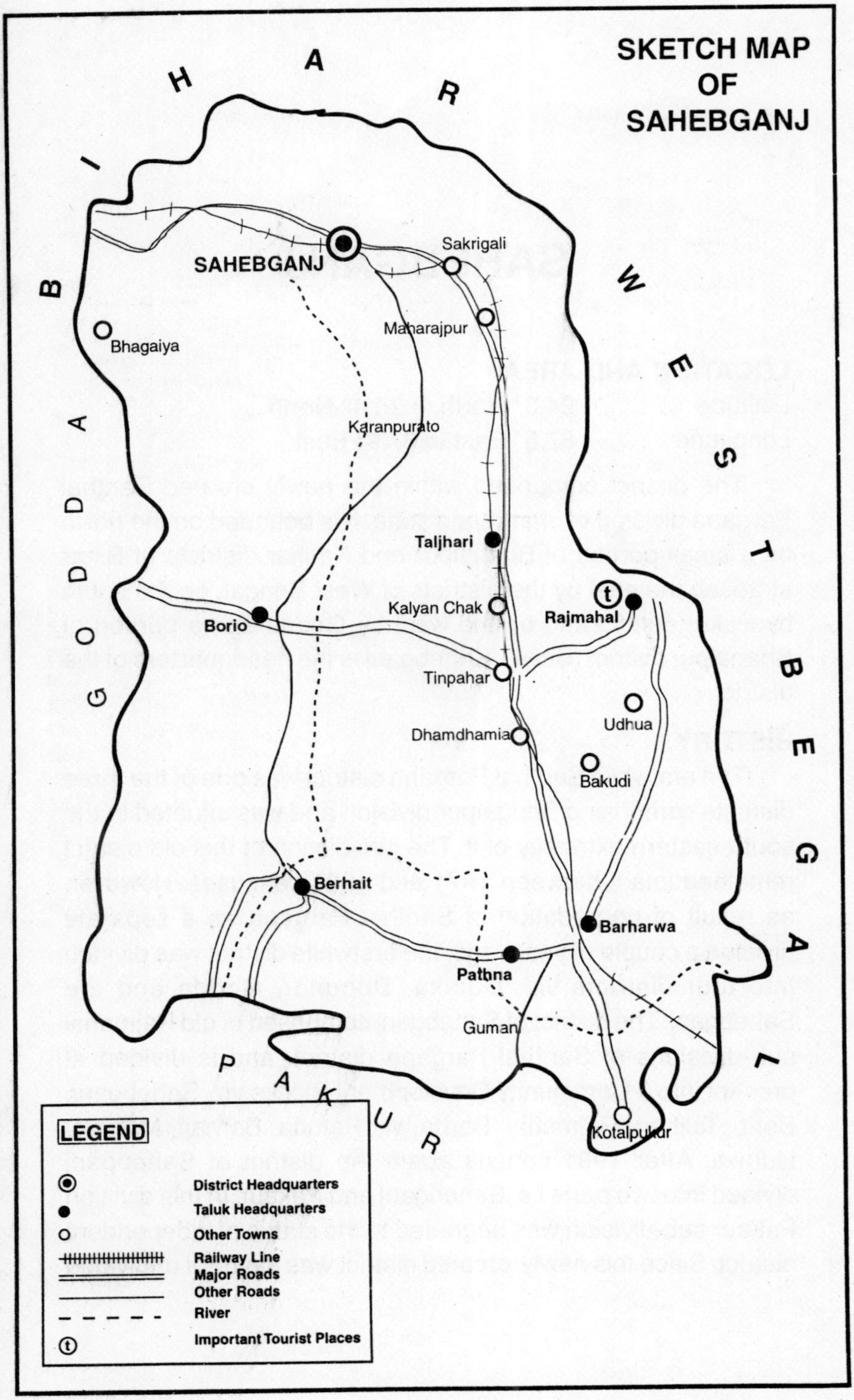
SKETCH MAP OF SAHEBGANJ
B I H A R
W E S T B E N G A L
G O D D A
P A K U R
SAHEBGANJ
Sakrigali
Maharajpur
Bhagaiya
Karanpurato
Taljhari
Kalyan Chak
Rajmahal
Borio
Tinpahar
Udhua
Dhamdhamia
Bakudi
Berhait
Barharwa
Pathna
Guman
Kotalpukur
LEGEND
District Headquarters
Taluk Headquarters
Other Towns
Railway Line
Major Roads
Other Roads
River
Important Tourist Places

SAHEBGANJ

LOCATION AND AREA

Latitude : 24.8° North to 25.4° North
Longitude : 87.5° East to 87.9° East

The district comprised within the newly created Santhal Pargana division of Jharkhand state. It is bounded on the north by a small portion of Bhagalpur and Katihar districts of Bihar state, on the east by the districts of West Bengal, on the south by Pakur district and on the west by Godda and a portion of Bhagalpur district (Bihar). Sahebganj is the headquarters of the district.

HISTORY

The erstwhile Santhal Pargana district was one of the three districts comprising Bhagalpur division and was situated in the south eastern extremity of it. The jurisdiction of this old district remained intact between 1971 and 1981 censuses. However, as result of upgradation of Santhal Pargana as a separate division a couple of years ago, the erstwhile district was divided into four districts viz. Dumka, Deoghar, Godda and the Sahebganj. The district of Sahebganj comprised of old Rajmahal sub-divisions of Santhal Pargana district, and is divided at present into 9 Community Development Blocks viz. Sahebganj, Borio, Taljhari, Rajmahal, Barharwa, Pathna, Barhait, Mandro, Udhwa. After 1991 census again the district of Sahebganj divided into two parts i.e. Sahebganj and Pakaur. In this division Pakaur sub-division was upgraded to the status of independent district. Since this newly-created district was a part of undivided

Santhal Pargana, the historical past of Sahebganj district is the same as of its parent district which has been narrated in detail in the Dumka district.

POPULATION (GENERAL, SC/ST)

Total population of the district according to 2001 census is 736835 persons. Rural population of the district is 829,481 persons and urban population is 98,103 persons.

The Community Development Block-wise, population distribution with sex ratio and literacy rate of this district is given below:

	Sex ratio		Literacy rate		Population	
C.D. Block	Rural	Urban	Rural	Urban	Rural	Urban
SAHEBGANJ DISTRICT	**951**	**879**	**33.64**	**72.09**	**829481**	**98103**
Sahibganj	901	872	37.99	75.02	59,619	80,129
Mandro	978	-	33.87	-	59742	-
Borio	975	-	27.46	-	82,021	-
Barhait	965	-	28.46	-	109,417	-
Taljhari	971	-	34.68	-	64,126	-
Rajmahal	931	912	36.45	58.54	113,280	117,974
Udhwa	943	-	26.98	-	130,280	-
Pathna	974	-	33.17	-	67,718	-
Barharwa	941	-	42.87	-	143,402	-

The Scheduled Castes and Scheduled Tribes population of the district as per 1991 census is 49304 persons and 228990 persons respectively. The rural-urban breakup of these population is indicated below:

Rural	(i)	Scheduled Castes	:	42411
	(ii)	Scheduled Tribes	:	228076
Urban	(i)	Scheduled Castes	:	6893
	(ii)	Scheduled Tribes	:	914

The decennial growth rate of population of the district as a whole in relation to the state between the period 1991 and 2001 is presented below:

State/ District	Decennial growth rate of population (per cent) 2001		
	Total	Rural	Urban
Jharkhand	23.19	21.62	28.99
Sahibganj	25.89	24.16	42.67

LANGUAGES AND RELIGION

Hindi is the principal language spoken in the district.

Religionwise breakup of population is indicated below as per 1991 census:

Hindus: 892511, Muslims: 366961, Christians: 35269, Sikhs: 311, Buddhists : 8, Jains: 77, Other religions and persuasions: 5951, Religion not stated:—.

GEOGRAPHY AND PHYSICAL FEATURES

Annual Rain fall : 1575.0 mm
Temperature : Max. 44.40°C and Min. 6.80°C

The district comprises of hilly portions stretching from the bank of the Ganges in the north to the borders of Bengal in the south. It contains the Rajmahal Hills and other hill ranges and covers the entire Damin-i-Koh area. The principal ranges in the district are that of the Rajmahal Hills which rise abruptly to some 1000-2000 ft on the southern bank of the river Ganges. These hills stretch southward almost up to the Bengal border and form the backbone of the district. The hill ranges bifurcate near Borio in Rajmahal sub division. The hills and slopes are covered with forests once dense but scanty now.The valleys have cultivable lands. yielding mostly paddy. A narrow strip of low, fertile, alluvial plain lying between the Ganges and the hills passes along the loop line of the Eastern Railway.

RIVERS, CANALS AND WATERWAYS

The river Ganges forming the northern boundary of the

district enters it at its north-western corner and journeys eastward upto Sakrigali. Here it takes a turn to the south and then forward forming the southern boundary of the district upto a little beyond Radhanagar in Rajmahal sub-division. Other rivers in the district lying east of the Rajmahal hill ranges are Gumani, Banslvi, Palsi and Brahmani.

TOWNS, VILLAGES AND AMENITIES

The district, at present comprises of one sub-divisions, 9 Community Development Blocks. It has 2 towns.

The urban population of the district as percentage of total population in the census years 2001 is indicated below. It also shows the sex ratio (females per 1000 males) and density (population per sq km) in the urban population of the district in relation to state:

State/ District	*Urban population as percentage of total population*	*Sex ratio, 2001 (Females per 1000 males)*			*Density (Population per sq km)*
	2001	*Total*	*Rural*	*Urban*	
Jharkhand	22.25	966	973	931	338
Sahebganj	10.58	943	951	879	580

Amenities

Number (with percentage) of. villages having one or more amenities in the district as per 1991 census is given below:

Sl. No.	*Amenities*	*Number of inhabited villages*	*Percentage*
1.	Education	1352	56.22
2.	Medical	314	13.06
3.	Drinking Water	2405	100.00
4.	Post and Telegraph	158	6.57
5.	Market/Hat	174	7.23
6.	Communications	257	10.69
7.	Approach by Pucca Road	365	15.14
8.	Power Supply	286	11.89

COMMUNICATIONS

The district is served by a well connected network of roads. All the Community Development Block headquarters are connected with the district headquarters by black-topped roads. The Jamtara-Dumka-Sahebganj road provides a link with Assam after ferry across the Ganges and is quite busy. Sahebganj the district and Sakrigali are the railway stations on the loop line of the Eastern Railway. The only navigable waterway is the river Ganges. The railway maintains a ferry steamer service between Maharajpur Ghat (Sakrigali Ghat) and Manihari Ghat (Purnia). The Zila Parishad of Sahebganj district has three ghat ferries on the Ganges at Rajmahal, Sakrigali ghat and Maharajpur ghat. Large cargo boats ply on the Ganges and are used throughout the year. Smaller boats are also used for ferrying people across.

AGRICULTURE AND IRRIGATION

Paddy and maize are important crops grown in the district. Linseed, groundnuts, sweet potatoes and khesari are other crops grown widely in Rajmahal and its adjoining areas. Jute is cultivated in parts of Rajmahal sub-division. Irrigational facilities are not adequate in this district. The most common source is the well, but this is not a very dependable source of irrigation. The major part of the district being rockey in nature, it is difficult to dig wells. The undulatory nature of land makes it possible to store rain water by bunding. Seepage ponds are also found. Apart from being dependent upon rains, these are by no means adequate. The result is that failure of rains invariably involves failure of crops except in small pockets.

ANIMAL HUSBANDRY

The livestock population of the district include cows, buffaloes, sheep, goats and pigs, apart from poultry birds. The State Government is making all efforts to improve the breed of the cattle by way of distribution of stud bull of Haryana and Tharparkar varieties. A number of veterinary hospitals and dispensaries are working in the different parts of the district for the welfare of livestock.

The extensive bed of the river Ganges at Sahebganj and Rajmahal offers one of the best fields in the state for collection of fish-spawn and fishing. There are a number of displaced fishermen who are experts in their line. The spawn of rah, ketla, mirgal, catfish and hilsa is collected from the Ganges in the flood season. The collected fish spawn is in great demand in other parts of Jharkhand and West Bengal. Fish spawn collected is stocked in specially prepared nursery tanks. The fish trade of Rajmahal and Sahebganj has considerable turnover. It has an assured market in Kolkata. There has, however, been very little of fishing development in the big tanks of the district.

INDUSTRIES

Among the large industrial establishments of the district, mention may be made of the following:

1. Metal Press Works, Sahebganj.
2. Tincan Manufacturing Co., Sahebganj
3. China-clay factories, Mangalhat (Rajmahal)

Besides the above, a number of small scale industries have also been set up in the district. The availability of China-clay, fire clay, sabai grass and bamboos underscores the industrial potentiality of the district. The traditional cottage and village industries practised by the Santhal and the Paharias constitute tassar, rearing, bidi making, rope making, handloom weaving etc.

MINERALS AND ORES OCCURRENCES

Abrasives

Flint pebbles have been obtained from Burhait (24.9, 87.7).

Bentonite

Bentonite is reported to occur at Tinpahar (24.9, 87.6) in the Rajmahal Hills.

Building Materials

Trap is being quarried all along the eastern margin of the

hills from Burharwa (24.9, 87.8) to Maharajpur (25.2, 87.8). The largest quarries are near Burharwa, Bakudi and Taljhari. Near Taljhari, the pitch stone, which is easy to break is quarried on a large scale. Several small quarries have been opened in the Rajmahal hills for road metal.

Sandstones in considerable variety are obtainable in the northern and southern portions of the Rajmahala hills. Some of the intertrappean beds would also supply useful flagstones, and have been used for bridge building near Burio (25.1, 87.6) in the centre of the hills.

Coal

The coal seams are less than 4 ft. in thickness at some places in Rajmahal.

Fire-clay

Boraghat (25.01, 87.43), Chilgo (24.55, 87.5), Sima (25.03, 87.4).

Gemstone (Agate)

Near Burhait (24.9, 87.66), Taljhari (25.08, 87.75), Kheroa (24.9, 87.63), Chutio (24.93, 87.96), Pachauri (24.53, 87.5).

Gemstone (Amethyst)

Near Burhait (24.9, 87.66).

Gemstone (Opal)

Opal occurs in the trap of Rajmahal hills (25.05, 87.83) and near Sahibganj Railway station (25.23, 87.63).

TRADE, COMMERCE AND EXPORT

The district has a good system of roadways which are very important for trade and commerce. The river Ganges provides water link also for such purposes. The chief centre of wholesale business is Sahebganj, where trading in foodgrains is carried on on a large scale. The chief imports of the district are sugar, cement, coal, kerosene oil, diesel, cloth, rice and iron. The chief exports are semal cotton, green mango, mustard oil, stone chips, lac, bidi, fish, sabie-grass etc. The table given below lists the most important commodities manufactured, exported from and imported in the towns of this district:

Name of the town	*Most important commodities*			*Banks*
	Manufactured	*Exported*	*Imported*	
Rajmahal	China clay, utensils, Electrical equipment, mango	Silica-sand and china clay, tomato and parwal	Kerosene oil, diesel, cloth	3
Sahebganj	Oil mill, machinery, mango products, plastic products	Fish, parwal, sabie-grass	Rice cloth, iron	5

TOURISM

Bhagnadir. The village lives in Barhait block. It is the birthpiace of the famous Santhal brothers—Sidhu, Kanhu, Chand and Bhairab, who led the Santhal rebellion of 1855.

Kanaiyasthan. Kanaiyasthan is situated 13 kms north-west of Rajmahal town on the bank of the Ganges. It derives its names from the temple of Lord Krishna located in the village. It is said that Chaitanya Mahaprabhu once stayed here on his way back from Bengal, and got the vision of Lord Krishna.

Sahebganj. Sahebganj is one of the main towns and administrative headquarters of the district bearing the same name. It is an important railway station on the loop line of the Eastern Railway. On the outskirts of the town, there are remains of the fortress named 'Sakrogarh'.

Rajmahal. Rajmahal is a small but historically impressive town. As its very name signifies, it was the seat of the Government during the Muslim period. Rajmahal was a place of importance during the Muslim period as well as the British administration. Even now relics of the old and prosperous Rajmahal are visible in this one-time capital of Bengal. The town contains the following important monuments: (i) Sang Dalan (stone verandah), (ii) Akbari Masjid (iii) Tomb of Maina Bibi, (iv) Tomb of Miran.

Sakrigali. The village is situated on the loop line of the Eastern Railway and had great of strategic importance in the olden days. As the name suggests, it is a narrow strip of plain land between the Ganges and the Rajmahal Hills, and served as a gateway of Bengal. It has been the site of many fierce battles. On the top of a nearby hill, there is the tomb of Syed Ahmed Makhdum, believed to have been erected by Shaista Khan, uncle of Aurangzeb.

Rampur. It is a village situated about 3 kms north of Sakrigali railway station on the loop line of the Eastern Railway. It contains the grave of a Muslim saint on an eight-foot high mound. This mound is believed to contain the ruins of an old temple of Lord Shiva and his consort, Parvati. Brick-gate with engravings and a stone door frame at the entrance to the grave are believed to be the remnants of the burried Shiva temple. According to a local story, a three foot high statue of Lord Vishnu shadowed by a five-hooded nag and a two and half feet long divine emblem *(lingam)* of Lord Shiva on a lotus flower base were found by a tiller of the mound. About 500 ft. off the holy grave stands a mosque said to have been built by Emperor Akbar.

Mangalhat. The village is situated about 10 kms west of Rajmahal. The place has a rich heritage. It has a temple and a mosque built by Man Singh. According to a story current in the locality, Man Singh had planned to erect a temple, but the matter was reported to Emperor Akbar, When Man Singh heard of it he apprehended the Emperor's displeasure. So he changed his idea and got a mosque (Jama Masjid} built. Another tradition says that he was building a place for himself when the matter was reported to the Emperor and to avert his anger he converted it into a mosque. Emperor Akbar it is said got a small Hindu temple built behind the mosque to appease the Hindu sentiment.

Shive Gadi. The place is located 8 kms north of Barhait in Rajmahal sub-division. It is situated 60 feet above the ground level and is surrounded by hills on three sides. The place is known for its cave temple of Lord Shiva. It has a waterfall nearby.

Udhua. The village is situated on the bank of the Ganges about 10 kms south-east of Rajmahal. The place has historical importance. After the battle of Palasi between Siraj-ud-Daula and Robert Clive, the next decisive battle was fought near the Udai or Udhua Nala. Signs of historic fight can still be seen here.

Damin-i-Koh. The vast tract of land enclosed between the hill ranges has been assigned this name. This is a Persian word meaning 'skirts of the hills'. The Damin area stretches from the loop line of the Eastern Railway in the extreme north of the district to the river Brahmi in the south, and covers parts of Rajmahal, Godda, Dumka and Pakaur sub-divisions. The history of the Damin-i-Koh is linked up with the struggle of the Paharias for freedom in the early days of British administration. Being the stronghold of the Santhals, the Damin area had become the nerve centre of the Santhal resurrection in 1855.

FAIRS AND FESTIVALS

Fairs and festivals are held regularly in the district. The most important seasonal fairs organised in the district are on the occasions of Shivratri and Shravana Sombari, apart from those held at the time of Durga Puja and Diwali. Hijala mela is held for seven days in the month of February every year in the adjoining Dumka district which is equally attended by the people of Sahebganj district.

EDUCATION

According to 2001 census, total literates (excluding the population in the age group of 0-6 years) in undivided district of Sahebganj is 279,980 persons. Of these, 184,378 are males and 95,602 are females. In the rural areas of the district 220843 persons (149,155 males and 71,688 females) are literates and in urban areas 59,137 persons (35,223 males and 23,914 females) are literates. The rate of literacy of this population to the total population, excludmg 0-6 years age group according to 2001 census are shown below:

	Persons	*Males*	*Females*
Total	37.91	48.33	26.78
Rural	33.64	44.19	22.48
Urban	72.09	80.14	62.80

Primary and middle schools are available in the towns. The following table gives the details of various types of educational institutions available in towns of this district including the number of stadia and public libraries .

Name of the town	*Educational institutions*	*Stadia*	*Public libraries, including reading rooms*
Rajmahal	One Secondary/ Matriculatlon and two Junior Secondary and Middle Schools	—	—
Sahebganj	One each Polytechnics, Shorthand and Typing Training Institute and Higher Secondary/ Intermediate School, 5 Secondary/Matriculation Schools and 12 Junior Secondary and Middle Schools.	—	PL. : 6

COLLEGES, 2000

B S K College, Barharwar, (Established 1978). Enrolment 561, Teachers 62. (Constituent Colleges)

Sahibganj College, Sahibganj, (Established 1953). Enrolment 2893, Teachers 81. (Constituent Colleges)

B L N Bohra College, Rajmahal, (Established 1980).

Enrolment 350, Teachers 66. (Affiliated College)

Bohra Sita Annapurna Mahila College, Barharwa, (Established1986). Enrolment 240. (Affiliated College)

Sahibganj Mahila College, Sahebganj (Established 1988). Enrolment 304, Teachers 21.(Affiliated College)

(Above named colleges belong to Siddhu Kanhu University, Dumka. Established 1992.)

MEDICAL

The table given below furnishes information regarding various types of medical institutions available in the towns of this district:

Name of the towns	*Medical institutions*	*Number of Beds*
Rajmahal	Hospital (1) :	12
	Family Planning Centre (1) :	—
Sahibganj	Hospital (1) :	25
	Family Planning Centres (2) :	—

ADMINISTRATION

(i) Administrative Divisions:

Sub-divisions: Sahebganj, Rajmahal.

Community Development Blocks: Sahebganj, Borio, Taljhori, Rajmahal, Barharwa, Pathna, Barhait, Mandro, Udhwa.

Towns and Urban Agglomerations with their Population, Sexratio, Decadal growth and Literacy rate (2001)

Town	Population	Percentage Decadal growth 1991-2001	Sex Ratio	Literacy Rate
Rajmahal (NA)	17,974	28.574	912	58.54
Sahibganj (M)	80,129	62.68	872	75.02

(ii) Parliamentary Constituencies and assembly segments:

No.* and *Name of Parliamentary Constituencies:

26-Rajmahal (ST) .

No.* and *Name of Assembly Segments:

147. Rajmahal—Rajmahal and Sahebganj police stations in Rajmahal sub-division.

148. Borio (ST)—Borio and Taljhari police stations in Rajmahal sub-division: and Boarijor police station (excluding G.Ps. Rajabhita, Kero, Kairasol, Bara Telo and Barapipra) in Godda sub-division.

149. Barhait (ST)—Barhait and Ranga police stations in Rajmahal sub-division; and Sundarpahari police station and G.Ps. Rajabhita, Kero, Kairasol, Bara Telo and Barapipra in Boarijar police station in Godda sub-division.

Rajmahal was in Purnea cum Santal Parganas Lok Sabha constituency in 1952. The communitywise breakup (OBE) in Rajmahal is Muslims (25 per cent). Scheduled Castes (5 per cent), and Scheduled Tribes (53 per cent). Of the Scheduled Tribes. Santals (42 per cent) are in clear majority. Kharwars are also found in small numbers among the Scheduled Tribes. Ahirs (5 per cent) are also present. Others like Brahmins and Telis are there only in small numbers.

DISASTROUS WEATHER EVENTS

Coldwave:

1st January 1982, Moderate.
29-30 November 1982, severe.
4-10 December 1982, severe.
2-14 January 1983, severe.
December 3rd and 4th week 1984, severe.
27-31 December 1989 severe.
1-10 January 1990, severe.
January 1st and 2nd week 1992.

Heatwave:

1-7 July 1982, Moderate to severe.

28 May to 2 June 1983, Moderate to severe.

6 June 1983, severe.

7 June 1983, moderate.

Drought:

August, and September 1st week, 1982. The drought was of moderate category. Transplantation of paddy badly affected.

Floods and Heavy Rains:

In August 3rd and 4th week this area witnessed heavy rains and flood.

July 4th week to October 2nd week 1987, this area witnessed heavy rains, damaged of property reported.

9 to 15 August 1995, there was severe flood at many places in the district. Several people died and cattleheads perished.

Thunder storm:

On 22 May 1988, there was a severe thunder storm in this area, caused heavy damage to property.

DISTRIBUTION OF *SCHEDULED CASTE* POPULATION BY SEX DISTRICTWISE (1991)

	POPULATION Total	Males	Females
SAHIBGANJ	70,788	36,611	34,177
Bantar	100	33	67
Bauri	3,852	1,858	1,994
Bhogta	85	52	33
Bhuiya	5,548	2,826	2,722
Chamar, Mochi	16,286	8,298	7,988
Chaupal	158	65	93
Dabgar	15	12	3
Dhobi	5,886	3,115	2,771
Dom, Dhangad	7,471	3,830	3,641
Dusadh, Dhari, Dharhi	8,607	4,584	4,023
Ghasi	159	63	96
Halalkhor	54	22	32
Hari, Mehtar, Bhangi	2,131	1,026	1,105
Kanjar	40	19	21
Kurariar	777	388	389
Lalbegi	19	13	6
Musahar	3,485	1,836	1,649
Nat	38	18	20
Pan, Sawasi	54	46	8
Pasi	1,318	716	600
Rajwar	6,559	3,436	3,123
Turi	5,589	2,934	2,655
Unclassified	2,557	1,419	1,138

DISTRIBUTION OF *SCHEDULED TRIBE* POPULATION BY SEX DISTRICTWISE (1991)

	POPULATION Total	Males	Females
SAHIBGANJ	5,07,321	2,57,135	2,50,186
Baiga	48	26	22
Bathudi	57	45	12
Bedia	5	1	4
Binjhia	20	16	4
Birhor	99	35	64
Chero	43	11	32
Chick Baraik	62	31	31
Gond	586	242	344
Gorait	52	31	21
Ho	57	16	41
Karmali	112	54	58
Kharia	202	89	113
Kharwar	14,950	7,637	7,313
Khond	309	158	151
Kisan	392	229	163
Kora	992	490	502
Korwa	339	255	84
Lohara, Lohra	5,925	2,992	2,933
Mahli	5,167	2,812	2,355
Mal Paharia	26,026	12,895	13,131
Munda	6,352	3,257	3,095
Oraon	7,118	3,293	3,825
Parhaiya	5,395	2,979	2,416
Santal	4,05,459	2,05,135	2,00,324
Sauria Paharia	27,504	14,393	13,111
Savar	28	13	15
Unclassified	22	0	22

SKETCH MAP OF EAST SINGHBHUM

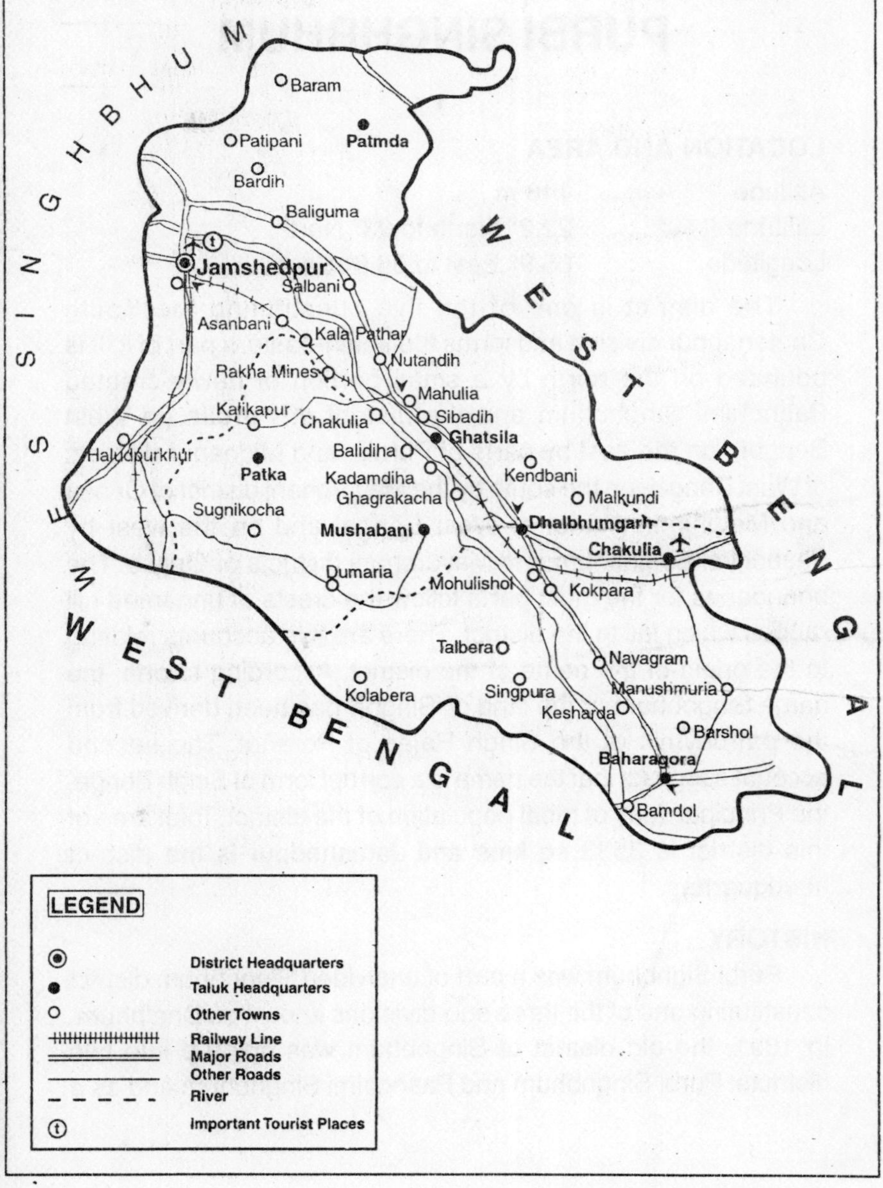

PURBI SINGHBHUM

LOCATION AND AREA

Altitude	:	148 m
Latitude	:	22.2° North to 23° North.
Longitude	:	85.9° East to 86.9° East.

The district is one of the five constituting the South Chotanagpur division and forms the south-eastern part of it. It is bounded on the north by a small portion of newly-created Pashchimi Singhbhum and the district of Purulia (in West Bengal), on the east by parts of Purulia and Midnapur districts of West Bengal, on the south by the Mayurbhanj district of Orissa and Medinipur district of West Bengal and on the west by Pashchimi Singhbhum and Mayurbhanj districts of Orissa. The boundaries for the most parts follow the crests of unnamed hill ranges which fall in the district. There are two accounts relating to the origin of the name of the district. According to one, the name Singhbhum or the land of 'Singhs' has been derived from the patronymic of the Singh Rajas of Porahat. The second account suggests that the name is a corrupt form of Singh Bonga, the Principal deity of tribal population of the district. Total area of this district is 3533 sq kms and Jamshedpur is the district headquarters.

HISTORY

Purbi Sighbhum was a part of undivided Singhbhum district constituting one of the three sub-divisions known as Dhalbhum. In 1991, the old district of Singhbhum was split up into two districts: Purbi Singhbhum and Pashchimi Singhbhum and as a result, the steel city Jamshedpur and its adjoining industrial areas fall in Purbi Singhbhum.

The early history of Singhbhum district is rather obscure although relics have been found within the district dating back to the stone age. The territory covered by Singhbhum district does not find any mention either in the Vedic texts or in *Puranic* literature. The earliest conjecture is in regard to the Gupta Emperor Samudragupta of Magadh. According to an inscription, his dominion included all the jungle countries from Baghelkhand to the Orissa coast including the present district of Singhbhum. According to a theory, when the northern and southern Bihar were annexed to the empire of the great Kushans, Orissa and the eastern seaboard were also conquered, implying that Singhbhum may also have lain in the conquered territory. The history of Singhbhum was influenced by the Hos who migrated from the Chotanagpur plateau and overcame the Bhuiyas who then held part of Singhbhum. The north of the district came under the rule of the Singh family of Forahat who claimed to be Rathor Rajputs and whose head was formerly known as the Raja of Singhbhum.

British relations with Singhbhum date back to 1767 when a small British force marched against the Raja of Dhalbhum, or as he is called in the early records of Midnapur, the Raja of Ghatsila. The district of Midnapur which included Dhalbhum, had been ceded to the East India Company in 1760. In 1818 Raja Ghanshyam Singh Deo of Porahat tendered allegiance to the British. His main objective was to be recognised as the Lord Paramount over the chiefs of Kharsawan and Seraikela and also to obtain assistance in reducing the Hos, whom he claimed as his subjects. The Hos resisted stiffly but their bows and arrows were of no match to the British equipment of war. In 1831 the Hos joined the rebellion (commonly called the Kol rebellion) of the Mundas of Chotanagpur. The insurgents went on burning villages, killing the people mercilessly and plundering property until the army was deployed to put down the rebellion. The rebellion was finally quelled after much bloodshed. The immediate result of these troubles and the Kol insurrections in Ranchi and other parts of Singhbhum was the establishment of the South West Frontier Agency by Regulation XIII of 1833. Dhalbhum, which had hitherto been included in Midnapur district, was transferred to the Manbhum division. After the conquest of the Kolhan in 1837, it was considered advisable to bring all the Ho *Pits* under the direct management of the British Government. A new district was consequently constituted to be known as Singhbhum with Chaibasa as its headquarters. In 1846 the district was enlarged by the transfer of Dhalbhum from Manbhum. When Act X of 1854 was passed, Singhbhum became a non-regulation district under the jurisdiction of the Lt. Governor of Bengal.

An era of peace and progress followed, to be broken almost forty years later by the Birsaite rising, the effects of which, however, were not very widespread or great. The history of the district in the present century is the saga of a powerful industrial revolution coming in the wake of the exploitation of the district's vast mineral resources. The inception and rapid development of Jamshedpur city bears ample testimony to the rapid strides the district has made in this regard.

POPULATION (GENERAL, SC/ST)

Total population of the district according to 2001 census is 1,978,671 persons, comprising of 1,024,945 males and 953,726 females. Rural population of the district is 891,013 persons (453,233 males and 437,780 females) and urban population is 1,087,658 persons (571,712 males and 515,946 females).

The Community Development Block-wise, population distribution with sex ratio and literacy rate of this district is given below:

C.D. Block	Sex ratio Rural	Sex ratio Urban	Literacy rate Rural	Literacy rate Urban	Population Rural	Population Urban
PURBI SINGHBHUM DISTRICT	**966**	**902**	**52.27**	**82.93**	**891013**	**1087658**
Patamda	972	-	48.36	-	131,646	-
Golmuri-cum-Jugsalai	936	902	59.59	83.37	91,049	982,583
Ghatshila	962	889	51.30	81.77	77,105	37,850
Potka	977	-	53.59	-	170,614	-
Musabani	980	905	51.13	78.16	50,677	52,895
Dumaria	994	-	43.15	-	53,581	-
Dhalbhumgarh	959	-	49.17	-	72,512	-
Chakulia	975	932	52.92	73.21	94,464	14,330
Baharagora	951	-	54.89	-	149,365	-

The Scheduled Castes and Scheduled Tribes popuiation of the district as per 1991 census is 77194 persons and 466572 persons respectively. The rural-urban breakup of this population is indicated below:

Rural	(i)	Scheduled Castes	:	33459
	(ii)	Scheduled Tribes	:	389226
Urban	(i)	Scheduled Castes	:	43735
	(ii)	Scheduled Tribes	:	77346

The decennial growth rate of population of the district as a whole in relation to the state between the period 1991 and 2001 is presented below:

State/ District	*Decennial growth rate of population (per cent)* 1991-2001		
	Total	*Rural*	*Urban*
Jharkhand	23.19	21.62	28.99
Purbi Singhbhum	22.66	16.75	27.97

LANGUAGES AND RELIGION

Main languages spoken in the district are Hindi, Bengali, Oriya, Punjabi and Urdu.

This district was since the part of erstwhile Singhbhum district till 1981 census, the religion wise break up of this newly created district is shown as recorded for Singhbhum district as per 1991 census:

Hindus: 1189510, Muslims: 130562, Christians: 21091, Sikhs: 31719, Buddhists: 505, Jains: 1156, Other religions and persuasions: 35235, Religion not stated: 58.

GEOGRAPHY AND PHYSICAL FEATURES

Annual Rainfall : 1434.0 mm
Temperature : Max. 44.50°C and Min. 6.40°C

The district forms part of the southern fringe of the Chotanagpur plateau and is a hilly upland tract. The regions of Kolhan and Porahat are comprised of mountainous tract of high hills alternating with steep valleys, particularly to the West Karo river. The plain land in the district is largely confined to the valleys of the South Koel river and the Subarnarekha river in Dhalbhum.

The district receives one spur emanating from the Chotanagpur plateau. The north-eastern spur contains the five principal peaks, viz Lopso (1612 feet), Okam (1398 feet), Chandar (1107 feet), Kapungadi (1651 feet) and Kurndi (1676 feet). To the south of the north-eastern spur, central Singhbhum is comprised of granitic gneiss surrounded by hills of the Dharwar system. The greater part of the district is covered by the iron-ore series and granite rocks. The minerals found in the district are uranium, chromite, copper, clay, gold, magnetite, manganese, kyanite, limestone, silica, asbestos and soap-stone.

RIVERS, CANALS AND WATERWAYS

The Subarnarekha and South Koel are the principal rivers of this district. The Subarnarekha rises near Ranchi town and enters Singhbhum from the north-west. It flows south-east through Dhalbhum for almost 112 kms. leaving the district at its south eastern extremity and flowing on through Midnapur district of West Bengal. Its bed is rocky and flow rapid. It contains gold in minute quantity whence the name. There are many tributaries of the Subarnarekha river, the main being the Kharkari which is formed by the two streams Torlo and Koranjai in the Kochan area. The river Sanjai rises from the hills of Porahat and after running 48 kms out of Kolhan, it meets the Kharkhari near Lungtasai. It is fed by several small streams. River Baitarani's course is only about 13 kms in the district. The Brahmani runs in the district for about 57 kms in a semicircular form. River Deo rising from Kolhan runs for about 56 kms while river Koina runs in the northerly direction covering about 58 kms in the district and meets river Koel at Manoharpur.

TOWNS, VILLAGES AND AMENITIES

The district is at present comprised of 2 sub-divisions, 9 Community Development Blocks namely, Patamda, Golmuri-cum-Jugsalai, Ghatshila, Potka, Musabani, Dumaria, Dalbhumgarh, Chakulia, Bahragora. It has 13 towns and 1750 villages (1576 inhabited villages and 174 uninhabited villages).

The urban population of the distlict as percentage of total population in the census years 2001 is indicated below. It also shows the sex ratio (females per 1000 males} and density (population per sq km) in the urban population of the district in relation to the state :

State/ District	*Urban population as percentage of total population*	*Sex ratio, 2001 (Females per 1000 males)*			*Density (Population per sq. km.)*
	2001	*Total*	*Rural*	*Urban*	
Jharkhand	22.25	941	963	870	338
Purbi Singhbhum	54.97	931	966	902	560

Amenities

Number (with percentage} of villages having one or more amenities in the district as per 1991 census is given below:

Sl. No.	Amenities	Number of inhabited villages	Percentage
1.	Education	947	60.09
2.	Medical	292	18.53
3.	Drinking Water	1576	100.00
4.	Post and Telegraph	138	8.76
5.	Market/Hat	99	6.28
6.	Communications	214	13.58
7.	Approach by Pucca Road	194	12.31
8.	Power Supply	415	26.33

COMMUNICATIONS

Purbi Singhbhum district is well-served by a network of good roads maintained by the Public Works Department, the Zila Parishad and the Forest Department. A good number of road maintained by the above departments are pucca roads of which some are also metalled. The National Highway runs through the district. Being the richest district in regard to minerals, the railway system has been suitably developed to ensure proper utilisation of minerals. The Tatanagar railway station of the South Eastern Railway serves the flourishing industrial area of Jamshedpur and is easily the most important railway station in the district.

The Howrah-Nagpur mainline of the South-Eastern Railway traverses the district from east to west for about 190 kms. Two branch line sections viz. Tatanagar-Gurhmahi-Sani- Badampahar and Raj-Kharsawan-Gua run to the southern fringes of the district.

The rivers of the district are not navigable as they dry up during the summer. Important ferries in the district are:

1. Mango ferry on river Subarnarekha near Jamshedpur,
2. Maubhandar ferry near Ghatshila on Subarnarekha river, and

Ferry services operate only in the rainy season.

Airways. Jamshedpur has an airfield owned by the Tata Iron and Steel Company. There is also a Pilot Baloon Observatory (D-type) of the Meteorological Department. There is also a big landing ground at Chakulia.

AGRICULTURE AND IRRIGATION

Rice is the main crop of the district. It accounts for more than three fourths of the gross area sown. Wheat comprises a very small proportion of the gross area sown. Among the non-food crops grown, oilseeds are the most important. Cauliflower, cabbage, tomato, raddish, carrot, beet etc, are some of the vegetables that are being grown now.

The rivers and streams of the district are hilly in character and are not much used for irrigation. The only way is to store their water for future use. The other sources of water supply are springs, tanks, wells, natural water reservoirs in depressions and ahars. The usual method of irrigation consists of the construction of embankments and bunds across the line of trench, i.e. at the upper end of a depression. Since independence there has been a concerted effort to increase the irrigation potential in the district and a number of minor irrigation schemes have been completed. The existing irrigation works, many of them constructed by the ex-landlords which had fallen into disrepair have also been repaired.

Prior to 1961, the area irrigated by Government canals or tube-wells was practically nil. Thereafter, some areas were brought under irrigation by these two means. In the recent past several schemes have been executed by the Government, the important among them being the Kaida, Brahmini, Sonua, Putangar, Rajaw Bandh, Torlow, Koro irrigation schemes. The district of Singhbhum still requires much greater facilities of irrigation. Given the terrain, it will be more worthwhile to construct a number of dams to harness the water resources and ensure irrigation as well as regular water supply for other purposes.

ANIMAL HUSBANDRY

The livestock in this district is generally of a poor variety. The local Hos, who constitute the majority of tribal population, are allergic to milk and its various preparations and take no interest in improving the breed. Pasturage is generally ample, for there are wide stretches of jungle and hilly areas and there is usually enough rain at intervals throughout the year to keep the grass and vegetation fairly green. In addition to the grass in the jungles and on the waste lands, cattle get pasturage in the rice fields also. Buffaloes and oxen are utilised for agriculture purposes.

There has been a concerted effort on behalf of the State Government to upgrade the cattle through the distribution of stud bulls of Haryana and Tharparkar types. In order to improve the breed of the cattle quickly and also at low cost, artificial insemination centres with sub-centres have been opened in the district. Distribution of frozen semen has also been introduced in the district.

There are a number of veterinary hospitals and dispensaries spread over the entire district. Treatment, prevention and eradication of diseases of the livestock are the main functions of the veterinary institutions.

The livestock population according of the district include cows, buffaloes, bulls and bullocks, sheep, goats and pigs. Poultry is an important activity in rural areas especially among the aboriginals who derive a side-income from it. Poultry farms have been opened at a number of places in the district and steps have been taken to improve the breed of the poultry in the district.

INDUSTRIES

The city of Jamshedpur and the areas upto Ghatsila form the main belt having some of the biggest factories of their kind in this country. The remaining portion consists of either agricultural or mining areas producing iron-ores and other ancilliary minerals for the manufacture of iron and steel. There are a few establishments both in the rural and urban areas of the district engaged in manufacturing tobacco products, flour mills, rice mills, saw mills, etc.

Among the large industrial establishments of the district, mention may be made of:

1. The Tata Iron & Steel Co. Ltd., Jamshedpur
2. The Tata Engineering & Locomotive Co. Ltd., Telco Works, Jamshedpur
3. Tinplate Co. of India (P) Ltd., Golmuri
4. The Indian Cable Co. Ltd., Golmuri
5. The Indian Copper Corporation Ltd., Moubhandar, Ghatsila
6. Indian Steel and Wire Products Ltd., Indernagar
7. The Indiana Tube Co., (1953) Ltd., Jamshedpur
8. The Tatanagar Foundry Co. Ltd., Burma Mines.

The Tata Iron and Steel* Co. *Ltd. Jamshedpur, Jharkhand.

To carry on the business of iron masters, steel converters, manufacturers, miners, smelters, engineers and iron plate makers. M/s. Tata Refractories Ltd., M/s Tata Pigments Ltd., M/s Kalimali Invt. Co. Ltd., M/s Special Steel Ltd. and M/s Tata Korf Engg. Services Ltd. are the subsidiary companies.

IVP Ltd. Golmuri, Jamshedpur-831003. Jharkhand.

Manufacturer: Vanaspathi, vegetable oil, minor chemicals, plasticizers, foundry chemicals; spark plugs and industrial ceramics.

IVP Ltd. 37-B, Adityapur Industrial Area, Jamshedpur-831003, Jharkhand.

Manufacturer: Vanaspathi, vegetable oil, minor chemicals, plasticizers, foundry chemicals, spark plugs and industrial ceramics.

Tata-Robins-Fraser Ltd. 11, Station Road, Burma Mines, Jamshedpur-831007.

Manufacturer: Material handling equipment such as idler rollers, vibrating screens, sectional and mine conveyors, industrial chains, wire screen cloth, winders, tipplers, crushers, ore and coal preparation equipment, and coal cutters and undertaking system contracts for such equipment including design manufacture, supply and installation of equipment.

Tata-Yodogawa Ltd. Adityapur Industrial Estate, Near Jam shedpur, Jharkhand.

Manufacturer: Steel mill rolls of all grades and types, cart gear wheels, rope drums, cart steel grinding media etc.

The Tinplate Company of India Ltd. Golmuri, Jamshedpur 831003, Jharkhand.

Manufacturer: Tinplate, blackplate and electrolytic tinplate.

The Tata Engg. and Locomotive* Co. *Ltd. (TELCO) Jamshedpur, Jharkhand.

Manufacturer: Light, medium and heavy commercial vehicles, passengers cars etc. and bodies thereon, marine engines, earth moving machinery, metal cutting and grinding machines steel castings, electronic equipments, electronic washing instruments, crane weighing instruments and equipment, spare parts for vehicles and other components.

Usha Martin Industries Ltd. Adityapur, Jamshedpur.

Manufacturer: Wire drawing and allied machines, wire rods, wire ropes, wires, billets, rolled products, hydraulic machines including presses, proof loading machines and accessories, equipment and materials for prestressed concrete system etc. M/s R.B. Agencies Ltd., M/s P.K. Estates Ltd., and M/s Umil Lease Finance Co. Ltd. are the subsidiary companies.

HANDICRAFTS

Cane and Bamboo works.

MINERALS AND ORES OCCURRENCES

Abrasive

Flint pebbles have been obtained along the streams in the neighbourhood of iron-ore hills in Kolhan and Dalbhum.

Garnet sands occur along the streams which traverse the mica-schists in north eastern Dhalbhum, and until recently, they were collected by the villagers near Malibani (22.4, 86.7). On the S.W. of Shirbai Dungri (22.3, 86.6).

Barytes

At Ghatsila (22.6, 86.5).

Building Materials

Around Dhalbhumgarh Railway station (22.5, 86.55) gravels cropout over a wide area, forming the base of the late Tertiary deposits. These gravels which consist very largely of quartz pebbles and boulders have been put to use as railway blast. A little further south from the gravels a line of massive quartz veins in the mica-schists has been excavated for road material. The Newer Dolerite dykes which traverse the Singhbhum granite can be used for railway blast and road metal.

Clay

White clay occurs near Nutandih (22.85, 86.3) and Chandrikol (22.8, 86.35).

Lime Stone

A form of calcareous tufa is found in the crevices of and as incrustations on quartzites; the material is locally known as ashurbar (demon bone.) Ball records one such deposit near Basadera (24.7, 86.5). Another deposit occurs in quartzite cropping out in *nalas* to the N.W. of Bakra Kocha (22.4, 86.5) and about 3 kms. N.W. of Khejurdari (22.4, 86.55).

Occurrence of lime stone have been reported from Mahulbasa (22.85, 86.3) and in the southern portion of Chagaltopa pahar (22.85, 86.33).

Manganese

Manganese-ore occurs in the ridge between mirgitanr (22.7, 86.5) and Basadera (22.7, 86.5) to the north of Ghatsila. Some of the manganese deposits on opening up were found to occur as lenticular masses interbedded with phyllites and majority of them rapidly thin out. Manganese also occurs at Jhatijharna

(22.7, 86.55). Manganese ore associated with phyllites and hamatites-quartz rocks is found at Lahkaisini Pahar (22.7, 86.6) and near Hatibari (22.6, 86.39).

Mica

Books of muscovite measuring up to 3 ins. by 2 ins. occur in a small pegmatite vein at Laubera (22.5, 86.7).

Ochere

Ochere is obtained from ferruginous phyllites occurring near Mangru (22.5, 86.26), Maheshpur (22.67, 86.5) and Labari (22.6, 86.7). Clays at Meteabandi (22.55, 86.6) at Khari Dungri (22.5, 86.75) and near Dharadih (22.71, 86.53) are used as colour wash.

Lime

Apetite veins rich in magnatite occur at Patharghara (22.53, 86.45). From this locality and extending upto Khariatola (22.53, 86.46) apatite veins occur within mylonitised granite. Here veins up to a thickness of 20 ft. are met with. Apatite veins are also encountered around Mosabani (22.5, 86.46). Apetite veins are well developed to the east of Badia and again to the south of Bhadua (22.46, 86.5). Veins of apatite are again found near Kanjaluka (22.5, 86.5) and Sunrgi (22.45, 86.53).

Pyrrhotite

Pyrrhotite is a common accessory of the copper-ores at Mosabani (22.51, 86.46), Badia (22.5, 86.46), Patharghara (22.53, 86.43), etc.

Torbernite

Specimen of torbernite have been recorded at Sungri (22.45, 86.55) along with a little uranium Ochre. The minerals are associated with apetite-magnetite rocks.

Steatite

At Tikri (22.63, 86.46), Dari (22.7, 86.25) Muttagora (22.65, 86.37), Domapal (22.45, 86.6) are important centres, where pot stone was worked. It also occurs at Narsinghpur (22.73, 86.43).

Extensive deposits of massive choloritic talc rock are reported from near Mahespur (22.4, 86.5). Burudih (22.37, 86.5) and Dongadah (22.35, 86.6).

Tungsten

At Kalimati (22.76, 86.3). It occurs in pockets and is associated with quartzites.

Vanadium

In Singhbhum vanadium bearing iron-ores occurs as veins in gobro principally around Dublabera (22.5, 86.3) and its neighbour hood in the Dhalbhum sub division. Vanadium -ore is also located at Dhenga-Am-Kudar Sahi (22.47, 86.27), Khariadih (22.5, 86.3). Kotwar Pahar (22.5, 86.3). The total reserve of the Ore in the area have been estimated to be large.

Xenotime

A mineral intermediate in composition between monazite and Xenotime and associated with apatite has been reported from Aruburu near Kanyaluka (22.5, 86.5).

Fire-clay

Deposits of fire-clay which on investigation may prove to be suitable for manufacturing fire bricks occur at Matiabandi (22.55, 86.63) and Kharki Dungri (22.53, 86.75).

Garnet

Garnets shed from the mica-schist are found in the river sands. In the north eastern part of Dhalbhum, certain of the stream sands consist almost entirely of garnet crystals.

Gemstone (Jasper)

Attractive specimens of jasper are found associated with lavas and tuff of the iron ore series of S. Singhbhum, in the vicinity of the iron ore mines.

Iron

At Kudlun (22.78, 86.38), Basadera (24.66, 86.5), Samram (22.73, 86.06), Jaikan (22.72, 86.11), Binaburu (22.68, 86.2), Udal (22.53, 86.28), Turamdih (22.71, 86.25), and Hakigora (22.68, 86.21), Shamadanga (22.7, 86.53), Ghaghra (22.58,

86.65), Dublabera (22.48, 86.28), Sindurpur (22.46, 86.25), Jobhi (22.58, 86.68) and Dublakonda (22.6, 86.75), Ramchandra Pahar (22.72, 86.21), Kudana (22.7, 86.2), Patharghara (22.53, 86.45), Mosaboni (22.51, 86.46), Khejurdari (22.4, 86.56)

Kyanite

At Pakhamines (22.63, 86.35), Bhatin (22.66, 86.35), Surda (22.55, 86.43), Badia (22.48, 86.46), Bakra (22.48, 86.48), Kanyaluka (22.46, 86.51), Shirbai (22.33, 86.66), Dalbhum Railway Station (22.5, 86.55), Mohanpur (22.56, 86.53), Chirugora (22.55, 86.51), Dobha (22.53, 86.51), Bhatar (22.38, 86.6), Daonatanri (22.5, 86.15).

Gold

At Kamesara (22.25, 86.71), Bhitardari (22.7, 86.2), Digarsai (22.6, 86.25).

Kaolin

At Sini (23.8, 86.92), Chapra (22.7, 86.01), Koludih (22.71, 86.11), Samram (22.74, 86.74), Rangamatia (22.75, 86.03), Khari Dungri (22.53, 86.75).

TRADE, COMMERCE AND EXPORT

Purbi Singhbhum district is singularly fortunate in the richness of natural resources. These resources are mostly minerals.

The table below lists the most important commodities manufactured. exported from and imported in the towns of the district:

Name of the town	*Most important commodities*		
	Manufactured	*Exported*	*Imported*
Ghatshila	Copper	Copper	Salt
Jadugora	—	Uranium	Rice
Jamshedpur	Steel	Steel	Machinery
Jugsalai	Plastic bag	Plastic bag material	Plastic raw
Mango	Iron goods	Timber	Foodgrains
Musabani	—	Copper	Rice

Jamshedpur, chiefly a steel production centre, has steel as the most important commodity manufactured as also the most important commodity exported to other places. Copper is the chief item manufactured as also exported from Ghatshila town where a very large copper factory, viz. the Indian Copper Corporation Ltd. is located. Plastic bags are the main items manufactured and exported from Jugsalai town.

TOURISM

Baruni. It is a village situated about 5 kms from the block headquarters at Bahara—gora on the southern bank of the river Subarnarekha. According to a local legend, the Pandavas spent a part of their period of incognito exile in village Pandra, across the river. The village has a waterfall named as Baruni Kund. It is said about this Kund that Kunti, the mother of the Pandavas, wanted to offer Ganges water to Lord Shiva. Her sons accordingly set up five *Shivalingas* and Arjun created the waterfall with his arrow, bringing the *Patalganga* to surface. A. big annual fair is held on the occasion of Madhubamsha *Trayodashi* in the month of *Chaitra* (March-April).

Kokpara. The village is situated in Dhalbhum block on the northern bank of the Subarnarekha. It is noted for its historical associations. It has a temple of Lord Shiva with a deity known as Kapileshwar. The image is said to have been partly destroyed by Kalapahar, the legendary Muslim ruler of the past who is said to have played havoc with places of Hindu worship.

Chitreshwar. The village which is situated about 11 kms from the block headquarters at Baharagora, is noted for its temple of Mahashambhu, traditionally believed to be about 3000 years old and finding mention in the Skandha-purana.

Dharagiri. It is a beautiful waterfall on the Ghatshilla-Phuljhore forest road, situated about 18 kms from Ghatshila. The perennial waterfall attracts many visitors.

Rhoinibera. The village, which lies in Potka block, is noted for the temple of Goddess Rankini. According to the prevalent legend, the goddess while fleeing from evil spirits, was saved by a washerman. The washerman subsequently became the founder of Dhalbhum estate.

Jamshedpur. It is the largest city in the district and one of the most important in the state of Jharkhand. The city is known all over the world as one of the largest steel producing centres in Asia. Established in 1907 by Sir Jamshedji Nusserwan Tata, the city has grown very rapidly and is continuing to expand with more industrialisation. It is situated about 64 kms north-east of Chaibasa. Tatanagar on the Howrah-Nagpur section of the S.E. Railway is the railway station for Jamshedpur. Besides the works of the Tata Iron and Steel Company, there are several important industries in the city such as the Tata Engineering and Locomotive Co., The Indian Tube Co. Ltd., Tin Plate Co. Ltd., Tata Yadogawas Ltd., etc.

ZOO

Tata Steel Zoological Park, Jamshedpur.

HOTELS (2000)

Centre Point, (Government Approved) 4 star at Jamshedpur. Access 4 kms. from Airport, 6 kms. from Railway station and walking distance fr,m Downtown area. Rooms: 45.

Hotel Siddharta (Government approved) 3 star, at Jamshedpur. Access 2 kms. from Air port, 2.5 kms. from Railway station, 2 kms. from Sakchi. Rooms: 35.

Mansarovar Hotel, (Government approved) 3 star, at Jamshedpur. Access 4 kms. from Airport, 4 kms. from Railway station, 1 km. from Bus stand. Room: 41.

The Boulevard Hotel, (Government approved), 2 star, at Jamshedpur. Access: 4 kms. from Airport, 4.5 kms. from Railway station, 4 kms. from Bus stand. Rooms: 16.

FAIRS AND FESTIVALS

Important fairs and melas organised in various parts of the district are mentioned below:

Dussehra and Divali mela, Sankranti mela, Chaitra Sankranti mela, Rajashwala Sankranti mela, Shivratri mela, Mahadeo puja mela.

EDUCATION

According to 2001 census, total literates (excluding the population in the age group of 0-6 years) is 1,184,657 persons. Of these, 708,476 are males and 476,181 are females. In the rural areas of the district 392,841 persons (258,161 males and 134,680 females) are literates and in urban areas 791,816 persons (450,315 males and 341,501 females) are literates. The rate of literacy of this population to the total population, excluding 0-6 years age group according to 2001. census is shown below:

	Persons	*Males*	*Females*
Total	69.42	80.08	57.95
Rural	52.27	67.55	36.45
Urban	82.93	89.61	75.50

There are as many as 947 villages accounting for 60.09 per cent of the total number of inhabited villages in the district where educational facility is available.

Facilities of primary and middle schools are generally available in all the towns. The table furnished below gives details of different categories of educational institutions per ten thousand population in different towns of the district.

Name of the town	*Number per ten thousand population*			
	Higher Secondary/ Inter/PUC/ Junior College	*Secondary/ Matriculation*	*Junior Secondary/ Middle*	*Primary*
Bagbera	—	0.47	1.64	4.92
Chakulia	—	3.44	3.44	6.88
Gadhra	—	0.95	1.91	4.73
Ghatshila	0.40	1.19	2.38	3.18
Jadugora	0.87	0.87	0.87	3.47
Jamshedpur	0.02	0.70	1.66	1.60
Jugsalai	—	0.59	1.17	1.47
Mango	—	0.30	1.49	1.93
Musabani	—	0.34	1.70	2.38

MEDICAL

The availability of medical amenity in the villages is *very* low and only 18.53 per cent villages have it.

The table below furnishes information regarding availability of beds in the medical institutions in the urban areas of the district. .

Name of the towns	*Number of beds in medical institutions per 1000 population*
Bagbera	—
Chakulia	0.69
Gadhra	—
Ghatshila	1.83
Jadugora	4.77
Jamshedpur	4.50
Jugsalai	0.12
Mango	0.12
Musabani	5.27

COLLEGES (2000)

Behragora College, Behragora, (Established 1969) (Constituent College).

Ghatsila College, Ghatsila, (Established 1967) (Constituent College).

Graduate School/College for Women, Jamshedpur (Established 1971) (Constituent College)

Jamshedpur Cooperative College, Jamshedpur (Established 1954) (Constituent College)

Jamshedpur Women's College, Jamshedpur (Established 1950) (Constituent College).

Jamshedpur Workers College, Jamshedpur (Established 1960) (Constituent College).

Janata Parikh College, Jamshedpur (Established 1972) (Constituent College).

L B S M College, Jamshedpur. (Constituent College).

A J K College, Jamshedpur. (Affiliated College)

B D Sant Lal Chariti Trust Mahila Mahavidyalaya, Ghatsila (Established 1983). (Affiliated College)

J K S College, Mango, Jamshedpur (1983-84). (Affiliated College)

Karim City College, Jamshedpur (Established 1965). (Affiliated College)

Karim College of Education, Jamshedpur. (Affiliated College)

Loyola BEd. College, jamshedpur. (Affiliated College)

M G M Medical College, Jamshedpur (Established 1961). (Affiliated College)

(Above named colleges belong to Ranchi University, Established 1960).

MEDIA

Newspapers information.

ADMINISTRATION

(i) Administrative Divisions :

Sub-divisions : Dhalbhum, Ghatshila.

Community Development Blocks: Patamda, Golmuri-cum-Jugsalai, Potka, Dumaria, Musabani, Ghatshila, Dhalbhumgarh, Chakulia, Baharagora.

Towns and Urban Agglomerations with their Population, Sexratio, Decadal growth and Literacy rate (2001)

JAMSHEDPUR UA

Adityapur (NA); Jamshedpur (NA&OG); Jamshedpur (NA); Tatanagar Rly-colony (OG, Mango (NA); Jugsalai (M); Bagbera (CT); Haludani (CT); Sarjamda (CT); Gadhra (CT) Chhota Gobindpur (CT); Ghorabandha (CT).

Town	Population	Percentage Decadal growth 1991-2001	Sex Ratio	Literacy Rate
Chakulia (NA)	14,330	12.69	932	73.21
Chhota Gobindpur (CT)	24,751	27.79	875	86.36
Bagebera (CT)	67,100	17.64	916	77.32

Ghatshila (CT)	37,850	16.76	889	81.77
Gadhra (CT)	15,742	7.92	903	75.85
Ghorabandha (CT)	14,751	54.74	911	86.12
Haludbani (CT)	19,933	34.41	944	79.99
Jugsalai (M)	46,061	19.26	917	83.09
Jamshedpur (NA)	570,349	23.83	901	85.57
Jadugora (CT)	19,003	15.13	885	81.48
Mango (NA)	166,091	53.65	902	81.29
Musabani (CT)	33,892	-8.17	916	76.30
Sarjamda (CT)	18,373	77.72	961	70.76

(ii) Parliamentary Constituencies and assembly segments:

No.* and *Name of Parliamentary Constituencies:

50-Jamshedpur.

No.* and *Name of Assembly Segments:

287. Bahragora—Bahragora and Chakulia police stations in Dhalbhum sub-division.

288. Ghatsila (ST)—Ghatsila police station and Musabani police station (excluding G.Ps. Palasbani, Asta Koyali, Nunia, Kumarasol, Barakanjiya, Bomaro Bangoriya and Damudih) in Dhalbhum sub-division.

289. Potka (ST)—Potka police station, G.Ps. Palasbani, Asta Koyali, Nunia, Kumarasol, Barakanjiya, Bomaro Bangoriya and Damudih in Musabani police station,BagberaTown and G.Ps. Karandih-Purihasa, Hargarghutu, Bagbera and village 1167— Kitadih in Jugsalai police station in Dhalbhum sub-division.

290. Jugsalai (SC)—Jugsalai police station (excluding Bagbera Town and G.Ps. Karandih-Purihasa, Hargarghutu, Bagbera and village (1167) Kitadih); Golmuri and Patamda police stations in Dhalbhum sub-division.

291. Jamshedpur East—Census wards 20 and 23 to 40 in Jamshedpur Notified Area Committee in Dhalbhum sub-division.

292. Jamshedpur West—Jamshedpur Notified Area Committee (excluding census wards 20 and 23 to 40) in Dhalbhum sub-division.

OBSERVATIONAL ORGANISATION

Surface Observatories

Jamshedpur has this facility. This area lies under Meteorological subdivision, Bihar Plateu. The instrument lies in

Latitude	:	22.8° North
Longitude	:	86.2° East
Altitude	:	129 m
Date of starting	:	21-12-1922.

Hydrometeorological Stations for Climatological Purposes

This instrument lies in

Latitude	:	22.6° North
Longitude	:	86.5° East
Altitude	:	91 m
Date of starting	:	3-2-1971

Upper Air Observatories

These observatories record and report information about upper winds. This information is of vital importance not only for forecasting purposes but also to pilots of air craft, who must have knowledge of the speed and direction of winds at various levels in the atmosphere. Jamshedpur has this facility.

Meteorological Organization for Aviation

This facility is available in Jamshedpur.

DISASTROUS WEATHER EVENTS

Coldwave:

1st January 1982 moderate
29-30 November 1982, severe.
4-10 December 1982, severe.
2-14 January 1983, severe.

December 3rd and 4th week 1984, severe.

27-31 December 1989, severe.

1-10 January 1990, severe.

January 1st and 2nd week 1992.

Heatwave:

1-7 July 1982, moderate to severe.

28 May to 2 June 1983, moderate to severe.

6 June 1983, severe.

7 June 1983, moderate.

12 June 1985, severe.

Hail Storm:

30 April, 1987, Fall abundant to whiten ground and large stones, TV Transmission tower of Jamshedpur Doordarshan Kendra damaged resulting in cancellation of all the TV programmes.

Heavy Rains:

July 4th week to October 2nd week 1987, this area witnessed moderate to heavy rains. Crops badly damaged.

On 19th June 1988, this district witnessed heavy rains, specially in Jamshedpur city 3 persons killed and several people injured due to wall collapse.

On 8 July 1994, there was heavy rains in this area. Four women and 2 children died at Jamshedpur.

Lightning:

On 6 June 1995, Jamshedpur area witnessed lightning. Due to this, the reservation counter of Tata Railway station damaged. On 12 June 1995 again the disastrous lightning repeated due to this 3 Jawans died and 2 other injured.

Floods and Heavy Rains:

During 9 to 15 October 1995, there was severe flood at several places in this district, which resulted casualties and good number of cattle head perished.

ARCHAEOLOGICAL SITE

Barbil	Dt Singhbhum East	Dolmenoid structures and menhirs (4.17.4). IAR 1961-2.
Barda bridge	Dt Singhbhum West	Palaeoliths (4.2). near Chakradharpur. IAR 1959-60.
Bardha	Dt Singhbhum East	Palaeotiths (4.2) and microliths (4.5). IAR 1960-1
Bardugua	Dt Singhbhum East	Three shouldered celts of copper (4.11) Patna Museum Collection.
Ghatsila	Dt Singhbhum East	Microlithic tools and neoliths (4.6.4). IAR 1959-60
Hirjihati	Dt Singhbhum East	Early and Middle Stone Age (Lower and Middle Palaeolithic (4.2.3.) tools and microliths (4.5). IAR 1962-3.
Jagannathpur	Dt Singhbhum East	Site with Early and Middle Stone (Lower and Middle Palaeolithic [4.2.2,3]) Age and microlithic (Mesolithic (4.5) tools. IAR 1962-3.
Jamshedpur	Dt Singhbhum (Purbi)	Neolithic (4.6.5) site situated near the confluence of the Subarnarekha and the Kharkai within the town of Jamshedpur. IAR 1972-3.

DISTRIBUTION OF *SCHEDULED CASTE* POPULATION BY SEX DISTRICTWISE (1991)

	POPULATION		
	Total	Males	Females
PURBI SINGHBHUM			
	77,194	39,838	37,356
Bantar	96	77	19
Bauri	1,906	1,024	882
Bhogta	53	21	32
Bhuiya	14,097	7,336	6,761
Chamar, Mochi	8,207	4,516	3,691
Chaupal	120	61	59
Dabgar	63	37	26
Dhobi	12,919	6,856	6,063
Dom, Dhangad	8,714	4,446	4,268
Dusadh, Dhari, Dharhi	2,054	1,141	913
Ghasi	10,272	5,038	5,234
Halalkhor	57	17	40
Hari, Mehtar, Bhangi	6,785	3,426	3,359
Kanjar	60	50	10
Kurariar	498	166	332
Lalbegi	102	57	45
Musahar	1,321	665	656
Nat	75	28	47
Pan, Sawasi	6,044	2,997	3,047
Pasi	914	501	413
Rajwar	579	287	292
Turi	1,724	782	942
Unclassified	534	309	225

DISTRIBUTION OF *SCHEDULED TRIBE* POPULATION BY SEX DISTRICTWISE (1991)

	POPULATION		
	Total	Males	Females
PURBI SINGHBHUM			
	4,66,572	2,36,318	2,30,254
Asur	167	64	103
Baiga	71	15	56
Banjara	58	5	53
Bathudi	1,414	778	636
Bedia	941	549	392
Bhumij	81,002	41,189	39,813
Binjhia	150	71	79
Birhor	361	201	160
Birjia	203	108	95
Chick Baraik	129	46	83
Gond	2,166	1,127	1,039
Gorait	203	85	118
Ho	37,947	19,054	18,893
Karmali	136	92	44
Kharia	11,305	5,437	5,868
Kharwar	3,572	1,799	1,773
Khond	212	123	89
Kisan	97	35	62
Kora	1,386	652	734
Korwa	484	270	214
Lohara, Lohra	9,882	4,881	5,001
Mahli	9,494	4,721	4,773
Mal Paharia	326	179	147
Munda	41,423	20,978	20,445
Oraon	9,749	5,049	4,700
Parhaiya	105	80	25
Santal	2,49,731	1,26,835	1,22,896
Sauria Paharia	329	181	148
Savar	3,509	1,710	1,799
Unclassified	20	4	16

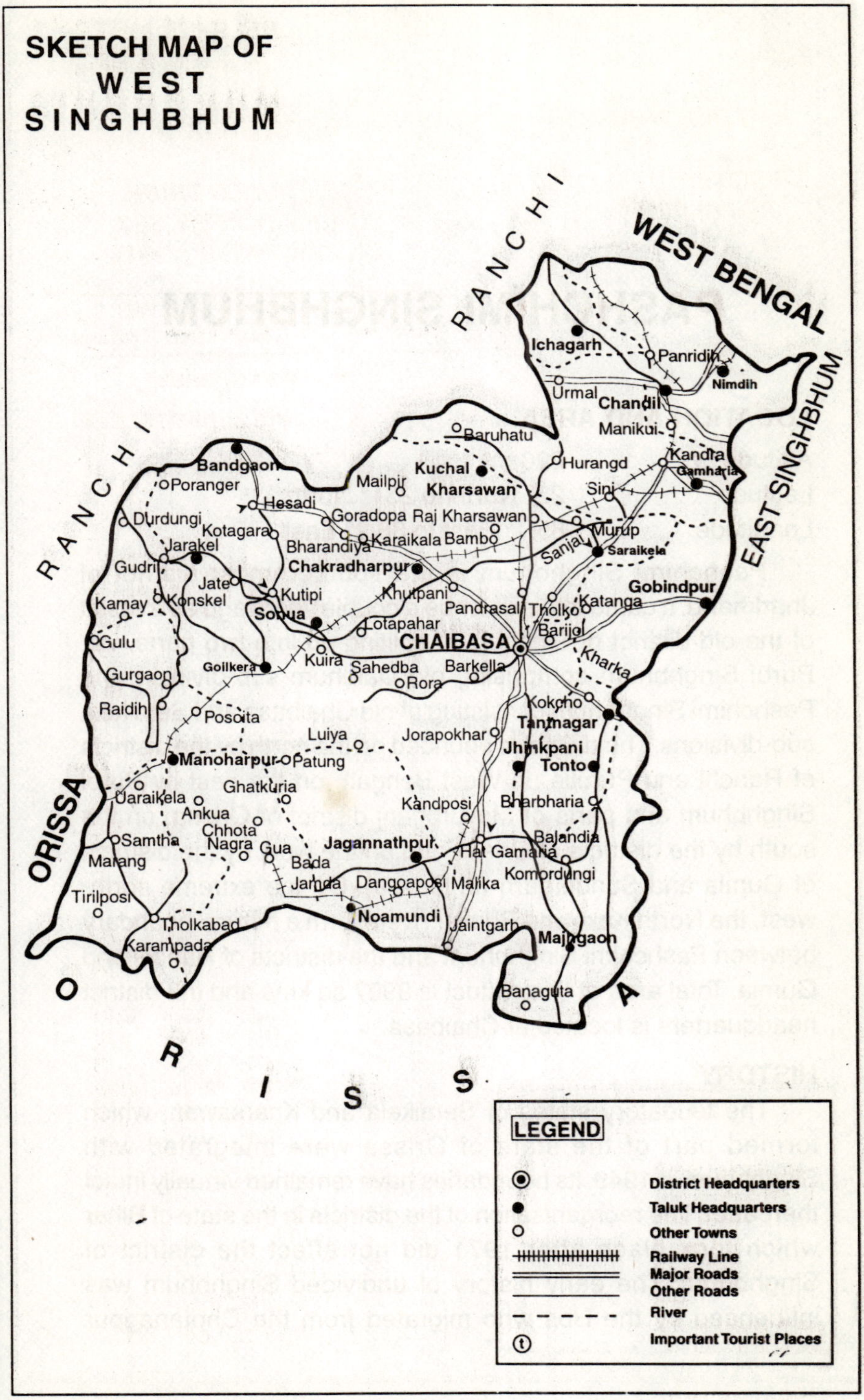
SKETCH MAP OF
WEST
SINGHBHUM
RANCHI
RANCHI
WEST BENGAL
EAST SINGHBHUM
ORISSA
ORISSA
Ichagarh
Panridih
Nimdih
Urmal
Chandil
Manikui
Baruhatu
Hurangd
Kandra
Gamharia
Bandgaon
Poranger
Mailpir
Kuchal
Kharsawan
Sini
Hesadi
Durdungi
Goradopa
Raj Kharsawan
Kotagara
Bambo
Murup
Jarakel
Bharandiya
Karaikala
Sanjai
Saraikela
Gudri
Chakradharpur
Jate
Kutipi
Khutpani
Gobindpur
Kamay
Konskel
Sonua
Pandrasali
Tholko
Katanga
Lotapahar
Gulu
CHAIBASA
Barijol
Goilkera
Kuira
Sahedba
Barkella
Kharka
Gurgaon
Rora
Raidih
Posoita
Kokcho
Tantnagar
Luiya
Jorapokhar
Jhinkpani
Manoharpur
Patung
Tonto
Ghatkuria
Uaraikela
Ankua
Kandposi
Bharbharia
Chhota
Nagra
Samtha
Gua
Jagannathpur
Bajandia
Marang
Bada
Hat Gamaria
Jamda
Dangoaposi
Malika
Komordungi
Tirilposi
Noamundi
Tholkabad
Jaintgarh
Majhgaon
Karampada
Banaguta
LEGEND
District Headquarters
Taluk Headquarters
Other Towns
Railway Line
Major Roads
Other Roads
River
Important Tourist Places

PASHCHIMI SINGHBHUM

LOCATION AND AREA

Altitude	:	226 m
Latitude	:	22° North to 231° North
Longitude	:	85.1° East to 86.2° East

Pashchimi Singhbhum is the southernmost district of Jharkhand. It came into existence a couple years ago as a result of the old district of Singhbhum spliting up into two parts, viz. Purbi Singhbhum comprising old Dalbhum sub-division and Pashchimi Singhbhum consisting of old Chaibasa and Seraikela sub-divisions. The district is bounded on the north by the districts of Ranchi and Purulia (in West Bengal), on the east by Purbi Singhbhum and parts of Mayurbhanj district of Orissa, on the south by the districts of Orissa and on the west by the districts of Gumla and Sundergarh (in Orissa). On the extreme north-west, the North Karo and Phuljar rivers form a natural boundary between Pashchimi Singhbhum and the districts of Ranchi and Gumla. Total area of this district is 9907 sq kms and the district headquarters is located at Chaibasa.

HISTORY

The feudatory states of Seraikela and Kharsawan, which formed part of the state of Orissa were integrated with Singhbhum in 1949. Its boundaries have remained virtually intact thereafter. The reorganisation of the districts in the state of Bihar which took place after 1971 did not affect the district of Singhbhum. The early history of undivided Singhbhum was influenced by the Hos who migrated from the Chotanagpur plateau and overcame the Bhuiyas who then held part of Singhbhum. The Hos successfully maintained their independence in the south of the district. The north of the district came under the rule of the Singh family of Porahat who claimed to be Rathore Rajputs, and whose head was formerly known as the Raja of Singhbhum. It is said that their ancestors were three brothers in the bodyguard of Akbar's general, Man Singh who supported the Bhuiyas against the Hos. At one time the Singh Rajas also ruled over the country included in the states of Seraikela and Kharsawan and claimed suzerainty over the Kolhan, a claim which the Hos deny. During the Mohammedan period, the Hos were left alone more or less by the Mohammedans although nominally they had the whole of the Jharkhand country stretching from Rohtasgarh to the frontiers of Orissa. British relations with Singhbhum date back to 1767 when a small British force marched against the Raja of Dhalbhum. The district of Midnapur which included Dhalbhum had been ceded to the East India Company in 1760. In 1765, a force was sent against the neighbouring Zamidars, but it could not subdue the Raja of Dhalbhum. After this expedition another force was sent under John Ferguson in 1767. He commenced his march from Jambuni to Ghatsila. The enemy had, however, retreated and the fort of Narsinghgarh had been destroyed by them earlier. However, the Raja was captured and sent to Midnapur in confinement. His nephew Jagannath Dhal was installed on the throne on a promise to pay an annual revenue of Rs 5,500 to the British. Jagannath Dhal could not have an easy time. He fell into arrears of yearly revenue and there was an expedition against him. Jagannath Dhal attacked his successor, Baikunth Dhal with a large force. Eventually in 1777, Jagannath Dhal was reinstated in the estate on payment of revenues due to him and in 1800 the estate was permanently settled at an assessment of Rs 4,267. In 1818 Raja Ghanshyam Singh Deo of Porahat tendered allegiance to the British. His main object was to be recognised as the Lord Paramount over the chiefs of Kharsawan and Seraikela and also to obtain assistance in reducing the Hos. The Hos resisted stiffly but their bows and arrows were of no match to the British equipment of war. In 1831 the Hos joined the rebellion of the Mundas of Chotanagpur. The immediate result of these troubles and the Kol insurrections in Ranchi and other parts of Singhbhum was the establishment of the South West Frontier Agency by Regulation XIII of 1833. Dhalbhum, which had hitherto been included In Midnapur district, was transferred to the Manbhum division. After the conquest of the Kolhan In 1837, it was considered advisable to bring all the Ho Pirs under the direct management of the British Government. A new district was consequently constituted to be known as SInghbhum with Chaibasa as its headquarters. In 1846 the district was enlarged by the transfer of Dhalbhum from Manbhum. When Act X of 1854 was passed, SInghbhum became a non-regulation district under the jurisdiction of the Lt. Governor of Bengal.

The Indian forces stationed at Hazaribagh had rebelled, soon to be followed by a detachment of the Ramgarh Battalion sent from Ranchi to quell the rising at Hazaribagh. The PrIncipal Assistant Commissioner fled and sought the protection of the Raja of Seraikela. The insurgent forces raided the treasury and broke open the jail. They then sought to proceed to Doranda but were prevented by the flooded river Sanjai. They were given refuge by Arjun Singh, Raja of Purahat, who was proclaimed a rebel by the British AdmInistration. On 16 September 1857 the new Principal Assistant Commissioner Lt. Birch reached Chaibasa with the Rajas of Seraikela and Kharsawan and Kol forces. Ultimately, Arjun Singh and his followers surrendered in February 1859. An era of peace and progress followed, to be broken almost forty years later by the Birsaite rising, the effects of which, however, were not very widespread or great. The history of the district in the present century is the saga of a powerful industrial revolution coming in the wake of the exploitation of the district's vast mineral resources.

POPULATION (GENERAL, SC/ST)

Total population of the district according to 2001 census is 2,080,265 persons, comprising of 1,052,711 males and 1,027,554 females. Rural population of the district is 1,729,598 persons (867,723 males and 861,875 females) and urban population is 350,667 persons (184,988 males and 165,679 females) .

The Community Development Block-wise, population distribution with sex ratio and literacy rate of this district is given below:

	Sex ratio		Literacy rate		Population	
C.D. Block	Rural	Urban	Rural	Urban	Rural	Urban
PASHCHIMI SINGHBHUM DISTRICT	**993**	**896**	**44.65**	**78.92**	**1729598**	**350667**
Sonua	999	-	40.99	-	81,266	-
Bandgaon	990	-	38.53	-	65,287	-
Chakradharpur	1,017	921	46.90	83.75	113,764	55,158
Kuchai	985	-	35.94	-	50,910	-
Kharsawan	981	915	51.73	77.21	63,099	6790
Chandil	949	919	53.69	73.00	111,979	4,341
Ichagarh	957	-	46.53	-	93,832	-
Nimdih	970	-	49.95	-	89,729	-
Adityapur	956	870	57.48	77.80	101,572	129,822
Seraikela	982	888	48.31	79.97	60,667	18,749
Gobindpur	998	-	50.44	-	116,817	-
Khuntpani			42.05	-	63,544	-
Goilkera	999	-	32.65	-	76,535	-
Manoharpur	987	946	44.69	67.44	99,147	3,949
Noamundi (Barajamda)	999	920	31.54	74.33	48,578	51,234
Tonto	1,003	-	31.12	-	53,911	-
Chaibasa	999	892	53.41	84.17	72,391	63,615
Tantnagar	1,012	-	41.17	-	48,654	-
Manjhari	1,022	-	35.03	-	54,093	-
Jhinkpani	1,023	968	37.56	64.76	61,066	11,835
Jagannathpur	1,010	897	45.82	78.50	79,391	51,74
Kumardungi	1.034	-	35.94	-	66,696	-
Majhgaon	1,027	-	40.87	-	56,670	-

The Scheduled Castes and Scheduled Tribes population of the district as per 1991 census are 89496 persons and 978069 persons respectively. The rural-urban breakup of this population is indicated as follows:

Rural	(i)	Scheduled Castes	:	68713
	(ii)	Scheduled Tribes	:	922017
Urban	(i)	Scheduled Castes	:	20783
	(ii)	Scheduled Tribes	:	56052

The decennial growth rate of population of the district as a whole in relation to the state between the period 1991 and 2001 is presented below:

State/ District	Decennial growth rate of population (per cent) 1991-2001		
	Total	Rural	Urban
Jharkhand	23.19	21.62	28.99
Paschimi Singhbhum	16.35	14.88	24.17

LANGUAGES AND RELIGION

Main language spoken in the district is Hindi.

Religion-wise breakup of population is indicated below as per 1991 census:

Hindus: 1018492, Muslims: 42936, Christians: 52960, Sikhs: 2284, Buddhists: 132, Jains: 436, Other religions and persuasions: 670598, Religions, not stated: 117.

GEOGRAPHY AND PHYSICAL FEATURES

Annual Rainfall	:	1314.4 mm
Temperature	:	Max. 44.90°C and Min. 7.30°C

The district forms part of Chotanagpur plateau and is a hilly upland tract. The south-west portion of the district consists of a group of hills known as the Suranda or seven hundred hills. The plain land in the district is largely confined to the valleys of the south Koel river and the Subarnarekha river in Dhalbhum. The district receives north-western spur which constitutes the northern boundary of the district. Its ranges include the Dalma range near Chancil, the trap range and the quartzite range. The chief peaks of the trap range are Bicha (2776 feet), Tatkoral (2910 feet), and Narji (2491 feet) along the northern border of the district. The quartzite range contains the Dharagiri (1738 feet) and Lakshini (1636 feet) peaks. Forests in the district cover approximately one-fifth of the total area of the undivided Singhbhum. Three types of forests are (i) dry thorny type, (ii) semi-evergreen type and (iii) most tropical deciduous type. Sal is the main tree species in all types of forests in the district. Other tree species found associated with sal are asan, dhaura, Jamun, bija, karam, simal, kendu, arjun, gamhar and bamboos. In the dry open hills salai, jhingam and bamboos are commonly found. Mahua and kusum are found near the cultivable lands. The greater part of the district is covered by the iron-ore series and granite rocks.

RIVERS, CANALS AND WATERWAYS

The principal rivers of this district are Subarnarekha and South Koel. The Subarnarekha rises near Ranchi town and enters the district from the north-west. There are many tributaries of the Subaranarekha river in the district.

TOWNS, VILLAGES AND AMENITIES

The district, at present comprises of 3 sub-divisions, 23 Community Development Blocks. It has 17 towns and 2859 villages, (2780 inhabited villages and 79 uninhabited villages).

The urban population of the district as percentage of total population in the census years 2001 is indicated below. It also shows the sex ratio (females per 1000 males) and density (population per sq km) in the urban population of the district in relation to the state:

State/ District	Urban population as percentage of total population	Sex ratio, 2001 (Females per 1000 males)			Density (Population per sq. km.)
	2001	Total	Rural	Urban	
Jharkhand	22.25	941	963	870	338
Pashchimi Singhbhum	16.86	976	993	896	210

Amenities

Number (with percentage) of villages having one or more amenities in the district as per 1991 census is given below:

Sl. No.	Amenities	Number of inhabited villages	Percentage
1.	Education	2016	72.52
2.	Medical	450	16.19
3.	Drinking Water	2780	100.00
4.	Post and Telegraph	184	6.62
5.	Market/Hat	218	7.84
6.	Communications	337	12.12
7.	Approach by Pucca Road	314	11.29
8.	Power Supply	456	16.40

COMMUNICATIONS

The district is well served by a network of good roads. the National Highway No. 33 runs through the district, comprising sections on the Chaibasa-Chakradharpur-Ranchi and Chaibasa-Haludpokhar road covering about 140 kms. The following are a few important roads in the district maintained by various departments:

State Highways. Chaibasa-Ranchi, Chaibasa-Jaintagarh, Chaibasa-Halud-pokhar, Chaibasa-Seraikela-Chandil, Serai-kela-Kharsawan, Kharsawan-Amda.

Zila Parishad. Chaibasa-Bharanadia, Chak-radharpur-Sonua. Chaibasa-Bhoya etc.

The Hawrah-Nagpur mainline of the South-eastern Railway traverses the district from east to west. As regards the Airways, there are small air strips at Chaibasa and Noamundi. Important ferry service operative in the district is Anandpur ferry on river Koel on Anandpur-Manoharpur .

AGRICULTURE AND IRRIGATION

Agricultural conditions vary considerably in different parts of the district. The district may be divided into three tracts, first comparatively level pains then hills alterna ting with open valleys and lastly, the steep forest clad mountains. The inhabitants of the district have almost changed their nomadic life and have taken up cultivation on a more permanent basis. The soil of the district has been classified into two groups viz. red soil and yellowish grey. Red soil is spread throughout the district. It is sandy and loamy and has poor fertility. Only kharif crops are grown here. Paddy is grown in the low lands where irrigation is possible. Yellowish grey and grey soils are found in the plains especially in the Seraikela and its adjoining areas.

Paddy is the main crop of the district. Wheat comprises a very small proportion of the gross area sown. Among the non-food crops grown, oilseeds are the most important. The usual method of irrigation consists of the construction of embankments and bunds across the line of trench i.e. the upper end of a depression.

ANIMAL HUSBANDRY

Cows, buffaloes. bulls and bullocks, sheep and goats are the main livestock of the district. Poultry birds are also found in quite good numbers. There are a number of veterinary institutions such as hospitals and dispensaries opened by the Animal Husbandry Department. Treatment and prevention of diseases of the livestock are the main functions of these veterinary institutions.

INDUSTRIES

The major portion of this district consists of either agricultural or mining areas producing iron-ores and other ancilliary minerals for the manufacture of iron and steel. The other important industrial activities are biri-making at Chakradharpur and shellac manufacture at Chandil. There are a few establishments both in the rural and urban areaṣ of the district engaged in manufacturing tobacco products, flour mills, rice mills, saw mills etc. Some of the large industrial establishments found in the district are mentioned below:

1. S.E. Railway Engineering Workshop, Sini.
2. The Associated Cement Gays Ltd. Chaibasa.
3. Cement Works. Jhinkpani.
4. The Seraikela Glass Works (P) Ltd. Kandra.

MINERALS AND ORES OCCURRENCES

Abresive

Beds of impure chert are abundant North of Chandil (22.95, 86.1). In southern Singhbhum there are beds of pure white chert in the Iron-Ore series, particularly to the N.E. of Jamda (22.2, 85.43) and pebbles shed from these strewn along the stream courses would be suitable for use in grinding mills.

Asbestos

Occurrences of asbestos in Seraikela, the most important of these being at Bara Bana (22.6, 85.9) Patka (22.6, 85.9) and Chotta Doana (22.6, 85.9) Occurrences of asbestos have also been reported from Saranghos (22.65, 85.99), Bhrudih-Bhrusa (22.63, 85.95), Joddiha (22.6, 85.90), Chilma (22.6, 85.9) Patakocka (22.6, 86.1).

Barytes

Barytes occurs in discontinuous lenticular patches at Pradhanpali (22.33, 85.1) and Dhanpal (22.3, 85.1). Veins of barytes with steep dip towards S.E. occur half a mile S.W. of Kalpotka (22.66, 85.1), near Saraikela station on the S.E. Railway. The southern zone contains workable veins.

Building Materials

Sandstones and sandstone-quartzite of the iron ore series

are quarried for local building purposes, particularly near Barijal (22.56°, 85.55°). N.E. of Chaibasa.

Chromite

Deposit of chromite occur between 22.47 and 22.5° North and 85.6° East to 85.66° East in the Jojohatu area. The ore occurs as veins or bands in serpentinized ultrabasic rocks. At Sura Pass (22.55, 85.7) to the west of Chaibasa.

Copper

At Duarpuram (22.76, 85.5) near Bamaini River.

Limestone

Occurrence of magnesiam limestone from Putada springs north of Chaibasa (22.55°, 85.8°). A lime stone in fault breccia to the north of Lota Pahar Railway staiton (22.6°, 85.56°) was quarried and calcined at one time. A dark bluish massive limestone at Ghat Kuri (22.3, 85.4) and a more extensive bed of magnasiam lime stone cropping out across Karo river south of Patang (22.4, 85.4) are also reported by him.

Limestones belonging to the Kolhan series extend from Chaibasa to Jagannathpur (23.2, 85.65) for a total distance of about 50 kms. The bands are variable thickness and pinches out completely at places. The lime stone is about 40 ft. thick near Rajanka (22.43°, 85.73°).

Rutile

Rutile occurs in association with Kyanite rocks in the Lapsa Buru (22.8, 85.75) area.

Manganese

Occurrence of magniferous hematite and limonite in a ridge to the south of Chaibasa town. The ores are of a lateritic character developed on the out crop of Dharwar phyllites, sandstone, quartzites and grits. Deposit have been located at Bistampur or Matagota (22.45, 85.85), Gitilpi (22.5, 85.87), Kalenda (22.5, 85.87), Lagia (22.53, 85.77), Madkamhatu (22.53, 85.85). Tekrasai (22.5, 85.87), Tutugutu (22.5, 85.83) and Leda Hill (22.47, 85.43).

Vanadium

An occurrence of magnetite containing traces of vanadium has been noted between chilma (22.6, 85.9) and Arahasa (22.6, 85.9). This is a local segregation of the ore in an ultrabasic rock.

Gemstone (Tourmaline)

Tourmaline of blue and brown colour occurs near Lapsa Buru (22.8, 85.73). A white aplete with streaks of blue tourmaline occurs at Jhanda Buru (22.1, 85.7).

Gemstone (Idocrase)

Idocrase occurs in small grains in granites near Jiling Bera (22.8, 85.15).

Iron

At Chaibasa (22.55, 85.86), Noamundi (22.13, 85.46), Gua (22.21, 85.38), Salai (22.33, 85.33), Chiria (22.3, 85.28), Baraiburu (22.15, 85.36), Jamda (22.16, 85.43), Marang Ponga (22.23, 85.23), Pechahatu (22.26, 85.36), Lipunga (22.25, 85.45), Saranda (22.63, 85.2), Lukud Buru (22.66, 85.45).

Kaolin

Occurrence of Kaolin at Amda (22.74, 85.83), Ghirudih (22.75, 85.74), Ragunathpur (22.78, 85.98), Ghagi (22.73, 86.00), Bharatpur (22.7, 86.8), Majri (22.7, 85.66), Choenhatu (22.61, 85.8), Keshumandu (22.16, 85.75), Mahuldiha (22.23, 85.68), Telaipi (22.41, 85.91), Karanjia (22.2, 85.68), Bhonda (22.16, 85.83), Raikhomon (22.13, 85.9), Dumaria (22.2, 85.8), Juldiha (22.16, 85.9), Libraria (22.26, 85.7) and Guli (22.4, 85.93), Pandrasali (22.61, 85.8), Madhkamhatu (22.53, 85.8), Gundiposi (22.5, 85.7), Matiabandi (22.55, 85.63), Dharadih (22.71, 85.53).

Kyanite

Kayanite occurs at Lapsa Buru (22.8, 85.75), Hatitand (22.8, 86.00), Tirildih (22.8, 86.01), Jhar Gobindapur (22.8, 86.08), Ghagidih (22.75, 86.18), Kacha (22.75, 86.16), Padampur (22.78, 85.93), Chaori Buru (22.81, 85.93), Sarengda (22.8, 85.95), Biday (22.71, 85.5), Kuku Dungri (22.78, 86.01), Sirum (23.11,

86.03), Kukru (23.1, 85.98), Sapada (23.11, 85.93), Haitiral (23.1, 86.5), Bandudih (23.8, 86.1), Inchadih (23.8, 86.16), Benryadih (23.1, 86.18), Juradih (23.7, 86.23), Salbani (23.6, 86.26)

Gold

At Pahardia (22.5, 85.26), Sausal (22.63, 85.5), Dhipa (22.43, 85.26)

TRADE, COMMERCE AND EXPORT

The table furnished below lists the most important commodities manufactured, exported from and imported in the towns of the district :

Name of the town	*Most important commodities*		
	Manufactured	*Exported*	*Imported*
Adityapur	Cycle parts	Chemicals	Iron
Chaibasa	Timber	—	Rice
Chakradharpur	Bidi	Bidi	Tobacco
Chiria	—	Iron ore	Rice
Gua	—	Iron ore	Cereals
Jhinkpani	Cement	Cement	M. Oil
Kharsawan	—	Tassar	Cloth
Kiriburn	—	Iron Ore	Cereals
Noamundi	—	Iron	Cereals
Seraikela	Silver	Kyanite	Cloth
Sini	—	Lac	Cloth

While bidi is the most important commodity manufactured as also exported to other places from Chakradharpur town, cement is the main item manufactured and exported from Jhinkpani. Pashchimi Singhbhum is equally fortunate in the richness of natural resources. These resources are mostly minerals. Chakradharpur being an important railway centre, has a very big business in timber, bamboo, biri and shellac. Gua, Noamundi and Manoharpur export iron ore and timber.

Barajamada is the centre for manganese ore, iron ore and forest produce. Sonua and Goelkera are noted for timber trade.

TOURISM

Bidri. The village lies in Manjhari development block. It has a small lake on its outskirts with a hillock to the east. The Forest Dak Bungalow situated west of the lake commands a fine scenic view. The Thakora waterfall is about 6 kms away.

Hirni. The village is situated 40 kms north of Chakradharpur on the Ranchi-Jamshedpur road. It contains a beautiful waterfall in the midst of dense forest. It is a popular picnic spot.

Jojohatu. The village is situated 22 kms west of Chaibasa amid forests. It is noted for its chromite deposits and iron-ore mined by the Singhbhum Chromite Company and the Tata Iron and Steel Company.

Lupunggutu. It is a small village situated only 2 kms west of Chaibasa town. It has a perennial natural spring which is a popular picnic spot.

Kharsawan. It is a small town situated on the bank of river Sona (which rises near the Ranchi-Singhbhum border). Presently headquarters of the block bearing the same name. It used to be the headquarters of the erstwhile Kharsawan Raj.

Bandgaon. It is a small village in Chakradharpur block lying on the Ranchi-Chaibasa road. It is noted for its annual fair held on the occasion of Asadh Dwadashi (April-May) and Baisakh Purnima (June-July).

Chakradharpur. It is the largest town in the district, lies on the Ranchi-Chaibasa highway and is also a rail head on the Howrah-Nagpur section of the South-eastern Railway. The town was an erstwhile seat of the Porahat Raja and contains a Palace known as Rajabari.

Tholkobad. The village lies 46 kms. south of the block headquarters at Manoharpur. It is scenically situated amid forests at an elevation of 1800 feet and draws many visitors, particularly for game.

Hotel 2000

Name of the City	*Name of the Hotel*	*Star Category*	*No. of Rooms*
Jamshedpur	1. Centre Point	4	40

FAIRS AND FESTIVALS

Important fairs and melas organised in various parts of the district are mentioned below:

Asadh Dwadasi, Baisakh Purnima, Shiva Chaturdasi, Chaitra Sankranti, Shivaratri and Makar Sankranti.

EDUCATION

According to the 2001 census, total literates (excluding the population in the age group of 0-6 years) is 871,410 persons. Of these, 575,772 are males and 295,638 are females. In the rural areas of the district 631,705 persons (435,048 males and 196,657 females) are literates and in urban areas 239,705 persons (140,724 males and 98,981 females) are literates. The rate of literacy of this population to the total population, excluding 0-6 years age group according to 2001 census is shown below:

	Persons	*Males*	*Females*
Total	50.70	66.23	34.81
Rural	44.65	61.38	27.85
Urban	78.92	87.61	69.17

There are as many as 2016 villages in the district where educational facility is available. Facilities of primary and middle schools are generally available in all the towns. The table given below provides details of different categories of educational institutions per ten thousand population in different towns of the district:

Name of the town	Number per ten thousand population			
	Higher Secondary/ Inter/PUC/ Junior College	Secondary/ Matriculation	Junior Secondary/ Middle	Primary
Adityapur	—	0.19	1.50	1.87
Chaibasa	—	1.75	2.40	4.81
Chakradharpur	—	1.57	2.92	1.80
Chhota Gobindpur	—	1.33	2.00	1.33
Gua	—	0.94	0.94	3.77
Jhinkpani	—	0.96	2.87	1.91
Kharsawan	—	1.96	3.92	7.83
Kiriburn	1.11	1.11	1.11	2.21
Noamundi	—	0.70	1.39	4.17
Saraikela	—	1..27	2.54	6.36
Sini	—	1.67	1.67	3.34

COLLEGES (2000)

Ghatsila college, Ghatsila (Established 1967) (Constituent College).

Gyanchand Jain Commerce College, Chaibasa (Established 1973) (Constituent College).

Jawaharlal Nehru College, Chakardharpur, (Established 1968) (Constituent College).

K S College, Saraikela, (Constituent College).

Singhbhum College, Chandil, (Constituent College).

Tata College Chaibasa (Established 1970) (Constituent College).

Womens College Chaibasa (Established 1970) (Constituent College)

St. Augustine College, Manoharpur (Established 1983). (Affiliated College)

S. K. Bage College, Kolibira, Gumia, (Affiliated College)

PUAEM College, Chainpur, (Affiliated College)

Smt Roop Lata Law College, Chaibasa. (Affiliated College)

R.I.T. Jamshedpur, (Affiliated College)

A B M College Jamshedpur, (Affiliated College)

(Above mentioned colleges belong to Ranchi University, Established 1960.

MEDICAL

The availability of medical amenity in the villages is very low and only 16.19 villages have it. The table below furnishes information regarding availability of beds in the medical institutions in the urban areas of the district :

Name of the town	*Number of beds in medical institutions per one thousand population*
Chaibasa	2.23
Chakradharpur	4.09
Gua	5.65
Jhinkpani	3.34
Kharsawan	0.78
Kiriburn	2.77
Noamundi	5.56

ADMINISTRATION

(i) Administrative Divisions:

Sub-divisions : Singhbhum Sadar, Seraikela, Chakradharpur.

Community Development Blocks : Bandgaon, Chakradharpur, Sonua, Goilkera, Manoharpur, Noamundi (Barajamda), Jagannathpur, Majhgaon, Kumardungi, Manjhari, Tantnagar, Jhinkpani, Tonto, Khuntpani, Chaibasa, Gobindpur (Rajnagar), Adityapur (Gamharia), Seraikela, Kharsawan, Kuchai, Chandil, Ichagarh, Nimdih.

Towns and Urban Agglomerations with their Population, Sexratio, Decadal growth and Literacy rate (2001)

CHAKRADHARPUR UA

Chakradharpur(M&OG)
Chakradharpur (M)
Chakradharpur Rly. Colony (OG)

Town	Population	Percentage Decadal growth 1991-2001	Sex Ratio	Literacy Rate
Adityapur (NA)	119.221	53.23	867	77.56
Barajamda (CT)	7,691	-	907	62.89
Chaibasa (M)	63,615	12.14	892	84.17
Chiria (CT)	3,949	-	946	67.44
Chandil (CT)	4,341	-	919	73.00
Chakradharpur (M)	38,352	17.15	925	83.21
Danguwapasi (CT)	5,174	1.77	879	78.50
Gua (CT)	10,891	13.35	927	73.18
Jhjinkpani (CT)	11,835	7.17	968	64.76
Kandra (CT)	6,815	4.03	886	70.84
Kalikapur (CT)	3,786	-	929	96.36
Kharsawan (NA)	6,790	18.40	915	77.21
Kiriburu (CT)	9,545	5.55	914	77.97
Megnahatuburu Forest Village	6,879	-	886	85.74
Noamundi (CT)	16,228	6.14	939	73.37
Sini (CT)	6,489	-4.09	893	81.05
Seraikels (M)	12,260	9.68	886	79.39

(ii) Parliamentary Constituencies and assembly segments:

***No.* and *Name of Parliamentary Constituencies* :**

49-Ranchi, 51-Singhbhum (ST), 52-Khunti (ST).

No.* and *Name of Assembly Segments Jamshedpur:

It is one of those constituencies where community wise break up (OBE) in difficult to establish because of a big change in the last couple of decades. However, for Muslims (7 per cent), Scheduled Castes (5 per cent), Scheduled Tribes (36 per cent), the figures are fairly reliable. Of the Scheduled Tribes, Santals (16 per cent), Hos (9 per cent), Mundas (5 per cent) and Bhumijs (4 per cent) are dominant. Other communities like Ahirs, Brahmins, Rajputs, Tantis, Kurmis, Kayas-thas are also found.

Ranchi

293. Ichagarh—Ichagarh, Chandil and Nimdih police stations in Seraikella sub-division.

Singhbhum (ST)

294. Seraikella (ST)—Seraikela municipality and G.Ps. Govindpur, Pandra, Manik Bazar, Tangrani, Pathanmara, Jordiha, Gurgudia and Badakakda in Seraikela police station, Rajnagar police station (excluding village 98-Dighi) and Adityapur police station in Seraikela sub-division.

295. Chaibasa (ST)—Chaibasa Sadar and Jhinkpani police stations and Chaibasa Mufassil police station (excluding G.Ps. Bhoya, Keadchalam, Domra-Parnia, Lota; Thakuragutu, Dopai-Gamhariya, Sarda, Matkamhatu Khuntpani, Chiru and Rajabasa) in Chaibasa Sadar sub-division.

296. Majhgaon (ST)—Majhgaon and Manjhari police stations in Chaibasa Sadar sub-division.

297. Jaganathpur (ST)—Naomundi and Gua police stations and G.Ps. Kurtabera, Urkiya, Makaramda, Thalkobad (Part I) and Chhotanagra (Part I) in Manoharpur police station in Chaibasa Sadar sub-division.

298. Manoharpur (ST)—Manoharpur police station [excluding G.Ps. Kurtabera, Urkiya, Makaramda,Thalkobad (Part I) and Chhotanagra (Part I)] and G.Ps. Beralumin, Jojoda, Serengda, Orenga, Jhilrua, Goilkera, Kuria, Kadamdiha, Dalaikela, Sonua-Jorapokhar, Porahat, Sogoisai, Gudri Jarakel, Asantaliya, Dalki-Gobindpur, Bhalurangi, Harimara, Tunian Gajpur, Bandu, Poronger, Koloeda, Kulda, Bari, Lonjo, Bera Kayam, Mamail, Piring, Komrora, Komrora-Dariyo, Dura-Jante and Banskata in Chakradharpur police station in Chaibasa Sadar sub-division.

299. Chakradharpur (ST)—Chakradharpur police station (excluding G.Ps. Beralumin, Jojoda, Serengda, Orenga, Jhilrua, Goilkera, Kuira, Dadamdiha, Kalaikela, Sonua-Jorapokhar, Porahat, Sogoisai, Gudri Jarakel, Asantaliya, Dalki-Gobindpur, Bhalurangi, Harimara, Tunian-Gajpur, Bandu, Poronger, Koloeda, Kulda, Bari, Lonjo, Bera Kayam, Mamail, Piring.

Komrora, Komrora-Dariyo, Dura Jante and Banskata) in Chaibasa Sadar sub-division.

Khunti (ST)

300. Kharsawan (ST)—Kharsawan and Kuchai police stations and Seraikella police station (excluding Seraikella municipality and G.Ps. Govindpur, Para, Manik Bazar, Tangrani, Pathanmara, Jordiha Gurugudia and Badakakda) and village 98-Dighi in Rajnagar police station in Seraikella sub- division; and G.Ps. Bhoya Keadchalam, Domra-Parnia, Lota, Thakurgutu, Dopai-Gamhariya, Sarda, Matkamhatu-Khuntpani, Chiru and Rajabasa in Chaibasa Mufassil police station in Chaibasa Sadar sub-division.

The communitywise break up (OBE) in Singhbhum is Muslims (3 per cent). Christians (4 per cent) Scheduled Castes (4 per cent) and Scheduled Tribes (65 per cent), Of the Scheduled Tribes. Hos (35 per cent), Mundas (9 per cent). Santals (10 per cent) and Bhumijs (7 per cent) are the largest groups. Among other communities. Tantis. Ahirs and Kurmis are present in small numbers.

OBSERVATIONAL ORGANISATION

Surface Observatories

This facility is available at Chaibasa. This area lies in Meteorological sub-division: Bihar Plateau. The instrument lies in

Latitude	:	22.55° North
Longitude	:	85.81° East
Altitude	:	226 m
Date of starting	:	21-8-1983.

Hiydrometeorological Stations for Climatological Purposes

At Manoharpur, this facility is available. The instrument lies in

Latitude	:	22.16° North
Longitude	:	85.16° East
Altitude	:	
Date of starting	:	22-10-1968

DISASTROUS WEATHER EVENTS

Coldwave:

1st January 1982, moderate.
29-30 November 1982, severe.
4-10 December 1982, severe.
2-14 January 1983, severe.
December 3rd and 4th week 1984, severe.
27-31 December 1989, severe.
1-10 January 1990, severe.
January 1st and 2nd week 1992.

Heatwave:

1-7 July 1982, moderate to severe.
28 May to 2 June 1983, moderate to severe.
6 June 1983, severe.
7 June 1983, moderate.
12 June 1985, severe.

Hailstorm:

30 April 1987, Adityapur, Saraikela, Gamharia and Chandil Area witnessed heavy hailstorm, damages to properly reported.

Heavy Rains:

July 4th week to October 2nd week 1987, this area witnessed moderate to heavy rains. Paddy crops badly damaged.
On 19th June 1988, this district witnessed heavy rains, houses collapsed, several people reported killed.

Flood and Heavy Rains:

During July 2nd week 1994, at several places in the district, there was flash flood and at some places severe flood. There was severe flood in the Swarnrekha river caused damaged to the crops and road communications.
On 8 July 1994, there was heavy rains at some places caused damage to the property.

Lightning:

On 31st August 1995, there was lightning in this area. Three tribals reported died and 7 other injured at village Losoiki.

ARCHAEOLOGICAL SITE

Amainagar	Dt Singhbhum West	Lower Palaeolithic site.
Andhari	Dt Singhbhum West	Six shouldered copper celts (4.11) found in a pit. Patna Museum collection
Bholadih	Dt Singhbhum West	Microliths (4.5). IAR 1963-4.
Chaibasa (22°36', 85°48°)	Dt Singhbhum West	Palaeololiths (4.2-4) and microliths (4.5) IAR 1960-1
Chakulia	Dt Singhbhum West	Microliths (4.5) and neoliths (4.6.4) IAR 1959-60
Chandil	Dt Singhbhum West	Microliths tools (4.5) and neoliths (4.6.4). IAR 1959-60.
Chewra	Dt Singhbhum West	Microliths (4.5). IAR 1963-4.
Dahigara	Dt Singhbhum West	Lower Palaeolithic (4.2) site.
Dobo	Dt Singhbhum West	Microlithic tools (4.5) were found. IAR 1959-60.
Doran	Dt Singhbhum West	Microlithic (4.5) stie. IAR 1963-4.
Dugni	Dt Singhbhum West	Neolithic (4.6.4.) site on the Sanjai also yielding palaeoliths and microliths (4.5). IAR 1972-3.
Galudih	Dt Singhbhum West	Lower Palaeolithic (4.2) site.
Garadi	Dt Singhbhum West	Cemetery consisting of 12 urn burials (4.17.4) see Dhalbhum.
Ghoranagi	Dt Singhbhum West	Lower Palaeolithic (4.2) and Upper Palaeolithic (4.4) site in the Suvarnarekha valley, also yielding Neolithic (4.6.5) celts and mace-heads. IAR 1975-6.
Gopalpur	Dt Singhbhum West	Early and Middle Stone Age (Lower and Middle Palaeolithic [4.2.3] tools and microliths (4.5). IAR 1962-3.
Guriadi	Dt Singhbhum West	Dolmenoid structures and menhirs (4.17.4). IAR 1961-2.
Haribera	Dt Singhbhum West	Neolithic (4.6.4) site. AI, 9, 1953, p.77
Harindubri	St Singhbhum West	Early and Middle Stone Age (Lower and Middle Palaeolithic (4.2.3) tools and microliths (4.5) . IAR 1962-3.

Jaganathpur	Dt Singhbhum West	Site with Early and Middle Stone (Lower and Middle Palaeolithic [4.2.2.3] Age and microlithic (Mesolithic [4.5] tools. IAR 1962-3.
Kendposi	Dt Singhbhum West	Dolmenoid structures and menhirs [4.17.4]. IAR 1961-2.
Kera	Dt Singhbhum West	A Shouldered copper celt [4.11]. Patna Museum collection.
Kharsote	Dt. Singhbhum West	Lower Palaeolithic site.
Kuju	Dt Singhbhum West	Microlithic tools (of unspecified nature). IAR 1959-60.
Lokjuria	Dt Singhbhum West	Lower Palaeolithic [4.2] site.
Lotapahar	Dt Singhbhum West	Of the two excavated trenches, one near the n.w. fringe of the Tantragupta hill on the left bank of the Sanjai at Govindpur and the other on the right bank of the same river at Dalki, the first revealed two Pds. Pd I was character ized by Upper Palaeolithic tools [4.4] represented by scrapers and Pd II by microliths of both geometric and non-geometric varieties. The second trench revealed only one cultural Pd associ ated with microlithic tools, both geomet ric and non-gemetric. Besides a few Lower Palaeolithic [4.2] tools were found embedded the on surface of the first trench. Two Neolithic [4.6.5] celts and a polished roller had been previ ously found. IAR 1959-60; 1966-7.
Murganhata	Dt. Singhbhum West	Early and Middle stone age, IAR 1962-3.
Narsinghgarh	Dt. Singhbhum West	Lower Palaeolithic (4.2) site.

DISTRIBUTION OF *SCHEDULED CASTE* POPULATION BY SEX DISTRICTWISE (1991)

	POPULATION		
	Total	Males	Females
PASHCHIMI SINGHBHUM			
	89,496	45,482	44,014
Bantar	84	31	53
Bauri	768	354	414
Bhogta	507	275	232
Bhuiya	33,106	16,549	16,557
Chamar, Mochi	4,952	2,578	2,374
Chaupal	51	34	17
Dabgar	74	38	36
Dhobi	6,874	3,695	3,179
Dom, Dhangad	8,838	4,518	4,320
Dusadh, Dhari, Dharhi	1,504	817	687
Ghasi	13,939	6,937	7,002
Halalkhor	266	146	120
Hari, Mehtar, Bhangi	523	233	290
Kanjar	34	19	15
Kurariar	205	88	117
Lalbegi	33	10	23
Musahar	6,644	3,341	3,303
Nat	108	51	57
Pan, Sawasi	7,367	3,987	3,380
Pasi	735	414	321
Rajwar	409	194	215
Turi	1,713	799	914
Unclassified	762	374	388

DISTRIBUTION OF *SCHEDULED TRIBE* POPULATION BY SEX DISTRICTWISE (1991)

	POPULATION		
	Total	Males	Females
PASHCHIMI SINGHBHUM			
	9,78,069	4,88,892	4,89,177
Asur	31	18	13
Baiga	242	118	124
Bathudi	225	63	162
Bedia	5,086	2,821	2,265
Bhumij	72,990	36,249	36,741
Binjhia	71	17	54
Birhor	535	256	279
Birjia	14	6	8
Chero	580	239	341
Chick Baraik	1,629	693	936
Gond	11,545	5,891	5,654
Gorait	443	162	281
Ho	5,89,109	2,95,736	2,93,373
Karmali	642	318	324
Kharia	1,846	865	981
Kharwar	549	299	250
Khond	517	243	274
Kisan	493	282	211
Kora	2,067	982	1,085
Korwa	1,123	535	588
Lohara, Lohra	7,846	4,083	3,763
Mahli	9,116	4,363	4,753
Mal Paharia	710	368	342
Munda	1,33,129	66,349	66,780
Oraon	31,483	15,802	15,681
Parhaiya	111	45	66
Santal	1,04,777	51,585	53,192
Sauria Paharia	867	346	521
Savar	255	136	119
Unclassified	38	22	16